ABSTRACTS

of

LINCOLN COUNTY NORTH CAROLINA DEEDS

- 1786-1793 -

(Volume #1)

Compiled by:
Dr. A.B. Pruitt

Southern Historical Press, Inc.
Greenville, South Carolina

Please direct all correspondence and book orders to:
www.southernhistoricalpress.com
or
SOUTHERN HISTORICAL PRESS, Inc.
1071 Park West Blvd.
Greenville, SC   29611

Southernhistoricalpress@gmail.com

Introduction

This book contains abstracts of deeds of Lincoln County, NC, recorded between January 1786 and October 1793. These deeds are in the following deed books: "new" Book 3, p. 1-546 (same as "old" Book 13, p. 272-290, "old" Book 14, p. 1-273, & "old" Book 15, p. 1-256), "new" Book 4, p. 1-162 (same as "old" book 15 p. 257-383 and 11 later deeds), and Book 16.

Lincoln County was formed, along with Rutherford County, by the break up of Tryon County in 1779. In 1782 part of Burke County was added to Lincoln County. Subsequently, Lincoln County was divided into the following: part of Cleveland County in 1842, Catawba County in 1842, and Gaston County in 1846. Therefore, the land described in the deeds in this book is primarily in the present counties of Catawba, eastern part of Cleveland, Gaston, or Lincoln. Some of the land in Catawba County is described as being "formerly in Burke and now Lincoln Co". There is one deed for land in Bladen County (#584) and one for land in Tennessee (#758). In addition to land, some "deeds" describe sales of slaves, household articles, houses, and crops. Also there is one deed for part of what began as speculation land of Lewis Beard. Two town are mentioned:

(1) Lincolnton, the county seat. Joseph Dickson, county clerk, obtained the grant for this land on Dec. 14, 1785 (in grant book 61 p. 21). The land was first divided into 100 lots; 48 lots were 72 square poles each and 52 lots were 84 square poles each. These lots were sold in a lottery. Later, in 1816, 60 lots of varying sizes were added and sold at an auction.

(2) Ulricksburg (or Crowdertown) which was part of a grant to Ulrick Crowder or Whiteners Cr, a branch of South fork of Catawba R. Crowder moved to Wilkes Co, GA, and died before his town could succeed. More information about Ulricksburg can be found in The History of Catawba County edited by Charles J Preston jr (p. 370-373).

Abstract format

My abstracts are in the following format:

(1) a sequential number for each abstract; this number is used in the index;
(2) the date of the transaction;
(3) the name of the grantor (seller), his profession (if indicated in the deed), & his place of residence written in parenthesis; "NC" is omitted after the names of counties in North Carolina;
(4) following the word "to", is the name of the grantee (buyer), his profession, & place of residence; "same" indicates the grantee is from the same place as the grantor;
(5) the body of the abstract follows in the order: the amount paid, the number of acres, the creek or river or which the land is located, the neighboring land owners, & the title chain (if indicated);
(6) the name of the grantor as it was signed; I've not tried to duplicate individual marks of grantors who made marks rather than signed the deed;

(7) the names of the witnesses; sometimes the grantor and/or witness signed in old German, I've tried to translate these signatures using the sample old German handwriting in <u>A Genealogical & Demographic Handbook of German Handwriting</u> by N J Stones & L O Jenson; sometimes the clerk also wrote an anglicized version of the German names beside the old German signatures;   have mentioned these in the abstract if there was a significant difference between the German and anglicized versions (i.e. Zimmerman and Carpenter);
(8) the witness oath and/or dower oath are indicated on the rare occasions where they were written in the deed book; the names of witnesses giving oaths in court is most often in the court minutes and these have been or soon will be published;
(9) the date the deed was recorded;
(10) finally, the page numbers on which the deeds begin in the "old" and "new" deed books.

Brief History of Lincoln County Deeds

According to surviving papers in the North Carolina Archives (Miscellaneous Papers CR 060.428.6), the Lincoln County Court ordered the clerk to recopy "old" Books 2 and 9 because parts of these books were unintelligible.   This book became CR 060.401.10 in the NC Archives and included: Book 2 on p. 1-171, Book 9 on p. 172-184, and eleven deeds recorded in 1810 on p. 185-204.   Then in July 1838, the first fifteen original (or "old") books were recopied into four "new" books.   A bill presented in July 1840 by William H Lindsey indicates 2,202 "instruments of original record" were copied at 18 3/4 cents each, a total of $412.87. No amount was indicated for "altering the indexes by reversing surnames and making new indexes to show quantity of land at request of Mr. Wilson".   J. A. Ramsour and Tho G. Williamson composed the committee to compare the original books to the new books.

The following information is presented for the reader needing to locate the old or new deed books.   Most of this material was compiled by Mr. Mills Bridges.   New Books 1-3 and Book 16 are in the Lincoln County Court House in the Office of Register of Deeds.   The other books and microfilm are in the North Carolina Archives.   For archives material, "C" indicates microfilm call numbers and "CR" indicated call numbers for books.

<u>New deed Books 1-4 and Book 16</u>:
New Book 1 is in Lincolnton in two parts: p. 1-384 and p. 385-800; on microfilm it is on roll C 060.40230; this book includes the deeds in "old" Book 1 through "old" Book 8 p. 170.

New Book 2 is in Lincolnton in three parts: p. 1-274, p. 277-565, & p. 566-800; on microfilm it is on roll C 060.40231; this book includes the deeds in "old" Book 8 p. 171 through "old" Book 13 p. 271.

New Book 3 is in Lincolnton in two parts: p. 1-264 and p. 265-564; on microfilm it is on roll C 060.40232; this book includes the deeds in "old" Book 13 p. 272 through "old" Book 15 p. 256.

New Book 4 was lost some time between 1938 and about 1964; Book 4 is not on microfilm; this book included deeds in "old" Book 15 p. 257-383 and eleven deeds in CR 060.401.10 p. 185-203; these two "old" books do still exist in the archives; the grantor/grantee index cites deeds according to the page numbers in "new" Book 4 instead of the two "old" books; but, by reading my abstracts, the reader will find the page numbers for the old and new books as I have attempted to provide a cross link between the grantor/grantee index and the surviving copies of the deeds that were once in "new" Book 4.

Book 16 is in Lincolnton in one book p. 1-429; on microfilm it is on rolls C 060.40232 or C 060.400.04 (two copies of the same book).

<u>Old deed Books 1-15</u>:

Old Book 1 is in CR 094.401.8 except p. 1-8, 13-14, & 163-204 which are missing; on microfilm it is on roll C 060.40230 p. 1-106.

Old Book 2 p. 1-183 are in CR 094.401.2 and CR 060.401.10 p. 1-171; on microfilm it is on roll C 060.40230 p. 107-201 and C 094.4001.

Old Books 3 and 4 are in CR 094.401.3 p. 1-221; on microfilm they are on roll C 060.40230 p. 202-316.

Old Book 5 is in CR 094.401.4 p. 1-268; on microfilm it is on roll C 060.40230 p. 317-466.

Old Book 6 p. 1-245 are in CR 094.401.5 but p. 246-252 of this book are missing; on microfilm it is on roll C 060.40230 p. 467-604 and roll C 094.4002.

Old Book 7 p. 1-150 are in CR 094.401.1 but p. 151-153 of this book are missing; on microfilm it is on roll C 060.40230 p. 605-694.

Old Book 8 are in CR 094.401.6 except pages 1-3 and 262 which are missing; on microfilm p. 3-170 are on roll C 060.40230 p. 696-end and p. 171-261 are on roll C 060.40231 p. 1-56.

Old Book 9 p. 1-449 are missing but part is in CR 060.401.10 p. 172-184; on microfilm it is on roll C 060.40231 p. 57-314.

Old Book 10 p. 2-39 are missing but p. 40-187 are in CR 094.401.1 and p. 188-244 are in CR 094.401.7; on microfilm it is on roll C 060.40231 p. 315-453.

Old Book 11 p. 1-54 are on microfilm roll C 060.40231 p. 454-500.

Old Book 12 p. 1-135 are in CR 060.401.1; on microfilm it is on roll C 060.40231 p. 501-606.

Old Book 13 p. 1-291 are in CR 060.401.3; on microfilm it is on rolls C 060.40231 p. 607-799 and C 060.40232 p. 1-17.

Old Book 14 p. 1-273 are in CR 060.401.9; on microfilm it is on roll C 060.40232 p. 17-328.

Old Book 15 p. 1-2 are missing, but p. 3-383 are in CR 060.401.5; on microfilm p. 1-256 are on roll C 060.40232 p. 330-546; p. 257-383 of Book 15 are not on microfilm in the archives (these pages were the first part of "new" Book 4 which was lost before the books were microfilmed).

Tryon County microfilm in the North Carolina Archives also contains Lincoln County deeds; the following is a list for the two rolls:

Roll C 094.40001 contains (in order) old Book 7 p. 150, old Book 10

p. 40-187, old Book 2 p. 1-183, old Books 3 and 4 p. 1-221, and old Book p. 1-286.

Roll C 094.4002 contains (in order) old Book 6 p 1-252, old Book 8 p. 1-262, and old Book 10 p. 184-244.

Other Sources

Minutes for the Pleas and Quarter Sessions Court of Tryon County from 1768 to 1779 have been published by Virginia G DePriest and Lucille H Gardner; the minutes for Lincoln County from 1789-1796 have been published by Anne W McAllister and Kathy G Sullivan.   Abstracts of deeds in Lincoln County "new" Books 1 and 2 ("old" Book 1 through "old" Book 13 p. 271) were published by B. H. Holcomb.   Early land claims and surveys for Tryon, Lincoln, & Rutherford Counties have been published by Miles Philbeck.   Most of the land entries for Tryon and Lincoln Counties have been published by A. B. Pruitt.   Prior to the formation of Tryon County, this land was in Mecklenburg, Anson, & Bladen Counties.   Some of the surviving records of these counties have been published.   Present day Catawba County was previously in Burke and Rowan Counties, and some of the records of these counties have also been published.

For a brief definition of legal terms, the reader is referred to Appendix A of <u>North Carolina Research</u> by H F M Leary and M R Stirwalt. Also in this book, on pages 323-329 is a description of the early Superior or Supreme Court in North Carolina.   In the deeds, this court is referred to as the "Supreme Court at Wilmington for New Hanover, Bladen, Onslow, Duplin, & Cumberland Counties".

Index

The index of this book is in two parts: (a) first for people which includes slaves who were assigned the last name "Slave" and appear together under "S"; and (2) geographical locations--creeks, rivers, etc; "Lincoln County" and Catawba River" were omitted from the index because they appear so frequently.

Acknowledgements

The author wishes to thank the staff of the North Carolina Archives search room for their patience.   Also deserving thanks for their help and encouragement: Mrs. Grace Turner, Mr. Miles Philbeck, & Mrs. Anne McAllister.   A special thanks to Mr. Miles Y Bridges for sharing the results of his vast experience working with Lincoln County deeds.   Every county needs at least one researcher with a similar dedication to the job of locating records of genealogical interest.

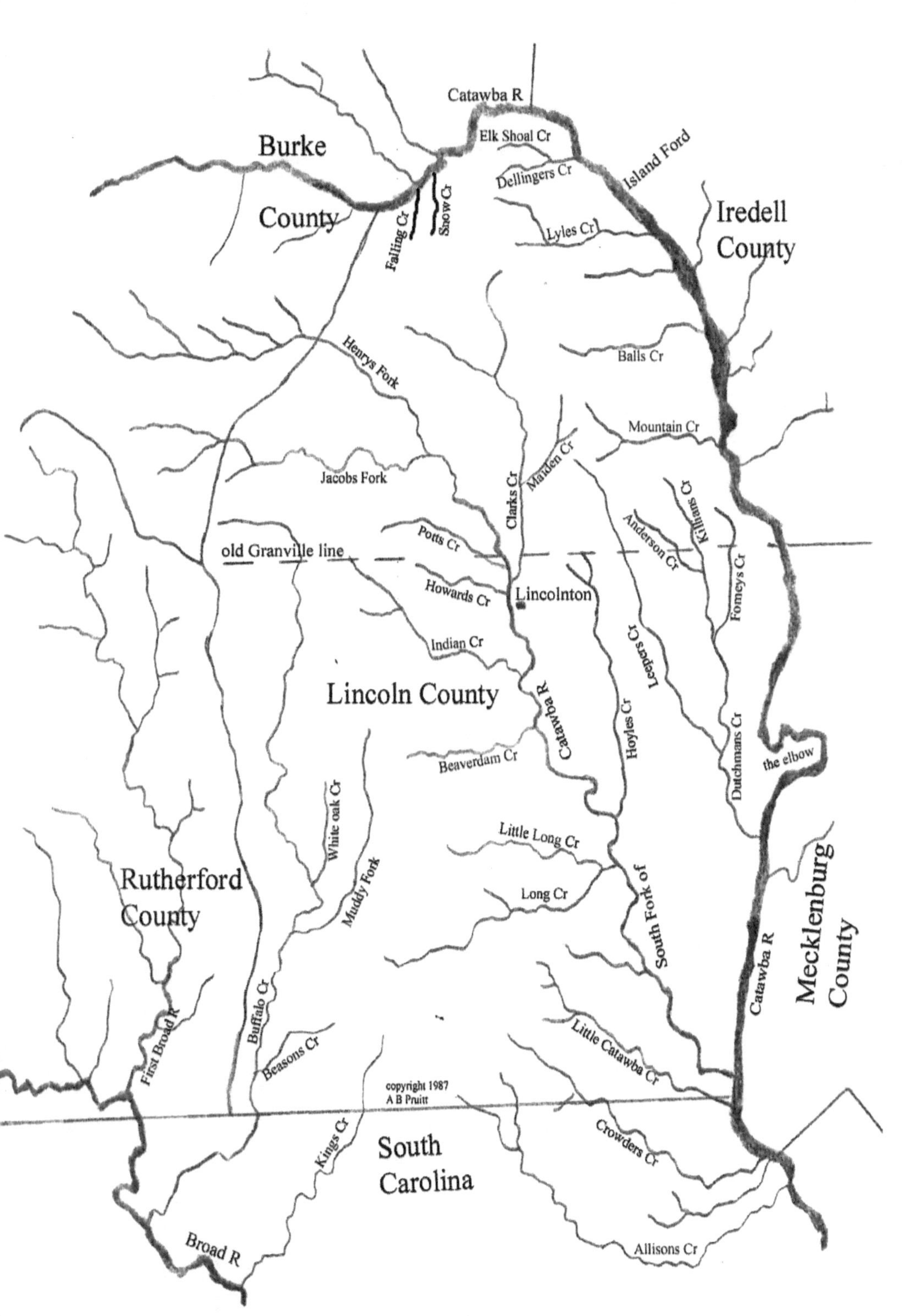

Burke County
Catawba R
Elk Shoal Cr
Dellingers Cr
Island Ford
Iredell County
Lyles Cr
Falling Cr
Snow Cr
Balls Cr
Henrys Fork
Mountain Cr
Maiden Cr
Clarks Cr
Killians Cr
Jacobs Fork
Anderson Cr
Fomeys Cr
Potts Cr
old Granville line
Howards Cr
Lincolnton
Indian Cr
Leepers Cr
Dutchmans Cr
Lincoln County
Hoyles Cr
the elbow
Beaverdam Cr
Catawba R
White oak Cr
Little Long Cr
Muddy Fork
Mecklenburg County
Rutherford County
Long Cr
South Fork of
Buffalo Cr
Catawba R
First Broad R
Beasons Cr
Little Catawba Cr
copyright 1987
A B Pruitt
Kings Cr
Crowders Cr
South Carolina
Broad R
Allisons Cr

Lincoln County, NC Deed book 3

Book 3 and Book 13

1. Oct. 13, 1785 James Logan (Rutherford Co) to Philip Mires (same); for 30£ sold 200 ac; granted Oct. 13, 1783 to James Logan; border: Carpenter. Signed James Logan (or Losan). Witness John Sloan & Walter Carruth. Rec. Jan. 1786. Book 3 p. 1; Book 13 p. 272

2. Mar. 25, 1785 John Pittillo (Lincoln Co) to Robert Cruthers (same); for 16£ NC money sold a Negro child Rachel, child of Negro wench Pat; John is to raise the child "on her mother's milk" and deliver the child to Robert when the child is 1.5 years old, and John loses everything is the child dies before then. Signed John Pittillo. Witness Fras McCorkle & Thomas Little. Rec. Jan. 1786. Book 3 p. 2; Book 13 p. 273

3. Dec. 23, 1785 John Simmerman (sic) (Lincoln Co) to Abraham Havener (same); for 10£ sold 200 ac on waters of Long Cr; border: Thomas Espey, "his" other line, & Ormand; granted Nov. 14, 1771 to John Summerman. Signed Jon Zenoreman. Witness Edward Hunter, Jacob Ramsour, & Henry Hoke. Rec. Jan. 1786. Book 3 p. 2; Book 13 p. 273

4. Nov. 14, 1793 John Pittilo (Lincoln Co) to Thomas Little (same); for "valuable consideration" gave a Negro boy Ben about 5 years old. Signed John Pittilo. Witness Fras McCorkel & Robert Cruthers. Rec. Jan. 1786. Book 3 p. 3; Book 13 p. 275

5. Nov. 29, 1785 John Harmon (Wilks Co) to Daniel Kingery (Richmond Co, Ga); for 19£ sold 130 ac on both sides of great road from Moses Moore's to Broad R and waters of Indian Cr; part of 350 ac grant to Davd. Huddlestone; border: Henry Randle and a hill. Signed John Harmon's mark. Witness David Ramsey & Willenelin Worlier(? german). Rec. Jan. 1786. Book 3 p. 4; Book 13 p. 275

6. Nov. 14, 1785 Thomas Robinson (Lincoln Co) to Peter Fite (same); for 350£ sold 621 ac between N & S forks of Catawba R; border: near waggon road to Tukasege ford and James Beatey; part of grant Jul. 17, 1778 to Thomas Robison (sic). Signed Thomas Robinson. Witness Joseph Henry, James Sumpter, & Thomas McGee. Rec. Jan. 1786. Book 3 p. 5; Book 13 p. 277
"reference being had to" p. 290 in "this book" for order of court Apr. 1792 [see deed No. 15 below].

7. Oct. 27, 1785 John Wallace, son of Hugh Wallace, (York Co, Cambden Dist, SC) to Edward Melon (Lincoln Co); for 80£ NC money sold 200 ac part in Lincoln Co and part in York Co on waters of Mill Cr; border: Robert Leeper and James Craigg; all of a grant Apr. 22, 1763 to Wm Dickson and sold Nov. 26, 1766 by Robert Harris and wife Margret to said John Wallace. Signed John Wallace. Witness John Gullick & John Gullick (sic). Rec. Jan. 1786. Book 3 p. 7; Book 13 p. 279

8. Nov. 3, 1785 Moses Scot & wife (Lincoln Co) to John Sumter (same); for 15£ NC money sold 100 ac on branch of Leepers Cr near George Rutledge; granted Jan. 30, 1773 to "said" John Cathy.   Signed Moses Scott (wife doesn't sign). Witness Robt Alexander & Jean Scott. Rec. Jan. 1786. Book 3 p. 8; Book 13 p. 281

9. Nov. 11, 1785 James Dozer & wife Mary (Lincoln Co) to James Hill (same); for 200£ sold 160 ac on bank of Cuttapaw R; border: "the" waggon ford; granted Sept. 29, 1750 to Samuel Coborn.   Signed James & Mrry Dozer. Witness A. Nelson, Robt Abernathy, & John Hill. Rec. Jan. 1786. Book 3 p. 9; Book 13 p. 282

10. Dec. 10, 1785 John Finger, farmer (Lincoln Co) to Jacob Finger (same); for 40£ sold 156 ac on Lick Br of Leepers Cr; border: Potts' new corner and Potts' corner; part of grant Apr. 22, 1763 to John Dellinger who sold Jul. 7, 1778 to John Finger.   Signed John Finger. Witness Robt Blackburn & William Blackburn. Rec. Jan. 1786. Book 3 p. 11; Book 13 p. 283.

11. Dec. 25, 1777 Jonathan Prince, sadler (Tryon Co) to John Skyles, planter (same); for $500 NC money sold 125 ac on branch of Kings Cr; includes Jonathan Prince's own improvments; border: Jacob Connel's "third" corner.   Signed Jonathan & Mary Prince. Witness Joseph Kuykendall & Jacob Huffstetler. Rec. Jan. 1786. Book 3 p. 12; Book 13 p. 285

12. Jan. 31, 1781 Thomas Hover, farmer (Burke Co) to John Jones, farmer (Rowan Co); for 200£ sold 135 ac; includes Solomon Hoover's improvements on W side of Cuttapa R; border: W side of N branch of Killions Cr, William Hager, "his" corner, & John Jewhart; granted Oct. 13, 1756 to Solomon Hoover.   Signed Thomas Hover(? german). Witness John Wilson and Danl McKisick. Rec. Jan. 1786. Book 3 p. 14; Book 13 p. 286

13. Jan. 3, 1786 Robert Allison, planter (in state of Franklin) to John McGill (Lincoln Co); for 20£ NC money sold 180 ac on N fork of Crowders Cr; border: above Charles McLean and up the river; includes mouth of Mine Br and "downwards"; granted Mar. 25, 1780 to Robert Allison.   Signed Robert Allison. Witness John Oats & Tho White. Rec. Jan. 1786. Book 3 p. 15; Book 13 p. 287

14. Nov. 5, 1785 John Carruth (Lincoln Co) to Henry Reynolds (same); for 60£ sold [ac omitted] on both sides of Lick fork of Indian Cr "above" and joins Hugh Pollock; granted Jan. 16, 1769 to John Sloan jr.   Signed John Carruth. Witness Wallace Beatey & Shadrick Reiche. Rec. Jan. 1786. Book 3 p. 16; Book 13 p. 289.

15. Apr. session 1792 ordered by court that it appears by oath of Thomas McGee and Alexander Nelson that the "figure 170" in location of tract sold by Thomas

Lincoln County, NC Deed book 3

Robinson "for" 621 ac is in error and aught to be 370; the figures ordered to be altered. [note: this refers to replacing 170 poles with 370 poles in one of the dimensions of the tract in deed No. 6].   Witness Jo Dickson, cc. Book 3 p. 17; Book 290

Book 3 and Book 14
April session 1786
16. Jan. 16, 1786 Henry Holman & wife Elisabeth (Lincoln Co) to Jacob Baker, blacksmith (same); for 400£ NC money sold 400 ac on S side of Cuttabaw R; border: said Baker; upper end of "plantation" said Holman purchased of Christopher Hainer.   Signed Henry Hollman & Elisabeth's mark. Witness Nathan Armitage & Elasebeth Jameson. Rec. Apr. 1786. Book 3 p. 17; Book 14 p. 1

17. Dec. 23, 1785 William Sherril, farmer, & wife Susana (Lincoln Co) to Jacob Baker, blacksmith (same); for 60£ NC money sold 50 ac on S side of Cuttabaw R; border: formerly Christopher Hainer's corner of "his" survey; granted Oct. 11, 1783 to William Shirl (sic). Signed William & Susanna Sherrill. Witness Henry Hollman & Jacob Sherrill. Rec. Apr. 1786. Book 3 p. 18; Book 14 p. 1

18. Aug. 30, 1785 Daniel Hudson (Lincoln Co) to Peter Myers (same); for 20£ NC money sold 100 ac on both sides of Indian Cr about a mile above "the" Scout Camp; border: Peter Johnston's entry, an old survey, & an open line.   Signed Daniel Hudson. Witness Lorans Yonts & Abraham Keener jr.   Rec. Apr. 1786. Book 3 p. 20; Book 14 p. 2

19. Feb. 3, 1786 Griffith Rutherford (Rowan Co) to Henry Rutherford, son of Griffith (same); for love and affection gave 410 ac on W side of Cuttabaw R; border: Adam Perkins, Robert Burchfield, James Holsclaw, & includes an island. Signed Griffith Rutherford. Witness John Johnston & Ad Osborn. Rec. Apr. 1786. Book 3 p. 21; Book 14 p. 3

20. Mar. 22, 1786 John Houke & wife Catharine (Lincoln Co, formerly Burke Co) to Jacob Weaver (same); for 70£ NC money sold 226 ac on E side of Jacobs fork of Cuttabaw R; border: Henry Whitner's corner; granted Oct. 11, 1783 to John Houke by "some freeman" of North Carolina.   Signed John & Catharine Houke's marks. Witness Martin Gronder [sic] & Conrod Goldman. Rec. Apr. 1786. Book 3 p. 22; Book 14 p. 5

21. Feb. 11, 1786 Philip & Elisabeth Fry, executors of Nicholas Fry desc, (Lincoln Co) to George Icard (same); for 10£ sold 240 ac in Lincoln formerly Mecklinburg Co on both sides of Hopp Cr; granted Apr. 28, 1768 to Nicholas Fry. Signed Philip Fry (german) and Elisabeth's mark. Witness George Fry, Peter Fry(? german), & Tho Whitson.   Rec. Apr. 1786. Book 3 p. 24; Book 14 p. 6

22. Feb. 11, 1786 Philip & Elisabeth Fry (Lincoln Co) to Peter Fry (same); for 10£ NC money sold 200 ac in Lincoln formerly Tryon Co on S side of Henrys fork of Cuttabaw R; granted Jul. 25, 1774 to Nicholas Fry. Signed Philip Fry (german) and Elisabeth's mark. Witness George Fry, Peter Fry(? german), & Tho Whitson. Rec. Apr. 1786. Book 3 p. 25; Book 14 p. 7

23. Feb. 11, 1786 Philip & Elisabeth Fry, executors of Nicholas Fry desc, (Lincoln Co) to Jacob Gortner (same); for 10£ NC money sold 150 ac in Lincoln formerly Tryon Co on both sides of S fork of Cuttabaw R; granted Jan. 5, 1773 to Nicholas Fry. Signed Philip Fry (german) and Elisabeth's mark. Witness George Fry, Peter Fry(? german), & Tho Whitson. Rec. Apr. 1786. Book 3 p. 26; Book 14 p. 8

24. Feb. 11, 1785 Philip & Elisabeth Fry, executors of Nicholas Fry desc, (Lincoln Co) to Martin Gortner (same); for 10£ NC money sold 240 ac in Lincoln formerly Mecklinburg Co on both sides of Hopp Cr; border: George Ichard and a conditional line; granted Apr. 25, 1767 to Nicholas Fry. Signed Philip Fry (german) and Elisabeth's mark. Witness Geroge Fry, Peter Fry (german), & Tho Whitson. Rec. Apr. 1786. Book 3 p. 27; Book 14 p. 8

25. Aug. 22, 1785 John Baldridge (Lincoln Co) on John Abernathy (same); for 5s sold [ac omitted] on S side of Leepers Cr; border: Sides and Baldridge; granted Oct. 28, 1782 to John Tucker. Signed John Baldridge. Witness John Tucker and Jos Abernathy. Rec. Apr. 1786. Book 3 p. 28; Book 14 p. 9

26. Dec. 14, 1785 Joseph Henry, sheriff (Lincoln Co) to Robert Abernathy jr (same); for 36£ sold 250 ac in Lincoln formerly Tryon Co on S side of Cattapaw R on middle fork of Killions Cr; sold due to a writ Oct. 8, 1784 from Lincoln Co court to levy on Thomas Clemons 35£ & 3£ 4s cost due to suit of Robt Abernathy jr; sale authorized by act of Assembly passed in Wilmington Oct. 25, 1764. Signed Joseph Henry. Witness James Kirkpatrick, Sarah Wilson, & Jno Wilson. Rec. Apr. 1786. Book 3 p. 29; Book 14 p. 10

27. Apr. 6,1786 Peter Johnston, executor of John Kirkconnel desc, (Lincoln Co) to John Dickson (same); for 5s sold 500 ac on both sides of Kings Cr; border: Francis Beattey on upper side; includes an old mill seat; granted Jul. 21, 1774 to Henry Wright and sold to John Kirkconnel. Signed Peter Johnston. Witness David Falls & Jno Wilson. Rec. Apr. 1786. Book 3 p. 30; Book 14 p. 11

28. Feb. 11, 1786 Philip & Elisabeth Fry (Lincoln Co) to Jacob Fry (same); for 10£ sold 228.25 ac in Lincoln formerly Mecklinburg Co on both sides of Clarks Cr; border: George Fry; part of grant Dec. 21, 1763 to John Wilkins who sold [no date] to John Clark who sold Aug. 15, 1765 to Nicholas Fry who willed it to Jacob Fry. Signed Philip Fry (german) and Elisabeth's mark. Signed George Fry, Nicholas Burns (german), & Tho Whitson. Rec. Apr. 1786. Book 3 p. 32; Book 14 p. 12

29. Feb. 1, 1786 Henry Dellinger (Lincoln Co) to Jacob Dellinger (same); for 40£ sold 185 ac; half of 370 ac grant Aug. 13, 1753 to Martin Dellinger who sold Sept. 3, 1757 to Philip Dellinger who sold May 29, 1783 to Henry Dellinger. Signed Henry Dellinger. Witness Jacob Ramsour, Henry Houke, & Joseph Henry. Rec. Apr. 1786. Book 3 p. 33; Book 14 p. 13

30. Jan. 10, 1786 Edward Hunter (Lincoln Co) to Frederik Hambright (York Co, SC); for 500£ in gold & silver sold three tracts on Long Cr and waters thereof: (1) 258 ac; border: James Wells, down Still House Br to Long Cr, & up the creek to Edwd Hunter's old line; (2) 258 ac; border: James Wells on Still House Br, Frederick Hambright's old line, & near Ferguson; & (3) 300 ac; border: Joseph Jenkins, Frederick Hambright's corner, John Rudissill, & Limeberger. Signed Edward Hunter. Witness Willis PreCoat (sic), Judith Scott Hunter, & Polina Hunter. Rec. Apr. 1786. Book 3 p. 34; Book 14 p. 14

31. Feb. 11, 1786 Philip & Elisabeth Fry (Lincoln Co) to George Fry (same); for 10£ NC money sol 228.25 ac in Lincoln formerly Mecklinburg Co on both sies of Clarks Cr; border: Philip Fry on W side of Clarks Cr; part of grant Dec. 21, 1763 to John Wilkins who sold [no date] to John Clark who sold Aug. 14, 1765 to Nicholas Fry who willed it to George Fry. Signed Philip Fry (german) and Elisabeth's mark. Witness Tho Whitson, Nicholas Burns (german), & Jacob Fry (german). Rec. Apr. 1786. Book 3 p. 36; Book 14 p. 16

32. Feb. 11, 1786 Philip and Elisabeth Fry (Lincoln Co) to Nicholas Fry (same); for 10£ NC money sold 200 ac in Lincoln formerly Tryon Co on N side of Henrys R; part of grant Jul. 21, 1774 to Nicholas Fry. Signed Philip Fry (german) and Elisabeth's mark. Witness George Fry, Peter Fry (german), & Tho Whitson. Rec. Apr. 1786. Book 3 p. 37; Book 14 p. 17

33. Sept. 6, 1786 James Henderson to William Bennett; for 35£ sold 200 ac on Juming Br of Big Long Cr; border: above his own land. Signed James Henderson. Witness Jamse(sic) Hillhouse & James Smith. Rec. Apr. 1786. Book 3 p. 38; Book 14 p. 18

34. Aug. 30, 1785 Daniel Hudson (Lincoln Co) to Lawrence Yontz (same); for 20£ sold 100 ac on both sides of Indian Cr above the Scout camps; border: Peter Myer's "third" corner and open line of a "former survey of which this is a part". Signed Daniel Hudson. Witness Abraham Keener & Peter Memv(? german). Rec. Apr. 1786. Book 3 p. 39; book 14 p. 18

35. Feb. 9, 1786 Francis Snell (Mecklinburg Co) to James Graham (Lincoln Co); for 40£ sold 150 ac on Dutchmans Cr waters of Cuttabaw R; border: "the" orphants line; granted May 24, 1773 to Leonard Webb who sold Sept. 19, 1777 to Willm Cathy who sold Mar. 22, 1780 to Francis Snell. Signed Francis Snell.

Witness George Graham & John McCall. Rec. Apr. 1786. Book 3 p. 40; Book 14 p. 19

36. Dec. 26, 1786 William Tankersly & wife Barbara (Lincoln Co) to Henry Roads (same); for 100£ sold 300 ac on or near Hoyles Cr a branch of S fork of Cuttapaw R; border: on W side of said creek a little below Saillers Br, Roads, & his other line; granted Mar. 2, 1775 to John Limeberger and went by descent to Lewis Limeberger, eldest son of John, and sold Aug. 5, 1778 by Lewis Limeberg & wife Barbara to William Tankersly.   Signed Barbara Tankersly & William's mark. Witness Jas Graham & Adam Stryue (german). Rec. Apr. 1786. Book 3 p. 41; Book 14 p. 20

37. Feb. 10, 1786 John Bullinger (Lincoln Co) to Jacob Bullinger (same); for 140£ sold [262 ac, part of 542 ac or "542 ac of two tracts 262 ac"] on Howards Cr as lower part of said land belonging to Jacob Bullinger "which division line will" show as it's to be drawn between land of Jacob Bullinger and David Bullinger. Signed Johann Bullinger (german). Witness James Nixon & Francis Bullinger (german). Rec. Apr. 1786. Book 3 p. 43; Book 14 p. 21

38. Feb. 10, 1786 John Bullinger (Lincoln Co) to David Bullinger (same); for 140£ sold [280 ac, part of 542 ac or "542 ac of two tracts 280 ac"] as upper part of said land belonging to David Bullinger which division line will show as it's drawn between David and Jacob Bullinger.   Signed Johann Bullinger (german). Witness Jo Dickson & James Johnston. Rec. Apr. 1786. Book 3 p. 44; Book 14 p. 23

39. Apr. 4, 1786 Michael Potts, farmer, & wife Catherine (Lincoln Co) to Philip Rudissell (same); for 80£ NC money sold 250 ac on E side of Clarks Cr about a mile E of Ramsour; border: a branch; granted Nov. 15, 1762 to William Welsh who sold Jul. 23 & 24, 1768 to George Shipe who empowered Henry Hollman to sell by power of atty Sept. 13, 1773 (recorded in Tryon Co Oct. term 1774), and sold May 7, 1782 by Henry Hollman to Michael Potts.   Signed Michel Botes(sic) & Cortsrnde Botzen(sic). Witness David Ramsey & Weiry Rudisell. Rec. Apr. 1786. Book 3 p. 45; Book 14 p. 24.

40. Jan. 28, 1786 James Rutledge (Lincoln Co) to Thomas McGee (same); for 35s paid by Samuel Johnston, late of this state, sold 50 ac on waters of Dutchmans Cr; border: Moses Williams' corner, said McGee's old line, & a stoney hill; part of 200 ac granted Jan. 30, 1783 to James Rutledge; land was purchased by said McGee from William Gent and by said Gent and his father Thomas Gent from Saml Johnston and said Johnston from said Rutledge.   Signed James Rutledge. Witness Samuel Rankin & Richard Santin. Rec. Apr. 1786. Book 3 p. 47; Book 14 p. 25

41. Aug. 13, 1785 Nicholas Leeper (Lincoln Co) to John Leeper (same); for 1s sterling sold 300 ac on NE side of South fork where "I" live; border: mouth of a

branch on the fork where "I" live and Alexander McLean. Signed Nicholas Leeper. Witness Joseph Henderson & Jane Howe. Rec. Apr. 1786. Book 3 p. 48; Book 14 p. 26

42. Nov. 2, 1785 George Lamkin (Lincoln Co) to Zachariah Spencer jr (same); for 30£ sold 100 ac on E side of S fork of Cuttabaw R; part of 392 ac grant to James Wyatt; includes Daniel Wyatt's improvement on said S fork.   Signed George Lamkin. Witness Vincent Wyatt & Charles Jones. Rec. Apr. 1786. Book 3 p. 49; Book 14 p. 28

43. Apr. 3, 1786 John Carpinter(sic) sr (Lincoln Co) to his son John Carpenter (same); for 10£ NC money sold 180 ac on branches of Beaverdam Cr of S fork of Cuttabaw R; border: a stoney hill, Jacob Carpinter; granted Mar. 2, 1775 to John Carpinter sr.   Signed John Carpinter's mark. Witness Jo Dickson & R Wood. Rec. Apr. 1786. Book 3 p. 50; Book 14 p. 28

44. Jul. 10, 1785 Richard Perkins, planter (Lincoln Co) to John Bordine (same); for 100£ sold 150 ac; border: Bigam Perkins on E side, William Gant on W side, down Flowers Br to Mountain Cr, & down Mountain Cr; granted Oct. 11, 1783 to Richd Perkins.   Signed Richard & Martha Perkins' marks. Witness Fras McCorkle & Filib Collingson (german).   Rec. Apr. 1786. Book 3 p. 52; Book 14 p. 30

45. Jul. 10, 1785 Richard Pirkins, planter (Lincoln Co) to Henry Loller (same); for 50£ sold 490 ac; border: Mountain Cr, Robert Bigam Pirkins, up the creek to mouth of Flowers Br, & up the branch to his own line; granted [no date] to Richard Pirkins.   Signed Richard & Martha Pirkins' marks. Witness Fras McCorkle & Filip Collingnr (german). Rec. Apr. 1786. Book 3 p. 53; Book 14 p. 31

46. Mar. 13, 1786 Joseph Henry, sheriff (Lincoln Co) to Robert Alexander esq (same); for 40£ sold 250 ac in Lincoln formerly Tryon Co on both sides of Camp Br of Indian Cr; border: Moses Moore; granted Jun. 12, 1772 to John Moore; sold due to writ Apr. 15, 1785 from Lincoln Co Pleas & Quarter Sessions Court to levy on John Moore & Jacob Shufert 112£ & 3£ 7s 7p cost due to suit of Robt Alexander esq; land is property of John Moore and sale authorized by act of Assembly Oct. 25, 1764.   Signed Joseph Henry. Witness James Johnston, James Rutledge, & Jno Wilson. Rec. Apr. 1786. Book 3 p. 54; Book 14 p. 32

47. Dec. 9, 1785 Joseph Henry, sheriff (Lincoln Co) to John Crawford (same); for 22£ sold 67 ac on W side of Cuttaba R and S side of Mountain Cr; border: the low ground and runs up the creek; part of tract sold by Abraham Collett to Henry Thomson [sic] sr who sold to Alexr Thompson and sold by Alexr & Henry sr Thompson to Henry Thompson jr who sold to Thomas Wheeler; sold due to a writ 1st Monday in Jul. 1785 from Lincoln Co court to levy 119£ 10s & 4£ 5p cost on Thomas Wheeler, Francis McCorkle, & James Fisher due to suit of John Cleveland; money to be returned to court 1st Monday Oct. "next"; land was

property of Thomas Wheeler and sale authorized by act of Assembly Oct. 25, 1764.   Signed Joseph Henry. Witness Wm Maclean(sic), Jno Wilson, & Robt Alexander. Rec. Apr. 1786. Book 3 p. 56; Book 14 p. 34

48. Feb. 14, 1786 John Martin, cooper (Lincoln Co) to James Martin, planter (same); for 100£ NC money sold 23 ac on S side of Cuttapaw R; border: Baldridge, Price, Nathan Mendinhall, Gingles, & Hill; granted Apr. 9, 1770 to John Martin "residue" covered by lines of older patents.   Signed John Martin. Witness Jno Barber & Jno Wilson. Rec. Apr. 1786. Book 3 p. 58; Book 14 p. 35

49. Feb. 10, 1786 John Finger (Lincoln Co) to Michael Potts (same); for 30£ sold (1) 100 ac on waters of Leepers Cr; border: Caun and corner of "the" old tract; granted May 20, 1772 to John Dellinger who sold Jul. 7, 1778 to John Finger; and (2) 144 ac part of another survey joining the above tract; border: point of a hill on SW side of a branch and Lick Run; part of a grant Apr. 23, 1763 to John Dellinger and sold Jul. 7, 1778 to John Finger.   Signed John Finger. Witness Robt Blackburn & William Blackburn. Rec. Apr. 1786. Book 3 p. 60; Book 14 p. 37

50. Jul. 22, 1782 Jonathan Jones, blacksmith (Burke Co) to Thomas Hoover, joiner (same); for 28£ NC money sold 40 ac in Burke Co on N side of Potts Cr; border: on Potts Cr at or near the old line; part of 400 ac granted Sept. 3, 1753 to Thomas Potts and Samuel Beason who sold to Joseph Milliken who died and willed half of land to daughter Catharine wife of said Jonathan Jones.   Signed Jonthan Jones. Witness Wm Dopens, Ja Smith (german), & _?_ Sumy (german). Rec. Apr. 1786. Book 3 p. 61; Book 14 p. 39

51. Apr. 1, 1786 Robert Alexander (Lincoln Co) to Wirely Rudissal (same); for 50£ NC money sold 93 ac on both sides of Dutchmans Cr known as Davis' mill place; part of grant May 6, 1769 to Joseph Davis desc.   Signed Robt Alexr. Witness Jo Dickson & Jno Wilson. Rec. Apr. 1786. Book 3 p. 63; Book 14 p. 40

52. Jan. 10, 1786 Moses Scott (Lincoln Co) to John Sumpter (Mecklenburg Co); for 25£ NC money sold 150 ac on waters of Cuttapaw R; border: David Philips and his own land; granted Nov. 5, 1779 to Moses Scott.   Signed Moses Scott. Witness Robt Alexander & Mary Alexander. Rec. Apr. 1786. Book 3 p. 64; Book 14 p. 41

53. Jan. 10, 1786 Moses Scott (Lincoln Co) to John Sumpter (Meclenburg Co); for 50£ NC money sold 200 ac on waters of Dutchmans Cr; includes "the" Flat rock that lies on the road to Miles Abernathy's mill; border: said Scott's corner, George Rutledge, & Hugh Jenkins; granted Nov. 4, 1779 to Moses Scott.   Signed Moses Scott. Witness Robt Alexander & Mary Alexander. Rec. Apr. 1786. Book 3 p. 65; Book 14 p. 42

54. Mar. 28, 1786 Michael Williams & wife Barbara (Lincoln Co) to Peter Mosteller (same); for 40£ NC money sold 140 ac on E side of S fork of Cuttabaw

R; border: Bickerstaff and William Wyatt. Signed Michael & Barbara Williams' marks. Witness Jo Dickson & R. Wood. Rec. Apr. 1786. Book 3 p. 66; Book 14 p. 43

55. Mar. 31, 1783 John West (state of South Carolina) to Daniel Smith (Lincoln Co); for 10s sterling sold 200 ac.   Signed John West's mark. Witness William Jenkins & Jonathan Price. Rec. Apr. 1784 (sic). Book 3 p. 67; Book 14 p. 44

56. Mar. 31, 1783 John West (96 Dist, SC) to William Jenkins (Camden Dist, SC); for 20£ sterling sold 200 ac in Lincoln Co.   Signed John West's mark. Witness Nicolus Whitsenhunt (german) & Daniel Smith.   Rec. Apr. 1786. Book 3 p. 68; Book 14 p. 55

July court 1786
57. Jun. 22, 1786 Peter Costner (Lincoln Co) to John Frunaberry (same); for 25£ NC money sold 50 ac on waters of Long Cr; part of land where Thomas Costner lives.   Signed Peter Costner's mark. Witness David Ramsey & T. V. Ray (or german). Rec. Jul. 1786. Book 3 p. 70; Book 14 p. 47

58. Jul. 2, 1786 William Fruneberry (Lincoln Co) to John Fruneberry (same); for 5£ NC money sold 64 ac on waters of Long Cr; part of land where William Fruneberry lives.   Signed William Fruneberry's mark. Witness David Ramsey & Thomas Costner. Rec. Jul. 1786. Book 3 p. 71; Book 14 p. 48

59. Sept. 3, 1786 William Sims, gent, & wife Susannah (Tryon Co) to David Jenkins, yeoman (same); for 100£ NC money sold 400 ac; border: on N side of Long Cr and crosses creek twice.   Signed William & Susannah Sims. Witness Ann Hendley Sims & Peggy Sims. Rec. Jul. 1786. Book 3 p. 72; Book 14 p. 49

60. Jan. 14, 1786 John Keeller to Christian Reignhart [sic]; for 60£ NC money sold 300 ac in Lincoln formerly Tryon Co on both sides of Hoyles Cr of S fork of Cutaba R; granted May 15, 1772 to John Keeler.   Signed John Keller & Jerusha's mark. Witness Robt Blackburn & Martin Goldman. Rec. Jul. 1786. Book 3 p. 73; Book 14 p. 50

61. Mar. 6, 1786 Christopher Walbert (Rutherford Co) to Jacob Carpinter (Lincoln Co); for 25£ sold 5 cows & 5 calves, a 2 year old heifer, a barren cow, & 4 sheep; cows branded on "off" side of rump with "CW" and marked on each ear with three "halfpennys" or marks on underside of ear; sheep marked with three marks on under side of each ear.   Signed Christopher Walbert. Witness Arthur Graham. Rec. Jul. 1786. Book 3 p. 75; Book 14 p. 52

62. Apr. 6, 1786 Christipher Walbert (Rutherford Co) to Jacob Carpinter (Lincoln Co); for 32£ sold (1) 2 horses: one is black horse about 14 hands high about 15 years old and other is sorrel "colour" 8 or 9 years old branded on near shoulder and buttock "CW"; and (2) 2 mares: one is a black mare and other is a bright bay

mare which formerly belonged to "one" Canacher; black mare is branded on near shoulder and buttock "CW" about 12 or 14 years old.   Signed Christopher Walbert. Witness Arthur Graham. Rec. Jul. 1786. Book 3 p. 75; Book 14 p. 53

63. Aug. 18, 1784 Martin Friday, farmer & wife Margaret (Lincoln Co) to Nicholas Friday (same); for 130£ NC money for 225 ac; border: James Wilson and Thomas Cohoon's old corner; land has been "transfered to several persons" the last by Amos Speace to Martin Friday.   Signed Martin Fritay and Margaret's mark. Signed Robt Blackburn & Robt McCasland. Rec. Jul. 1786. Book 3 p. 76; Book 14 p. 53

64. Jun. 26, 1786 Joseph Henry, sheriff (Lincoln Co) to George Wishenhunt (same); for 23£ sold 250 ac on both sides of Buffaloe Cr about a mile above Beattey; sold by James McEntire & wife to William Booth; sold due to writ Apr. 24, 1786 from Lincoln Co Pleas & Quarter Sessions Court to levy 20£ and 2£ 19s 3p cost from William Booth due to suit of Robert Wier; money to be returned to court first Monday of July "next" and sale authorized by act of Assembly on Oct. 25, 1764.   Signed Jos Henry. Witness R. Wood, Ad. Osborn, & Edward Hunter. Rec. Jul. 1786. Book 3 p. 77; Book 14 p. 55

65. Jun. 5, 1786 Joseph Henry, sherrif (Lincoln Co) to Robert Wier; for 180£ 1s sold 300 ac on both sides of Indian Cr; border: an old corner; part of 600 ac where Moses Moore lived granted Mar. 20, 1755 to Richard Reynolds who sold to Moses Moore who sold to Thos Robison who sold to Moses Moore; sold due to writ Apr. 24, 1786 from Lincoln Co Pleas & Quarter Sessions Court to leby 47£ 4s and 4£ 16s 9p cost from Moses Moore due to suit of Adolph Reap, admr; money to be returned to court first Monday of July "next" and sale authorized by act of Assembly on Oct. 25, 1764.   Signed Joseph Henry. Witness Wm Sharpe & Ad Osborn. Rec. Jul. 1786. Book 3 p. 79; Book 14 p. 56

66. Jul. 7, 1786 Robert Wier to Valentine Mauney; for 200£ sold 300 ac; border: an old corner on N side of Indian Cr and crosses creek; part of 600 ac where Moses Moore lately lived granted to Richd Reynolds; "note:" some "typo" type corrections made to the deed by order of court in Oct.   Signed Robert Weer. Witness Edward Hunter, Richd Singleton, & Absalom Bonham. Rec. Jul. 1786. Book 3 p. 81; Book 14 p. 58

67. Apr. 6, 1786 Jacob Horse, planter (Lincoln Co) to Adam Reep (same); for 10£ sold 70 ac on W side of S fork of Cutabaw R; border: said Horse; includes part of said Reep's improvement.   Signed Jacob Horse (german). Witness frentz(?) Horse (german). Rec. Jul. 1786. Book 3 p. 83; Book 14 p. 59

68. Mar. 20, 1786 Samuel Carpenter, planter (Rutherford Co) to Joseph Carpenter (same); for 25£ sold 300 ac on branches of Buffaloe Cr; border: a little below Collingwood.   Signed Samuel Carbender (sic). Witness Michael Eaker & Jonathan Mooney. Rec. Jul. 1786. Book 3 p. 84; Book 14 p. 60

69. Feb. 6, 1786 Peter Bumgardner, farmer (Lincoln Co) to Arthur Graham (same); for 20£ sold 150 ac on branch of Leepers Cr; border: Peter Telker (or Felker).   Signed Peter Bumgardner. Signed Jacob Bumgardner (german) & Mary Bumgardner. Rec. Jul. 1786. Book 3 p. 85; Book 14 p. 61

70. Aug. 1, 1785 Peter & Elisabeth Fry, heirs & executors of Nicholas Fry desc, (Lincoln Co) to John Fisher (same); for 18£ sold 150 ac on both sides of Frys Cr of S fork of Cuttabaw R; granted May 22, 1772 to Nicholas Fry.   Signed Philip & Elisabeth Fry. Witness Peter Iker & Abraham Moyer. Rec. Jul. 1786. Book 3 p. 86; Book 14 p. 62

71. Jun. 30, 1786 John Foreman & wife Margaret (Lincoln Co) to William Wittenburg, farmer (same); for 50£ NC money sold 161 ac on Moyers Br of Lyles Cr; border: Jacob Moyer's corner, Barnard Sigman, William Wittenburg, Henry Pope, Barnard Sigman's new entry, & George Deal; granted Oct. 28, 1782 to said John Foreman.   Signed John Foreman (german) & Margaret's mark. Witness George Smith (german) & Nathan Armitage. Rec. Jul. 1786. Book 3 p. 88; Book 14 p. 63

72. Jan. 24, 1785 Hugh Blair (Lincoln Co) to Jacob Hinkel (same); for 450£ sold two tracts on N side of Dutchmans Cr: (1) 280 ac; border: Abraham Kuykendal and James Kuykendall; and (2) [ac omitted]; border: tract 1 above and a branch; sold Dec. 17, 1781 by Moses Williams to Hugh Blair.   Signed Hugh Blair. Witness Robt Alexander, James Rutledge, & David Chirey. Rec. Jul. 1786. Book 3 p. 89; Book 14 p. 65

73. Feb. 16, 1786 Christian Reignhart to John Finger; for 66£ NC money sold 300 ac on both sides of Hoyles Cr of S fork of Cuttabaw R; granted May 15, 1772 to John Keller who sold Jan. 14, 1786 to said Christian Reignhart.   Signed Christian Renhart (german). Witness Henry Hoke & Jacob Ramsour. Rec. Jul. 1786. Book 3 p. 90; Book 14 p. 66

74. Jun. 19, 1786 Henry Whitener sr (Lincoln Co) to George Willfong (same); for 90£ NC money sold 134 ac on E side of S fork of Cuttabaw R and both sides of Finleys Br; border: said Whitener's SE corner, Martin Colter, & a ditch; part of 300 ac granted (#41). Apr. 19, 1763 to Henry Whitener.   Signed Henry Whitener. Witness Henry Whitener jr (german) & John Gross. Rec. Jul. 1786. Book 3 p. 92; Book 14 p. 67

75. Apr. 27, 1778 John Low, Lieut. in "the" Army, & wife Jane (Caswell Co) to Charles Alexander (Mecklenburg Co); for 100£ (400--lined out) NC money sold 300 ac in Tryon Co on waters of Little Long Cr of S fork of Cataba R; border: "flat piece of ground"; granted Feb. 28, 1775 to Frederick Hambright ("see Sec. book #16") surveyed by Jno Kirkonnel.   Signed John Low and Jane's mark. Witness Ephram Alexander, Archd. Murphy, & James Robison. Wit. oath Mar.

30, 1786 (Mecklenburg Co) by Jos Douglas (sic) for John Low & Archd Murphy and by Charles Alexander jr for Ephraim Alexander. Rec. Jul. 1786. Book 3 p. 93; Book 14 p. 68

76. Mar. 17, 1785 James Robinson, planter (Lincoln Co) to son David Robinson, planter (same); for love and affection "granted" 5 Negroes: a wench Limbo, a girl Luce, a boy Squash, a boy Dow, & a girl Fanny.   Signed James Robinson. Witness Joseph Steel & Danl McKisick. Rec. Jul. 1786. Book 3 p. 95; Book 14 p. 70

77. Mar. 17, 1785 James Robinson, planter (Lincoln Co) to son Jesse Robinson, planter (same); for love and affection "granted" 4 Negroes: a wench Febe, a boy Voll, a girl Patience, & a boy Jack.   Signed James Robinson. Witness Joseph Steel & Danl McKisick. Rec. Jul. 1786. Book 3 p. 95; Book 14 p. 70

78. Mar. 17, 1785 James Robinson, planter (Lincoln Co) to son John Robinson, planter (same); for love and affection "granted" 4 Negroes: a wench Jude, a boy August, [a girl] Hannah, & a boy Peter.   Signed James Robinson. Witness Joseph Steel & Danl McKisick. Rec. Jul. 1786. Book 3 p. 96; Book 14 p. 70

79. Apr. 20, 1786 Rodolph Huser (Lincoln Co) to Christian Carpinter (same); mortgage for 20£ to be paid by Apr. 20, 1792 or following is sold: (1) 124 ac on S side of Beaverdam Cr; border: Peter Eaker; (2) 150 ac joining tract where said Huson lives; (3) a horse 3 years old bay coloured & a white mare branded with swivel stirup; & (4) "my place" & tackings and all household goods.   Signed Rudolf Huser (german). Witness Michael Eake & Michael Carpenter. Rec. Jul. 1786. Book 3 p. 97; Book 14 p. 71

80. Dec. 30, 1785 John Rowland, yoeman (Rowan Co) to Jacob Ramsour (Lincoln Co); for 100£ NC money sold 200 ac in Lincoln formerly Tryon Co on Buffaloe fork of Indian Cr; border: a meadow; granted May 22, 1772 to Nicholas Welsh who sold to Jan. 20, 1779 to John Rowland.   Signed Johann Rowland (german). Witness Johann B (german) & _?_ Groff (german). Rec. Jul. 1786. Book 3 p. 97; Book 14 p. 71

81. Apr. 8, 1786 Philip Null (Lincoln Co) to Abraham Havener (same); for 40£ NC money sold 200 ac on both sides of a branch of S fork of Cuttaba R; border: Waddel.   Signed Phillip Null (german). Witness Edward Hunter & Johann Firgunrum(?) (german). Rec. Jul. 1786. Book 3 p. 99; Book 14 p. 73

82. Jan. 14, 1786 Peter Mull & wife Barbara (Lincoln Co) to John Gross (same); for 420£ sold 157.5 ac; border: Gasper Shell, George Willfong, & Martin Colter; part of 424 ac granted Apr. 28, 1768 to Peter Mull & regranted Oct. 11, 1783 to Peter Mull with addition of 76 ac.   Signed Peter Moll & Barbara's mark. Witness John Kennedy & John Willfong. Rec. Jul. 1786. Book 3 p. 100; Book 14 p. 74

83. Jun. 20, 1786 James Willson, planter (Lincoln Co) to John Boyd, planter (same); for 50£ sold 50 ac between Shady Br of Clarks Cr and heads of two branches of Allens Cr; border: Warleck, formerly Hugh Mills' corner now John Boyd, & "the" road; part of 310 ac granted Dec. 23, 1768 to James Willson. Signed James Willson. Witness Edward Hunter & Lamuel Patton. Rec. Jul. 1786. Book 3 p. 101; Book 14 p. 75

84. Feb. 7, 1785 James Huggins (Lincoln Co) to John Huggins sr (same); for 100£ sold [ac omitted] on both sides of Little Cuttabaw Cr; border: vacant land; part of 300 ac surveyed to Hugh Berry.   Signed James Huggins. Witness Robert Shannon, Samuel Knight, & William Huggins. Rec. Jul. 1786. Book 3 p. 102; Book 14 p. 76

85. Oct. 8, 1785 John Landdes, weaver (Lincoln Co) to Francis McNamir, blacksmith (same); for 86£ NC money sold 200 ac on S side of Indian Cr; border: Thomas Welsh.   Signed John Landes & Suzzanna's mark. Witness Forney Green Norman & Thomas Norman jr. Rec. Jul. 1786. Book 3 p. 103; Book 14 p. 77

October Court [1786]
86. Oct. 5, 1786 John McGaughy & wife Mary to Robert Wier; for 70£ sold a Negro boy Harry about 4 years old.   Signed John McGaughey & Mary's mark. Signed Edward Hunter, Jacob Ramsour, & Henry _?_ (german). Rec. Oct. 1786. Book 3 p. 105; Book 14 p. 78

87. Feb. 10, 1786 William McMullin, taylor (Burke Co) to John Bradbourn esq (same); for 50£ NC money sold 640 ac on both sides of forks of roads from Limestone Hills to Hill's iron works & to Charleston and from head of Cuttaba R to Sherrill's ford & to Salisburry; border: Horse ford Cr.   Signed William McMullen & Marthew's mark. Witness William Graham & John Carruth. Rec. Oct. 1786. Book 3 p. 105; Book 14 p. 78

88. Oct. 20, 1772 David Jenkins (Tryon Co) to William Cowan (Rowan Co); for 90£ sold 400 ac; border: on N side of Long Cr and crosses creek twice.   Signed David Jenkins. Witness Ben Cowan & Isaac Cowan. Wit. oath Jul. 21, 1786 (Rowan Co) by Isaac Cowan. Rec. Oct. 1786. Book 3 p. 106; Book 14 p. 80
89. Sept. 19, 1786 Henry Sudduth (Lincoln Co) to sond Elijah Sudduth; for love and affection gave 3 feather beds & furniture which are now in my house, 5 pewter dishes, 8 pewter plates, a bay horse, bridle & saddle, a Roan mare & horse colt, 2 cows & calves, an iron pot about 3 gallons, a frying pan, an iron skillett, 3 pewter basons, 2 ladles, 2 flesh forks, 2 pair of pot hooks, 2 chests, half dozen knives, 6 forks, 4 plates "Delfware", 6 pewter spoons, 2 stone cutter pots, & a looking glass.Signed   Henry Sudduth. Witness George Lamkin & Petter Rhyne. Rec. Oct. 1786. Book 3 p. 108; Book 14 p. 81

90. Oct. 6, 1786 Stephen Senter (Lincoln Co) to John Peter Baker (Chester Co, SC); for 30£ sold 100 ac on heads of Wiats Branches of S fork of Cuttaba R and

on N side of S fork; border: McKnitt's corner & "said" Wiatt; granted Nov. 10, 1784 to Daniel Wyatt.   Signed Stephen Senter. Witness Ruben Wood & Jo Dickson. Rec. Oct. 1786. Book 3 p. 109; Book 14 p. 81

91. Jul. 1, 1786 Michael Hoyle (Lincoln Co) to Philip Rine (same); for 100£ NC money sold 300 ac on both sides of Little Long Cr including "the" shoal; border: Peter Laboon.   Signed Mihel Hoyel (german). Witness Stephen Senter & John Fulenwider. Rec. Oct. 1786. Book 3 p. 109; Book 14 p. 82

92. Jul. 20, 1786 Henry Hollman & wife Elisabeth (Lincoln Co) to Jacob Sherrill (same); for 37£ NC money sold 37 ac on S side of Cuttabaw R on upper end of "plantation" where said Sherril lives and being lower end of land where said Hollman lives; border: Sherrill's upper corner, mouth of a branch, & Hollman. Signed Henry Hollman & Elisabeth's mark. Witness Nathan Armitage & Elisabeth Jameson. Rec. Oct. 1786. Book 3 p. 111; Book 14 p. 83

93. Sept. 18, 1786 John Hogan (Orange Co) to Charles McLain; for 50£ sold [ac omitted]; includes Cogdell's cabbin; border: Newman's old corner now Ferguson's.   Signed John Hogan. Witness Ad Osborn jr. Rec. Oct. 1786. Book 3 p. 112; Book 14 p. 85

94. Sept. 18, 1786 John Hogan (Orange Co) to John Oats; for 50£ sold [ac omitted]; border: Samuel Barnett.   Signed John Hogan. Witness Ad Osborn jr. Rec. Oct. 1786. Book 3 p. 114; Book 14 p. 86

95. Sept. 25, 1786 Jesse Johnston (Wilks Co, Ga) to Thomas Thomas (Lincoln Co); for 40£ sold 100 ac on S side of S fork of Cuttaba R; border: James Baird, includes Armstrong's ford on said river, & Armstrong; granted Oct. 13, 1783 to said Johnston.   Signed Jesse Johnson (sic). Witness William Ryndles & Jonn Gullick. Rec. Oct. 1786. Book 3 p. 115; Book 14 p. 87

96. Aug. 12, 1785 John Lawrence (Rowan Co) to Elisabeth Hegar (Lincoln Co); for 125£ sold a Negro wench Lid and child Jow 3 months old.   Signed Jno Lowrance (sic). Witness Wm Graham & Robt Lucky. Rec. Oct. 1786. Book 3 p. 116; Book 14 p. 88

97. Sept. 2, 1786 Thomas White (Lincoln Co) to John Woods; for 170 [blank] sold (1) 286 ac on waters of and in fork of Long Cr on W side of Cuttaba R; border: on W side of "South fork waggon road" near Adam Meek's corner and Thomas Welsh's line; granted Oct. 18, 1765 to Moses Ferguson who sold Oct. 13 (or 16), 1777 to John McMichael who sold Jun. 25, 1778 to John White who sold to Thomas White; and (2) 200 ac on head of Utleys Br of Long Cr; border: James White; granted Nov. 10, 1784 to Thomas White.   Signed Thomas White. Witness Benjamin Ormand & Jonn Gullick. Rec. Oct. 1786. Book 3 p. 117; Book 14 p. 88

Lincoln County, NC Deed book 3

98. Aug. 24, 1786 George Ewing, planter (Lincoln Co) to Hugh Ewing, planter (same); for 50£ sold 119 ac in forks of Cuttabaw R; branted to James Carter and taken by writ against James Carter by John Brandon in Feb. term in 32nd year of King George II reign [1758] at Supreme Court at Wilmington (for counties of New Hanover, Bladen, Onslow, Duplin, & Cumberland); writ was executed by John Hamar, sheriff to John Brandon who sold Jan. 6 & 7, 1763 to Thomas McKnight.   Signed George Ewing. Witness Joseph Henry & Andrew Barry. Rec. Oct. 1786. Book 3 p. 119; Book 14 p. 89

99. Oct. 26, 1779 John Hoyle (Lincoln Co) to Martin Hoyle (same); for 100£ NC money sold 20 ac on N side of S fork of Cuttabaw R; border: his father's old line; part of grant Apr. 6, 1765 to said John Hoyle.   Signed John Heyel. Witness Jonathan Gullick & Mihel Heyel (german). Rec. Oct. 1786. Book 3 p. 120; Book 14 p. 90

100. Dec. 26, 1785 Samuel Hollensworth (Lincoln Co) to Henry Moss (same); for 15£ NC money sold 50 ac on both sides of a branch of Mountain Cr; border: John Sneider's corner; part of grant to Samuel Hollensworth and where said Hollensworth lives.   Signed Samuel Hollensworth's mark. Witness Patrick Bryan & William Earwood. Rec. Oct. 1786. Book 3 p. 122; Book 14 p. 91

101. Jul. 7, 1786 John Harris (Lincoln Co) to Conrod Stotler (same); for 50£ sold 300 ac on waters of Indian Cr; border: Adam Wisenhunt, "his" new tract, & Howard; granted Nov. 20, 1771 to Philip Wisenhunt who sold to John Harris. Signed John Harris. Witness David Ramsey & O_?_ (german). Rec. Oct. 1786. Book 3 p. 123; Book 14 p. 92

102. Mar. 23, 1786 John Rudisell (Lincoln Co) to John Godfrey Arends (same); for 4£ NC money sold 10 ac on Leepers Cr; part of tract belonging to John Rudisell.   Signed John Rudisel. Signed Mehel Rudesil (german) & Henry Rudisealy (sic). Rec. Oct. 1786. Book 3 p. 124; Book 24 p. 93

103. Feb. 18, 1786 John Sloan (Lincoln Co) to John Woods (same); for 50£ NC money sold 200 ac on waters of Muddy fork of Buffaloe & Long Creks; border: land James Taylor lived on and George Trout; includes Warrick Woodard's improvements.   Signed John Sloan. Witness Robt Ligget & James Kirkpatrick. Rec. Oct. 1786. Book 3 p. 125; Book 14 p. 94

104. Sept. 26, 1786 John Moore (Lincoln Co) to William Moore (same); for 200£ NC money sold 250 ac on Deuharts Cr; border: Nathl Henderson and Davis; granted Nov. 9, 1764 to John McKnitt Alexander.   Signed John Moore. Witness John Moore sr & John Drohs(?). Rec. Oct. 1786. Book 3 p. 126; Book 14 p. 95

105. Feb. 7, 1785 John Winkler (Burke Co) to Philip Whitener (Lincoln Co); for 20£ sold 200 ac in Lincoln formerly Burke Co on both sides of Jacobs fork on S fork of Catawba R; includes mouth of Mountain Cr.   Signed Jan Wnker

(german). Witness Alex Erwin & William Bowman. Rec. Oct. 1786. Book 3 p. 127; Book 14 p. 96

106. Sept. 18, 1786 James Lockhart & wife Ann (Lincoln Co) to Andrew Wilson (same); for 100£ NC money sold 200 ac on both sides of Bets Br of Clarks Cr; part of a large grant Apr. 19, 1763 to William Welsh and by deed of gift Jul. 13, 1765 to Ann Mills now wife of James Lockhart; being middle lot of three "divisions" of said old survey.   Signed James Lockhart & Ann's mark. Witness Robt Blackburn & Martha Blackburn. Rec. Oct. 1786. Book 3 p. 129; Book 14 p. 97

107. Jul. 16, 1786 Joseph Dickson esq, proprietor in trust for commissioners appointed to lay off Lincolnton, (Lincoln Co) to Henry Dellinger (same); for 40s sold [ac omitted] lot No. 2 in SW of Lincolnton; lot is 6 by 12 rods.   Signed Jo Dickson. Witness Waightstile (sic) Avery, Edward Hunter, & Jos Henry. Rec. Oct. 1786. Book 3 p. 130; Book 14 p. 99

108. Jul. 8, 1786 Joseph Dickson, proprietor in trust for commissioners appointed to lay off Lincolnton, (Lincoln Co) to Margaret Bonham (same); for 40s sold [ac omitted] lot 14 in SE of Lincolnton; lot is 6 by 14 rods.   Signed Jo Dickson. Witness Jos Henry & Edward Hunter. Rec. Oct. 1786. Book 3 p. 131; Bok 14 p. 100

109. Oct. 4, 1786 Joseph Dickson esq, proprietor in trust for commissioners appointed to lay off Lincolnton, (Lincoln Co) to John Boyd (same); for 40s sold [ac omitted] lot 5 in SW of Lincolnton; lot is 6 by 12 rods.   Signed Jo Dickson. Witness Wm Sharpe, Wm Johnson, & Jos Henry. Rec. Oct. 1786. Book 3 p. 132; Book 14 p. 101

110. Jul. 8, 1786 Joseph Dickson esq, proprietor in trust for commissioners appointed to lay off Lincolnton, (Lincoln Co) to Joseph Henry (same); for 40s sold [ac omitted] lot 16 in NW of Lincolnton; lot is 6 by 14 rods.   Signed Jo Dickson. Witness Waightstile Avery & Edward Hunter. Rec. Oct. 1786. Book 3 p. 133; Book 14 p. 101

111. Jul. 13, 1786 Joseph Dickson esq, proprietor in trust for commissioners appointed to lay off Lincolnton, (Lincoln Co) to Joseph Henry esq (same); for 40s sold [ac omitted] lot 6 in NE of Lincolnton; lot is 6 by 12 rods.   Signed Jo Dickson. Witness Waightstile Avery & Edward Hunter. Rec. Oct. 1786. Book 3 p. 134; Book 14 p. 102

112. Jul. 23, 1786 Joseph Dickson esq, proprietor in trust for commissioners appointed to lay off Lincolnton, (Lincoln Co) to Daniel McKissick esq (same); for 40s sold [ac omitted] lot 15 in SE of Lincolnton; lot is 6 by 14 rods.   Signed Jo Dickson. Witness Wrightstile Avery & Reuben Wood. Rec. Oct. 1786. Book 3 p. 135; Book 14 p. 103

113. Jul. 20, 1786 Joseph Dickson esq, proprietor in trust for commissioners appointed to lay off Lincolnton, (Lincoln Co) to Absalom Bonaham (Burke Co); for 40s sold [ac omitted] lot 13 in SE of Lincolnton; lot is 6 by 14 rods.   Signed Jo Dickson. Witness Jos Henry & Edward Hunter. Rec. Oct. 1786. Book 3 p. 136; Book 14 p. 104

114. Oct. 5, 1786 Philip Null & wife Margaret (Lincoln Co) to Henry Cline (same); for 17£ sold [ac omitted] lot 2 in NE of Lincolnton; lot is 6 by 12 rods. Signed Philip Null & Margaret's mark. Witness John Dellinger & Jo Kennedy. Rec. Oct. 1786. Book 3 p. 137; Book 14 p. 105

115. Oct. 4, 1786 Phillip Null & wife Margaret (Lincoln Co) to John McGaughy (same); for 180£ sold [ac omitted] lot 1 in NE of Lincolnton; lot is 6 by 12 rods. Signed Philip Null and Margaret. Signed Saml Givens & Fors Cunningham. Rec. Oct. 1786. Book 3 p. 138; Book 14 p. 106

January Court 1787
116. Jan. 2, 1787 William Armstrong to William Smith; for 40£ NC money sold 250 ac on Uleys Br of S fork of Cuttabaw R; border: John Dudderoe and Hambright.   Signed William Armstrong. Witness Henrich Bellinger(?) (german), Jacob Huley(?) (german), Mehel Fry (german), & Jos Henry. Rec. Jan. 1787. Book 3 p. 139; Book 14 p. 107

117. Oct. 9, 1786 John Dellinger (Lincoln Co) to Samuel Givens (same); for 500£ sold 200 ac in Lincoln formerly Tryon Co on both sides of Indian Cr; border: John Alexander; includes "the" shoal and mill seat.   Signed John Dellinger. Witness Jo Dickson, Jos Henry, & Richard Johnalany. Rec. Jan. 1787. Book 3 p. 140; Book 14 p. 108

118. Mar. 13, 1786 Robert Burchfield, heir at law of Robert Burchfield sr who died intestate, (Burke Co) to William Allen (Lincoln Co); for 5s NC money and purchased of Robert Burchfield desc during his lifetime sold 290 ac on Isaacs Cr waters of Cuttaba R; border: near John Olivan's Road & "his" own former survey; grante Mar. 15, 1789 to Robert Burchfield desc.   Signed Robert Burchfield. Witness Thomas Little & B. Strother. Rec. Jan. 1787. Book 3 p. 141; Book 14 p. 109

119. Dec. 4, 1786 Jacob Seits (Lincoln Co) to John Edleman (or Eddleman) (same); for 5s sold 156 ac on both sides of Leepers Cr; border: Gerard Wills. Signed Jacob Seids (sic). Witness Jos Abernathy. Rec. Jan. 1787. Book 3 p. 142; Book 14 p. 110

120. Jul. 28, 1786 John Gross, miller (Lincoln Co) to Philip Rudysail (same); for 150£ NC money sold 163.75 ac; border: David Ramsaur, Baker, & Summerow; part of "a larger tract" granted to Thomas Welsh and "transfered to sunday

persons".   Signed John Gross's mark. Witness Martin Coulter & John Kennedy. Rec. Jan. 1787. Book 3 p. 143; Book 14 p. 111

121. Dec. 13, 1786 George Wilfong and Peter Moll, planter (Lincoln Co) to Casper Shell, farmer (same); for 89£ NC money sold 200 ac on N side of S fork of Cuttabaw R; border: Henry Whitener, Fisher, & a stoney hill; granted Oct. 26, 1767 to Geo Seits who sold Jan. 28, 1772 for 60£ to George Wilfong & Peter Moll.   Signed George Wilfong's mark & Peter Moll. Witness Christoph Ryder & John Wilfong. Rec. Jan. 1787. Book 3 p. 145; Book 14 p. 112

122. Dec. 2, 1786 William Sherrill & wife Agnes (Lincoln Co) to Jacob Sherril (same); for 350£ NC money sold 130 ac on S side of Cuttawba R; border: land formerly belonging to William Sherril jr; being lower most end of tract "taken up" by said William Sherrill, see deed dated Jan. 7, 1764 in Rowan Co Book 4 p. 579. Signed William & Agnes Sherrill's marks. Witness Joshua Sherrill & Adam Sherrill. Rec. Jan. 1787. Book 3 p. 147; Book 14 p. 114

123. Dec. 11, 1786 Joseph Henry, sheriff (Lincoln Co) to John Abernathy (same); for 25£ sold 600 ac on S side of Cuttawba R in Heslep's "bent"; border: James Freeman, Saml McCombs, "his" own land, William Bracher, & Vincent Cox; granted Oct. 9, 1783 to Baptist Scott; sold due to writ Jul. 12, 1784 from Mecklenburg Co Pleas & Quarter Sessions Court to levy 41£ 10s 2p and 3£ 11s 5p cost from Baptist Scott due to suit of William Alston; money to be returned to court 2nd Monday of Oct. "next" and sale authorized by act of Assembly on Oct. 25, 1764 at Wilmington.   Signed Jos Henry. Witness James Johnston & Robt Abernathy. Rec. Jan. 1787. Book 3 p. 148; Book 14 p. 115

124. Nov. 11, 1786 Joseph Henry, sheriff (Lincoln Co) to Alexander Gilliland (same); for 50£ sold 502 ac in two tracts on branch of Crowders Cr: (1) 202 ac border: Coborn & a new line, and (2) 300 ac border: Walker's corner & Coborn; each was granted and then conveyed "several" times until they were the property of Robt Parks; sold due to writ Jul. 24, 1786 from Lincoln Co Pleas & Quarter Sessions Court to levy 14£ 2s 3p and 2£ 14s 3p cost from Robert Parks (late of Lincoln Co) due to suit of James Baird, executor of John Baird; money to be returned 1st Monday of Oct. "next" and sale authorized by act of Assembly on Oct. 25, 1764 at Wilmington.   Signed Jos Henry. Witness Sarah Wilson, Mary Wilson, & Jno Wilson. Rec. Jan. 1787. Book 3 p. 151; Book 14 p. 117

125. Nov. 23, 1786 John & Mary McGaughey to William McCasland; for 120£ sold a Negro boy Tom about 11 years old.   Signed John & Mary McGaughey's marks. Witness Jo Kennedy & Nicholas Detter. Rec. Jan. 1787. Book 3 p. 153; Book 14 p. 119

126. May 24, 1778 John West (Tryon Co) to Samuel Kuykendall (or Cirkendol) (same); for 30£ sold 63 ac on W side of Cuttapaw R on Kuykendalls Cr; border:

William Moore, Bell, Kuykendall, & a hill.   Signed John West's mark. Witness Sarah Kuykendall & John Boyd. Rec. Jan. 1787. Book 3 p. 153; Book 14 p. 119

127. Dec. 12, 1786 Joseph Henry, sheriff (Lincoln Co) to John Cline jr (same); for 22£ NC money sold 144 ac on a branch of Clarks Cr; border: John Hannan's NE corner, Richd West, John Bennfield, & Saml Steel; sold due to writ Oct. 12, 1786 from Lincoln Co Pleas & Quarter Sessions Court to levy 17£ 11s 9p and 2£ 18s 7p cost from Christopher Cline due to suit of John Bennfield; sale authorized by act of Assembly on Oct. 25, 1764 at Wilmington.   Signed Jos Henry. Witness Joseph Steel, Simon Jonas, & Johann _?_ (german). Rec. Jan. 1787. Book 3 p. 154; Book 14 p. 120

128. Apr. 5, 1785 George Lamkin (Lincoln Co) to Robert Johnson (same); for 50£ sold 150 ac on branches and both sides of Keeners Cr; border: Johnston's N line; granted Nov. 1, 1784 to George Lamkin.   Signed Georg Lamkin. Witness James Henderson & Jas White. Rec. Jan. 1787. Book 3 p. 156; Book 14 p. 121

129. Jul. 10, 1786 Joseph Dickson esq, proprietor in trust for commissioners appointed to lay off Lincolnton, (Lincoln Co) to Joseph Henry esq (same); for 40s sold [ac omitted] lot 8 in SW of Lincolnton; lot is 6 by 12 rods.   Signed Jo Dickson. Witness James Moore & James Reid. Rec. Jan. 1787. Book 3 p. 157; Book 14 p. 122

130. May 20, 1785 Philip Bollinger & wife Elisabeth (Lincoln Co) to John Smyer (same); for 75£ NC money sold 300 ac on waters of Potts Cr; border: Jno Bradley's upper line, "his" corner, & runs down creek; granted Apr. 8, 1768 to Wm Reed who sold Aug. 13, 1784 to John Hiltebrand who sold Mar. 25, 1785 to Philip Bollinger.   Signed Filib Bollinger (german) & Elisabeth's mark. Witness Rudolph Conrad & Lorance Markle. Rec. Jan. 1787. Book 3 p. 158; Book 14 p. 123

131. Jan. 3, 1787 Joseph Dickson esq, proprietor in trust for commissioners appointed to lay off Lincolnton, (Lincoln Co) to John Hussenberry (blank county); for 6£ 1s sold [ac omitted] lot 6 in NW square of Lincolnton; lot is 6 by 12 rods. Signed Jo Dickson. Witness Jos Henry & James Moore. Rec. Jan. 1787. Book 3 p. 159; Book 14 p. 124

132. Oct. 9, 1786 Thomas Osborn (Abbevilla Co, SC) to Mary Hill (Lincoln Co); for 10£ NC money sold 25 ac; part of 100 ac grant to Thomas Osborn.   Signed Thomas Osborn's mark. Witness William Grant, John Michl Jollerton, & James Crowther. Rec. Jan. 1787. Book 3 p. 160; Book 14 p. 125

133. Dec. 15, 1786 Peter Clobb sr (Lincoln Co) to Peter Clobb jr (same); for 5s sold (1) 315 ac on both sides of Leepers Cr; border: a stoney hill; and (2) 100 ac on branches of Leepers Cr; border: Abernathy.   Signed Peter Clobb's mark.

Witness George Clobb & David Abernathy. Rec. Jan. 1787. Book 3 p. 162; Book 14 p. 125

134. Nov. 10, 1782 John Lowrance & Abraham Lowrance, exects of will of John Lowrance desc, (Rowan Co) to Andrew McCormick (Burke Co); for 1,510£ sold 300 ac in Burke Co on both sides of Liles Cr and both sides of N & S fork of said creek; border: Peter Lorance, Richard Lewis, & Ute Sherrill; granted Aug. 28, 1762 by Earl Granville to Joseph Lowrance.   Signed John & Abraham Lowrance. Witness David Crawford & Jacob Lorance. Rec. Jan. 1787. Book 3 p. 163; Book 14 p. 126

135. Mar. 6, 1786 John Walker (Lincoln Co) to Valentine Devalt (same); for 85£ sold (1) 175 (or 130) ac on waters of Dutchmans Cr; border: on E bank of creek and runs down creek; part of 154 ac grant May 5, 1769 to George Rutledge; and (2) 45 ac on E side of Dutchmans Cr near mouth of said Walker's Spring Br; border: Stophel Lifler; part of two grants: (a) 75 ac Jan. 25, 1773 to James Rutledge and (b) 100 ac Nov. 1, 1784 to James Rutledge.   Signed John Walker's mark. Witness James Rutledge and Johann Will (german). Rec. Jan. 1787. Book 3 p. 165; Book 14 p. 128

136. Sept. 23, 1786 John Fish sr (Lincoln Co) to John Moreland Bridges (same); for 30£ NC money sold 320 ac on Turkey fork of Bawls Cr about a mile above John Bridges; border: William Fish's "beginning" corner and a conditional line; part of 640 ac granted Apr. 6, 1765 to William Fawls who sold to Joseph Mercy who sold to John Fish sr.   Signed John Fish. Witness William Grant, John Ghent, & Cader Gant. Rec. Jan. 1787. Book 3 p. 166; Book 14 p. 129

137. (blank), 1776 William Berry & wife Elisbabeth (Tryon Co) to John Berry (same); for 10£ sold (blank) ac on a branch of Little Cuttabaw Cr; granted Apr. 25, 1767 to William Berry.   Signed Wm Berry & Elisabeth's mark. Witness John Brison, Robrt Martin, & John Gullick. Rec. Jan. 1787. Book 3 p. 168; Book 14 p. 130

138. (blank), 1776 William Berry & wife Elisabeth (Tryon Co) to Robert Berry (same); for 20£ sold 200 ac on waters of Mill Cr; border: Thomas Campbell, James Lewis, & Benjamin Davidson; granted Nov. 14, 1771 to William Berry. Signed Wm Berry & Elisabeth's mark. Witness John Brison, Robert Martin, & John Gullick. Rec. Jan. 1787. Book 3 p. 169; Book 14 p. 131

139. Dec. 16, 1786 William Sherrill (Lincoln Co) to sons Elisha & Moses Sherrill (same); for love & affection gave "my plantation" where I live after decease of wife Agnes and gave Elisha a Negro man Jack; remainder of estate, household "stuff", & furniture to beloved wife Agnes "all of which I give my two sons & wife" (sic).   Signed William Sherrill's mark. Witness Moses Sherrill & Nicholas Sherrill. Rec. Jan. 1787. Book 3 p. 171; Book 14 p. 132

140. Jan. 6, 1783 James Lewis (Campden Dist, SC) to John Lewis (Lincoln Co); for 500£ sold 279 ac on Mill Cr of Cuttapaw R; part of grant Apr. 7, 1752 to said James Lewis.   Signed Jas Lewis. Witness Andrew Sprott, William Robinson, & Jonn Gullick. Rec. Jan. 1787. Book 3 p. 171; Book 14 p. 138

141. Jul. 19, 1786 Joseph Dickson esq proprietor in trust for commissioners appointed to lay off Lincolnton, (Lincoln Co) to Joseph Henry (same); for 40s sold [ac omitted] lot 9 in SW of Lincolnton; lot is 6 by 12 rods.   Signed Jo Dickson. Witness James Moore & James Reid. Rec. Jan. 1787. Book 3 p. 173; Book 14 p. 134

142. Oct. 6, 1786 Joseph Dickson esq proprietor in trust for commissioners appointed to lay off Lincolnton, (Lincoln Co) to Andrew Hedricks (same); for 40s sold [ac omitted] lot 4 in SW of Lincolnton; lot is 6 by 12 rods.   Signed Jo Dickson. Witness Ad Osborn & Joseph Steel. Rec. Jan. 1787. Book 3 p. 174; Book 14 p. 135

143. Jan. 2, 1787 Michael Rudisail (Lincoln Co) to Philip Rudisail (same); for 10£ sold 200 ac on both sides of Long Cr waters of S fork of Cuttabaw R; border: Frederick Hambright; half of 400 ac granted Mar. 27, 1755 to William Adair. Signed Mihel Rudisile (german). Witness David Ramsey & Mihel Heyel (german). Rec. Jan. 1787. Book 3 p. 175; Book 14 p. 135

144. Aug. 21, 1786 James Henderson (Lincoln Co) to John Patterson (same); for 100£ sold (1) 200 ac on S side of S fork of Cuttabaw R; border: a branch and a new line; granted Apr. 25, 1767 to William Glen who sold Mar. 27, 1774 to James Henderson; and (2) 42 ac on W side of S fork of Cuttapaw R; part of grant Nov. 16, 1764 to Thomas McKnight.   Signed James Henderson. Witness Peter Fite & Lawson Henderson. Rec. Jan. 1787. Book 3 p. 176; Book 14 p. 136

145. Aug. 24, 1785 Robert Carruth (Lincoln Co) to John Huggins sr (same); for 50£ sold 100 ac on branch of Little Cuttabaw Cr; border: Barry.   Signed Robert Carruth. Witness William Huggins. Rec. Jan. 1787. Book 3 p. 178; Book 14 p. 137

146. Jul. 18, 1786 Nathaniel & Sarah Smith to John Reed; for 65£ NC money sold 150 ac on S side of Cuttabaw R and both sides of Horseford Cr; border: a fishing place; granted Oct. 28, 1782 to Nathaniel Smith.   Signed Nathaniel & Sarah Smith's marks. Witness John Kirkland & Jesse Hooper. Rec. Jan. 1787. Book 3 p. 179; Book 14 p. 138

147. Nov. 23, 1786 Jean (or Jain) Rutledge (Lincoln Co) to William Davenport (same); for 70£ NC money sold 200 ac on Leepers Cr "otherwise" Dutchmans Cr; granted Apr. 25, 1767 to Robert Walter who sold Apr. 18, 1768 to George Rutledge who willed it to son John Rutledge who sold Oct. 27, 1783 to Jain Rutledge; border: Andrew Hampton, old survey, & Heager.   Signed Jean

Rutledge's mark. Witness Thos Thomas, Geo Devenport, & William Patterson. Rec. Jan. 1787. Book 3 p. 180; Book 14 p. 140

April Court 1787
148. Feb. 27, 1787 Samuel Kuykendall (Lincoln Co) to Wirey Rudisale (same); for 50£ sold 340 ac on Beaverdam Cr on S side of Cuttapaw R; border: "beginning" corner of John Taylor's place granted to Saml Cobarn, Scott's line, Gleghorn, Davis, & mouth of Beaverdam Cr; part of three grants. Signed Saml Kuykendal. Witness Jo Dickson & Robt Alexander. Rec. Apr. 1787. Book 3 p. 182; Book 14 p. 141

149. Apr. 3, 1787 John Stamey (or Stemy) certifys it is false that Conrod Hiltebrant gave him money to seduce his wife and a story was "propogated" by John Stamey through "spite & malice". Signed John Stamey. Witness Robert Blackburn. Rec. Apr. 1787. Book 3 p. 183; Book 14 p. 142

150. Apr. 2, 1787 Peter Mull esq (Burke Co) to Jacob Yount (same); for 100£ NC money sold 87 ac on N side of Henrys fork of S fork of Cuttabaw R; border: Richard Johnston, old survey, a ridge, & John Shell's two surveys; part of 500 ac grant by state of NC to John Butt who sold Dec. 10, 1778 (#37--sic) to Peter Mull. Signed Peter Moll (sic). Witness John Shell & Peter Peterson. Rec. Apr. 1787. Book 3 p. 183; Book 14 p. 142

151. Aug. 1, 1786 Sarah Kuykendall (Wilks Co, Ga) to Samuel Kuykendall (Lincoln Co); for 200£ sold 340 ac on Beaverdam Cr on S side of Cuttabaw R; border: "beging" corner of John Taylor's place granted to Samuel Coborn, Scott's corner, Gleghorn, Davis, & mouth of Beaverdam Cr; part of three grants. Signed Sarah Kuykendall's mark. Witness Benjamin Newton & Thos Buchannan. Rec. Apr. 1787. Book 3 p. 185; Book 14 p. 143

152. Oct. 26, 1786 Nathaniel Porter (Lincoln Co) to James Alexander (same); for 60£ sold 92 ac on S side of Cutaba R; border: Cunningham, Beaty, Cathy, Barnet, & Hambright's old line; granted Oct. 30, 1765 to Roger Cook. Signed Natt Porter. Witness Robert Johnson. Rec. Apr. 1787. Book 3 p. 186; Book 14 p. 144

153. Mar. 28, 1787 John Bowers (Lincoln Co) to Jacob Forney (same); for 5s sold 300 ac on branch of Leepers Cr; border: Miller, Snider, & Bumgarner. Signed John Bowers' mark. Witness Jas Abernathy & Miles Abernathy. Rec. Apr. 1787. Book 3 p. 187; Book 14 p. 145

154. Mar. 24, 1787 Valentine Mauny & wife Caterine (Lincoln Co) to John Perry (same); for 270£ in gold & silver sold 370 ac on N side of Indian Cr on S branch of S fork of Cuttabaw R; border: Joseph Cloud desc; 170 ac was granted to & sold by John Moore desc to Jeremiah Potts who sold to "said" Moses Moore who sold to Valentine Mauny; 200 ac was granted Apr. 10, 1761 to Moses Moore. Signed

Vallentine Mauny & Caterine's mark. Witness _?_ (german) & Henry Landis. Rec. Apr. 1787. Book 3 p. 188; Book 14 p. 146

155. Oct. 23, 1786 Frederick Leinberger (Lincoln Co) to James Rutledge (same); for 100£ sold 300 ac on waters of Hoyls Cr of S fork of Cuttabaw r; border: Alexander & John Moore, David Abernathy, on S side of "the" road from Alexander Moore's to Thomas Rines, & Lewis Leinberger desc's 400 ac grant; part of 400 ac grant Nov. 1, 1784 to Lewis Leinberger desc.   Signed Fredriek Loeineberger. Witness John Carruth & James Dickson. Rec. Apr. 1787. Book 3 p. 190; Book 14 p. 148

156. Mar. 31, 1787 John Firtress (Lincoln Co) to Abraham Beackor (same); for 100£ NC money sold 120 ac on waters of Hayarts Cr; border: old "beginning" corner of said tract and a division; part of grant Mar. 28, 1755 to Thomas Potts. Signed Johann_?_ (german) & Catren Firtress' mark. Witness Philip Null & David Ramsey. Rec. Apr. 1787. Book 3 p. 191; Book 14 p. 149

157. Jan. 13, 1787 John Gross, planter (Lincoln Co) to Philip Rudissail, farmer (same); for 190£ NC money on 125 ac; border: John Gross, Christian Gross, Grisemore, Summerow, & Welsh's old line; part of grant Apr. 10, 1761 to Thomas Welsh who sold Aug. 10, 1773 to Henry Gross who sold May 17, 1776 to John Gross.   Signed John Groce's mark. Witness John Kennedy. Rec. Apr. 1787. Book 3 p. 192; Book 14 p. 150

158. Aug. 30, 1777 Michael (or Mehail) Keller (Tryon Co) to Christefor Arney (same); for 52£ sold 150 ac on N side of S fork of Cuttabaw R; border: Ramsour's survey; part of grant May 4, 1769 to Andrew Heddick.   Signed Michael Celler & Katren's mark. Witness David Ramsey & Henrih Bullinger (german). Rec. Apr. 1787. Book 3 p. 194; Book 14 p. 152

159. Feb. 6, 1787 Ebenezer Newton & wife Elisabeth (Lincoln Co) to Thomas Ryne (same); for 125£ sold 125 ac 2 roods & 20 poles; border: William Sterrett; part of grant Aug. 7, 1777 by William Sterrat (sic) to Ebenezer Newton on McNabbs Br "falling into" Cuttabaw R a little below Tukasegy ford.   Signed Ebenezer Newton & Elisabeth's mark. Witness Jo Dickson & Benjamin Newton. Rec. Apr. 1787. Book 3 p. 195; Book 14 p. 153

160. Feb. 17, 1787 Joseph Henry, sheriff (Lincoln Co) to Henry Dellinger (same); for 50£ sold 300 ac on both sides of Buffalow Cr of Broad R; between Francis Beattey's lower line and Carson; sold due to writ Jan. 19, 1784 from Lincoln Co Pleas & Quarter Sessions Court to levy 219£ 2s and 3£ 16s 3p cost from Samuel Bickerstaff (late of Lincoln Co) due to suit of Henry Dellinger; money to be returned to court 1st Monday of April "next" and sale authorized by act of Assembly on Oct. 25, 1764 in Wilmington.   Signed Jos Henry. Witness Jacob Carpenter, George Patterson, & James Palley. Rec. Apr. 1787. Book 3 p. 197; Book 14 p. 154

161. Mar. 21, 1785 Henry Savits & wife Catharine (Rowan Co) to Jesse Robison (Lincoln Co); for 100£ sold [ac omitted]; border: the river; part of tract that formerly belonged to Jacob Wilfong, see deed Nov. 29, 1762, and upper part of tract joining James Robison.   Signed Henrih Savits (german) & Catharine's mark. Witness Wm Erwin & Will Alexander. Rec. Apr. 1787. Book 3 p. 199; Book 14 p. 156

162. Sept. 14, 1782 Samuel Hunter (Lincoln Co) to Isaac Cooper (same); for 200£ "hard money" in gold & silver sold 200 ac where Robert Brown lives; bond for 400£ given if title isn't OK.   Signed Samuel Hunter's mark. Witness Thos McCorkle & Wm Beaty. Rec. Apr. 1787. Book 3 p. 200; Book 14 p. 157

163. Mar. 27, 1787 Andrew Floyd (York Co, SC) to William Crockett (Lincoln Co); for 180£ NC money sold 227 ac on S side of S fork of Cuttabaw R about 3 miles below "the lower mount"; part of grant Nov. 16, 1764 to Allen Alexander who sold to Nathl Henderson who sold to James Patterson who sold to David Elder who sold to Andrew Floyd.   Signed Anderw Floyd. Witness Sarah Wilson, Mary Wilson, & Jno Wilson. Rec. Apr. 1787. Book 3 p. 200; Book 14 p. 158

164. Nov. 18, 1786 George Pasehore, planter (Lincoln Co) to Peter Mason (same); for 20£ sold 100 ac on Kettles Shoal Br of S fork of Cuttabaw R; border: Peter Costner.   Signed George Pasehore's mark. Witness William Edwards, Peter Motelar, & Jesnmy Miller(?) (german). Rec. Apr. 1787. Book 3 p. 202; Book 14 p. 159

165. Mar. 16, 1787 Robert Alexander to Frederick Linebarger; for 20£ sold 200 ac on waters of Hoyles Cr; border: said Lineberger and Peter Smith.   Signed Robt Alexander. Witness James Henderson & Thos Flenenson (or Henenson). Rec. Apr. 1787. Book 3 p. 203; Book 14 p. 160

166. Mar. 31, 1787 Joseph Henry, sheriff (Lincoln Co) to Jane Brison (same); for 16£ sold 100 ac on S side of Little Cuttaba Cr; between John Breson and Saml Gingles; part of grant to John Gullick who sold to John Breson who sold to James Holland who sold to John McRandles; sold due to writ Oct. 12, 1786 from Lincoln Co Pleas & Quarter Sessions Court to levy 46£ 11s 6p and 2£ 18s 7p cost from John McRandles due to suit of Robert Mitchel; money to be returned to court 1st Monday of Jan. "next" and sale authorized by act of Assembly on Oct. 25, 1764 in Wilmington.   Signed Jos Henry. Witness Wm Berry, William Patterson, & Wm Rice.   Rec. Apr. 1787. Book 3 p. 204; Book 14 p. 161

167. Mar. 28, 1787 Jacob Forney (Lincoln Co) to Abraham Earhart (same); for 5s sold [ac omitted] on a branch of Killions Cr; border: Killions corner; granted Jul. 21, 1774 to Jacob Forney & George Hegar.   Signed Jo Dickson. Witness Jos Abernathy & Jacob Sides. Rec. Apr. 1787. Book 3 p. 205; Book 14 p. 163

Lincoln County, NC Deed book 3

168. Jan. 22, 1787 Peter Aker (Lincoln Co) to Michael Aker (same); for 100£ sold 300 ac on both sides of N branch of Beaverdam Cr; border: Christian Aker formerly Joseph Green; granted Apr. 10, 1761 to Elisabeth Freeland. Signed Peter Aker's mark. Witness Vallentine Mauny & Nathan Thompson. Rec. Apr. 1787. Book 3 p. 206; Book 14 p. 164

169. Jan. 2, 1787 Christian Carpenter (Lincoln Co) to son Jacob Carpenter (same); for 5£ NC money sold 300 ac on waters of Broad R on both sides of "a" main branch of Buffalow Cr; border: above Beattey; granted in 1769 to Christian Carpenter. Signed Christian Carpenter's mark. Witness Michael Carpenter & William Finn. Rec. Apr. 1787. Book 3 p. 207; Book 14 p. 164

170. Jan. 28, 1787 Jarrett Vinzantt (Lincoln Co) to William Tankersly (same); for 70£ sold 200 ac on NE side of S fork of Cuttabaw R; border: below Nicholas Srum and Christian Roads; part of grant Apr. 9, 1768 to Daniel McCarty and William Sym. Signed Garrat Vinzant. Witness David Ramsey & John Smith. Rec. Apr. 1787. Book 3 p. 209; Book 14 p. 165

171. May 28, 1782 Henry Hollman, farmer & wife Elisabeth (Burke Co) to Anthony Hollman (same); for 100£ NC money sold 200 ac in Burke Co on E side of Clarks Cr; border: on N & S sides of Lockharts Cr; part of grant Sept. 30, 1749 to Samuel Beason who sold Jan. 13 & 14, 1754 to John Ramsour and sold Nov. 21 & 21, 1767 by Jacob & David Ramsour, heirs of John Ramsour desc, to Henry Hollman. Signed Henry Hollman & Elisabeth's mark. Witness Nathan Armitage & William Sherrill. Rec. Apr. 1787. Book 3 p. 210; Book 14 p. 166

172. Mar. 29, 1787 Abraham Earhart (Lincoln Co) to Jacob Sides (same); for 5s sold [ac omitted] on branch of Killions Cr; border: Killion's old corner, Henry Sides, & widdow Hager; part of grant Jul. 21, 1774 to Jacob Forney and George Hager. Signed Abraham Earhart. Witness Jos Abernathy & Jacob Faruney. Rec. Apr. 1787. Book 3 p. 211; Book 14 p. 168

173. Jan. 2, 1787 Henry Reynolds (Lincoln Co) to John Seffret (same); for 60£ sold [ac omitted] on both sides of Lick fork of Indian Cr; border: above Hugh Poloak; granted Dec. 16, 1769 to John Sloan. Signed Henry Reynolds. Witness John Reynolds & Henry Landess. Rec. Apr. 1787. Book 3 p. 212; Book 14 p. 168

174. Dec. 19, 1786 Richard McRey (Wilks Co, Ga) to Henry Reynolds (Lincoln Co); for 60£ NC money sold [ac omitted] on Lick fork of Indian Cr; granted May 4, 1769 to David McRee. Signed Richard McRee. Witness John Seffret & Wm Kelly. Rec. Apr. 1787. Book 3 p. 213; Book 14 p. 170

July Court 1787
175. Apr. 10, 1787 Philip Null (Lincoln Co) to John Baily (same); for 130£ NC money sold a Negro boy Jack about 8 or 9 years old. Signed Philip Null. Witness Jos Henry. Rec. Jul. 1787. Book 3 p. 215; Book 14 p. 171

176. Jul. 2, 1787 Robert Abernathy jr (Lincoln Co) to Martin Rendleman (same); for 50£ sold 250 ac on middle fork of Kellions Cr; granted Mar. 24, 1754 to Leonard Killion.   Signed Robt Abernathy. Witness Danl McKisick & Robert Abernathy. Rec. Jul. 1787. Book 3 p. 215; Book 14 p. 171

177. Mar. 6, 1787 John Alexander (Lincoln Co) to Henry Wasson (late of Caswell Co); for 100£ NC money sold 400 ac on Cattail Br and Log Br of Crowders Cr; includes said John Alexander's improvements; border: Henry Vernor's corner, a hill, & near Wm Erwin; granted (#156) Feb. 28, 1775 to John Alexander.   Signed John Alexander. Witness Joseph Smith, John Wilson jr, & Jno Wilson. Rec. Jul. 1787. Book 3 p. 216; Book 14 p. 172

178. Jun. 5, 1778 Melcher Ayler (Tryon Co) to Christopher Cup (Rowan Co); for 117£ 4s sold 200 ac in Tryon Co on both sides of Indian Cr; granted in 1772. Signed Melcher Ayler's mark & Frances Aylly (sic). Witness Thos Poarson & John Arrawood. Rec. Jul. 1787. Book 3 p. 219; Book 14 p. 175

179. Jan. 18, 1787 Jacob Grisemore (Lincoln Co) to Henry Grisemore (same); for 50£ sold 300 ac on N side of S fork of Cuttabaw R; border: John Bradley and Christian Gross; part of grant to Jacob Grisemore.   Signed Jacob Grisemore (german). Witness Cristian Gross (german) & Robt Blackburn. Rec. Jul. 1787. Book 3 p. 219; Book 14 p. 175

180. Jan. 18, 1787 Jacob Grisemore (Lincoln Co) to Christian Braneman (same); for 50£ NC money sold 240 ac on N side of S fork of Cuttabaw R; border: Henry Grisemore, Jacob Grismore's old line, & Christian Gross; part of grant to Jacob Grisemore.   Signed Jacob Griseman (german). Witness Christian Gross (german) & Robt Blackburn. Rec. Jul. 1787. Book 3 p. 220; Book 14 p. 176
181. Sept. 11, 1778 Jacob McConnell, farmer (Tryon Co) to William Burk (Craven Co, 96 Dist, SC); for 180£ NC money sold 125 ac on a branch of Kings Cr; includes Jacob McConnell's improvements; border: John Skyles.   Signed Jacob McConnell. Witness Geo Barclay & Samuel Collins. Rec. Jul. 1787. Book 3 p. 221; Book 14 p. 177

182. Jan. 29, 1787 Garrett Vanzant (Lincoln Co) to John Smith (same); for 130£ NC money sold (1) [ac omitted] on SE side of S fork of Cuttabaw R; being the part that includes improvement he lives on; a grave yard excepted; border: Harl's corner and Jacob Costner; and (2) 100 ac joins above tract; border: Kender and Glance.   Signed Garratt Vanzant. Witness David Ramsey & _?_ Hovis (german). Rec. Jul. 1787. Book 3 p. 223; Book 14 p. 178

183. Mar. 3, 1781 Moses Henery (Lincoln Co) to Charles Hamilton (same); for 4£ sold 100 ac on branch of Crowders Cr; border: Gingles.   Signed Moses Henery. Witness David Miller & Joseph Henery. Rec. Jul. 1787. Book 3 p. 224; Book 14 p. 180

184. Mar. 25, 1780 grant #73 R. C. Caswell to Thomas McCormack; 100 ac in Tryon Co on waters of Shickles Cr; border: Solomon Hoover and Yohard (sic). Signed R. C. Caswell & A. Phillips, P Sec. Feb. 3, 1787 Joseph Henderson swears to Robt Alexander, JP that above is a true copy [signed] Josep Henderson. Rec. Jul. 1787. Book 3 p. 226; Book 14 p. 181

185. Feb. 1, 1785 William Hollett (Lincoln Co) to William Hamilton (same); for 20s NC money sold 150 ac on Thompsons Cabbin Br of Kings Cr; border: Arthur Patterson and on S side of said branch; includes Monohan's improvement; granted Oct. 9, 1783 to Jonathan Price.   Signed William & Massey Hullett's marks. Witness Samuel Collins & John Hambright. Rec. Jul. 1787. Book 3 p. 226; Book 14 p. 181

186. Mar. 9, 1787 William Hamilton (Lincoln Co) to John Hamilton (same); for 80£ NC money sold 150 ac on Thompsons Cabbin Br of Kings Cr; border: S side of a branch, Arthur Patterson, & Hoffstetler; includes Monohan's improvement; granted Oct. 9, 1783 to Jonn Price (#41).   Signed William Hamilton. Witness Wm Henry, John Wilson jr, & Jno Wilson. Rec. Jul. 1787. Book 3 p. 227; Book 14 p. 182.

187. Aug. 12, 1784 Jonathan Price (Lincoln Co) to William Hullett (same); for 5£ sold 150 ac on Thompsons Cabbin Br of Kings Cr; border: On S side of said branch and Arthur Patterson; includes Monohan's improvement; granted Oct. 9, 1783 to Jonathan Price.   Signed Jonathan Price. Witness Frederick Hambright, Arthur Patterson, & Jas Logan. Rec. Jul. 1787. Book 3 p. 229; Book 14 p. 183

188. Oct. 25, 1786 Thomas Espey, planted (Lincoln Co) to Samuel Espey (same); for 50£ sold 100 ac on waters of Crowders Cr known as "the big meadow"; granted Mar. 3, 1779 to Thomas Espey.   Signed Thomas Espey. Witness John Carruth & John Sloan. Rec. Jul. 1787. Book 3 p. 230; Book 14 p. 184

189. Feb. 16, 1787 Henry McMillian (SC) to Charles Williams (Lincoln Co); for 50£ sold (1) 200 ac on both sides of Doctors Br of Kellions Cr; and (2) 75 ac joins above tract; part of grant to Jacob Forney, David Crit, & Paul Wisnat; includes place Williams Abernathy lives on.   Signed Henry Mackmillan (sic). Witness John and Jos Abernathy. Rec. Jul. 1787. Book 3 p. 231; Book 14 p. 186

190. Jul. 2, 1786 Frederick Hambright, farmer (York Co and "New acquisition", SC) to Robert Gabie (Lincoln Co); for 30£ NC money sold 100 ac on branch of Kings Cr; border: William Sharp and Jacob Connell; includes a shoal; granted Nov. 1, 1784 to Frederick Hambright.   Signed Frederick Hambright. Witness Joseph Jenkins & Isaac Sellers. Rec. Jul. 1787. Book 3 p. 232; Book 14 p. 187

191. Feb. 11, 1786 John Butt (Lincoln Co "formerly called Burke Co") to Peter Mull ("same"); for 100£ NC money sold 100 ac on N side of Henrys fork of S

fork of Cuttabaw R; border: Peter Mull; being upper part of 500 ac "entered in late King's office" by William Butt of Pennsylvania and granted Dec. 10, 1778 "by representatives of freemen of this state" to John Butt.   Signed John Butt. Witness John Shell & Daniel Smith. Rec. Jul. 1787. Book 3 p. 233; Book 14 p. 188

192. May 7, 1787 Frederick Whittenberger (Greene Co, TN) to John Wason (Lincoln Co); for 57£ 10s sold 400 ac; border: Laurence Debung; includes head of Pinchgut Cr and crosses head waters of Hagines fork; granted Oct. 26, 1767 to Nicholas Grindstaff.   Signed Frederick & Margaret Whittenberger's marks. Witness Wm(?) Welk JP, Jas Peares JP, & Geog Smith (german). Rec. Jul. 1787. Book 3 p. 235; Book 14 p. 189

193. Oct. 11, 1786 William Patrick (Lincoln Co) to Thomas Buchannon (same); for 130£ NC money sold 210 ac on S side of S fork of Cuttaba R; border: James Baird's corner, William Patterson's corner, & Ratchford; granted Jan. 25, 1773 to William Patrick.   Signed William Pattrick. Witness Thomas Thomas, Joseph Neel, & Jonn Gullick. Rec. Jul. 1787. Book 3 p. 236; Book 14 p. 190

194. May 14, 1787 Joseph Dickson, commissioner in trust for Lincoln Co, to John Deeter (late of York Co, Pa); for 40s sold [ac omitted] lot 2 in NW square in Lincolnton; lot is 6 by 12 rods.   Signed Jo Dickson. Witness W. Moore, Henrich Rlein(?) (german), & Whieh Menett(?) (german). Rec. Jul. 1787. Book 3 p. 237; Book 14 p. 191

195. Oct. 3, 1786 Christian Mauney (Lincoln Co) to Joseph Cross (same); for 30£ sold 200 ac on Jacobs fork of Long Cr; border: a ridge; granted Mar. 28, 1775 to Jacob Hoffstetler.   Signed Christian Moni (german). Witness John Moore & Robt Blackburn. Rec. Jul. 1787. Book 3 p. 239; Book 14 p. 193

196. Dec. 12, 1785 Christopher Cup, potter (Lincoln Co) to Martin Chaitkel (Rowan Co); for 70£ NC money sold 200 ac on both sides of Indian Cr; granted in 1772. Signed Cristher Cott(?) (german). Witness Philip Cook, Jacob Wallis, & Gre_?_ (german). Rec. Jul. 1787. Book 3 p. 240; Book 14 p. 194

197. Jun. 26, 1787 Thomas Heslep (or Hestip) (Rutherford Co) to Mary Cherry (Lincoln Co); for 20£ NC money sold [ac omitted] on Suck fork of Buffaloe Cr; border: a stoney hill; includes Andrew Heslip's improvement; being 500 ac granted (#172) Feb. 28, 1775 to Andrew Heslip and "fell" to Thomas Heslep as Andrew's legatee.   Signed Thos Heslep. Witness Jonathan Hampton & David Chirry (sic). Rec. Jul. 1787. Book 3 p. 241; Book 14 p. 195

198. Jul. 4, 1787 Peter Johnston, surveyor & esecutor of John Kirkonnel desc, to William Oats (Lincoln Co); for 12£ sold 200 ac on both sides of Muddy fork of Buffaloe Cr; border: James Williams and James Kelly; granted Feb. 28, 1775 to

Lincoln County, NC Deed book 3

John Kerkonnel.   Signed Peter Johnston. Witness Jo Dickson & John Sloan. Rec. Jul. 1787. Book 3 p. 242; Book 14 p. 196

October Session 1787
199. Oct. 10, 1782 John Sloan (Lincoln Co) to James McGill (same); for 20£ NC money sold 154 ac on W side of Long Cr; border: crosses creek to Wm Fronabarrick's (sic) lower corner and Peter Summy; granted Apr. 5, 1767 to "said" John Sloan jr.   Signed John Sloan. Witness John Alexander & John Lequer. Rec. Oct. 1787. Book 3 p. 243; Book 14 p. 197

200. Aug. 28, 1787 Samuel Martin (Mecklenburg Co) to Barbara Ramsour & Sarah Ramsour, two of heirs of Jacob Ramsour desc (Lincoln Co); for 100£ paid by Jacob Ramsour during his lifetime sold 500 ac on N fork of Indian Cr near Peter Johnston; border: waters of Howards Cr, crosses head of a small branch, Hiltebrand's corner, & crosses "the" ridge.   Signed Sam Martin. Witness Wm Maclean, Joseph Henry, & Jno Rogers. Rec. Oct. 1787. Book 3 p. 244; Book 14 p. 198

201. Oct. 1, 1787 Alexander Gilliland (Lincoln Co) to James Graham (same); for 60£ NC money sold 137 ac in Lincoln formerly Tryon Co on both sides of ridge road between Falls Br and Crowders Cr; border: near John Smith; includes said James Graham's improvement; granted (#109) Mar. 25, 1789 to Alexander Gilliland.   Signed Alexr Gilliland. Witness James Willson. Rec. Oct. 1787. Book 3 p. 245; Book 14 p. 199

202. Oct. 27, 1784 James Graham (Lincoln Co) to James Wilson (same); for 5s sterling sold 250 ac on Walkers Br of Crowders Cr; border: on N end of Alexr Gilliland's entry and John Patterson's line; granted (#5) Oct. 9, 1783 to James Graham.   Signed James Graham. Witness Jas Henery & Jacob McFarlind. Rec. Oct. 1787. Book 3 p. 247; Book 14 p. 200

203. Jan. 27, 1774 James Thompson & wife Hannah (Craven Co, SC) to William Bryson (Rowan Co); for 20£ sterling sold 525 ac in Mecklenburg Co on head "draughts" of Keeners Cr and on both sides of road from John Beaty's ford across W end of "the" mountain to Jacob Egner's; granted Nov. 17, 1764 to James Thompson and enrolled in Mecklenburg Office Book #12 p. 125 (#231) Nov. 20, 1764.   Signed James Thomson & Hannah's mark. Witness Robert Adams & John Thomson. Rec. Oct. 1787. Book 3 p. 248; Book 14 p. 201

204. Sept. 26, 1787 John Davis (Lincoln Co) to Battee Abernathy (same); 50£ NC money sold 80 ac on W side of Cuttabaw R on waters of Coborns Cr; border: Hill, Dunkin, & "the" old line; granted Feb. 28, 1775 to John Stroud.   Signed John Davis's mark. Witness Jos Abernathy & Robt Abernathy. Rec. Oct. 1787. Book 3 p. 250; Book 14 p. 203

205. Sept. 19, 1787 Joseph Henry, sheriff (Lincoln Co) to John Shoeford sr; for 180£ sold 300 ac on Potts Cr; sold due to writ Jul. 17, 1787 from Lincoln Co Pleas & Quarter Sessions Court to levy 184£ and 3£ 12s cost from administrator of John Shoeford jr desc and in Jul. 1786 John Dellinger was appointed guardian by court and more cost of 4£ 1p is assessed; money to be returned to court in Oct. 1787 and sale authorized by act of Assembly on Oct. 25, 1764 in Wilmington.   Signed Joseph Henry; Witness Jesse Robinson, David Shuford, & James Johnson. Rec. Oct. 1787. Book 3 p. 251; Book 14 p. 204

206. Dec. 23, 1787 John Robinson (Abavale Co, SC) to Samuel Whitworth (Lincoln Co); for 40£ sold [ac omitted]; border: corner of original survey, Wm Simson (or Simpson), & down "the" river; includes "the" mountain and a small island.   Signed John Robinson. Witness Moses Sherrill & William Simpson. Rec. Oct. 1787. Book 3 p. 253; Book 14 p. 206

207. Mar. 25, 1787 John Smyth (Lincoln Co) to William Vernor (same); for 65£ NC money sold 263 ac on both sides of N fork of Crowders Cr; border: John Walker and Coburn; granted Apr. 29, 1768 to Henry Vernor who sold to Wm Vernor who sold to John Smyth.   Signed John Smyth. Witness Alexr Gilliland & John Chittam. Rec. Oct. 1787. Book 3 p. 254; Book 14 p. 207

208. Sept. 7, 1787 Rudolph Bew, planter (Lincoln Co) to John Kennedy, planter (same); for 95£ NC money sold 200 ac on both sides of Buffaloe Cr of Broad R; border: Christopher Carpinter on W side of creek and William Renolds' line on a branch.   Signed Rudolph Bew's mark. Witness Francis Guthrie & Hendrey Beaker. Rec. Oct. 1787. Book 3 p. 256; Book 14 p. 208

209. Oct. 8, 1785 Peter Johnston (Mecklenburg Co) to John Hiltybrand (Lincoln Co); for 100£ sold [ac omitted] in Lincoln formerly Tryon Co on both sides of Howards Cr; between Nicholas Fryday and Henry Hiltybrand; border: a gravelly hill and "his" old & new surveys.   Signed Peter Johnston. Witness Daniel Browne, Jos Henry, & Esther Kennedy. Rec. Oct. 1787. Book 3 p. 257; Book 14 p. 209

210. Dec. 23, 1787 John Robinson (Abavale Co, SC) to William Simpson (Lincoln Co); for 50£ sold [ac omitted]; border: second line of original survey; part of grant (#774) Nov. 9, 1784 to John Robinson.   Signed John Robinson. Witness Samuel Whitworth & Moses Sherrill. Rec. Oct. 1787. Book 3 p. 258; Book 14 p. 210

211. Oct. 1, 1787 John Thompson & wife Mary (Lincoln Co) to Thomas Bell (same); for 150£ sold two tracts on W side of Cuttaba R and S side of Mountain Cr: (1) 150 ac; border: Mountain Cr, Samuel Thompson, "the" marsh, & Henry Thompson jr's old tract; and (2) 60 ac; border: above tract, White's corner, Little, Reed, and old survey, & Samuel Thompson; granted Apr. 25, 1767 to Henry Thompson sr; both tracts were left to John Thompson by Henry Thompson sr's

will.   Signed John & Mary Thompson. Witness Samuel Thompson, Cornelius Clark, & William Thompson. Rec. Oct. 1787. Book 3 p. 259; Book 14 p. 211

212. Jan. 10, 1787 Michael Rudisealy to Henery Rudisealy; for 10£ NC money sold 200 ac; border: fork of a branch on "the" division line.   Signed Mihel Ruedisel (german). Witness Lemuel Sanders & John Godfrey Arendt. Rec. Oct. 1787. Book 3 p. 261; Book 14 p. 212

213. Mar. 25, 1785 John Hiltebrand & wife Barbary (Lincoln Co) to Philip Bollinger (same); for 70£ sold 300 ac on waters of Pots Cr; border: John Bradley's upper line and "his" line; granted Apr. 8, 1768 to Wm Reed who sold Aug. 13, 1784 to John Hiltebrant.   Signed John Hiltebrand & Barbary's mark. Witness Robt Blackburn, Jno Harris, & Lewis Warlick. Rec. Oct. 1787. Book 3 p. 262; Book 14 p. 213

214. May 20, 1787 Christian Money & wife Catharine (Lincoln Co) to Michael Williams (same); for 200£ NC money sold 200 ac on N side of S fork of Cuttabaw R; border: Aaron Biggerstaff and Saml Biggerstaff.   Signed Christian & Catharine Money's marks. Witness John Fulenwider & Jacob _?_ (german). Rec. Oct. 1787. Book 3 p. 264; Book 14 p. 214

215. Jul. 23, 1787 Miles Abernathy (Lincoln Co) to Battey Abernathy (same); for 5s sold 400 ac on a branch of Coborn's & Leepers Cr; border: a mill pond, John Hill, Coborn's old corner, Dunkin, & Stroud.   Signed   Miles Abernathy. Witness Jos Abernathy & John Farrar. Rec. Oct. 1787. Book 3 p. 265; Book 14 p. 215

216. Aug. 8, 1787 William Bryson & wife Susanna & Samuel Bryson (Lincoln Co) to Thomas Earwood (same); for 50£ sold 225 ac on head "draughts" of Keeners Cr; border: Samuel & James Bryson; part of grant Nov. 17, 1764 to James Thompson "enrolled in General Office" Nov. 20, 1764 & sold Jan. 7, 1774 to James Thompson to William Bryson.   Signed William, Susanna, & Samuel Bryson. Witness William Earwood & John Bryson. Rec. Oct. 1787. Book 3 p. 266; Book 14 p. 216

217. Jan. 31, 1778 George Miller, planter, & wife Mary (Tryon Co) to William McCormack, yoeman (same); for 600£ NC money sold 250 ac on Lick Run of Leopards Cr; border: Baker; includes said Miller's improvement; granted May 20, 1772 to George Miller.   Signed George Miller & Maria's mark. Witness _?_ Troutman (german), Martin Keener (german), & Michel _?_ (german). Rec. Oct. 1787. Book 3 p. 267; Book 14 p. 218

218. Sept. 10, 1787 Jenkin (or Jenkey) Jenkins (Lincoln Co) to Jacob McFarland (same); for 100£ NC money, paid half in had & half in "promisory" notes, sold 100 ac on both sides of Little Long Cr; border: near Anderson; granted Apr. 28,

1768 to Andrew Hoyle.   Signed Jinkey Jenkins. Witness Wm Vernor & Robert Aurmor (or german). Rec. Oct. 1787. Book 3 p. 269; Book 14 p. 219

219. May 1, 1787 Samuel McMin (Lincoln Co) to William Kinkead (same); for 5s sterling sold 150 ac on W side of Cattabaw R on waters of Siglas Cr; border: Abraham Wamock & Charles Regan.   Signed Samuel & Rachel McMin. Witness Jas Little & Jas Kincaid. Rec. Oct. 1787. Book 3 p. 271; Book 14 p. 221

220. Oct. 1, 1787 Isaac Lockerman (Lincoln Co) to John & David Lockerman (same); for 30£ NC money sold 200 ac on S side of (S fork of--lined out) Cuttapaw R & both sides of Little Cr of Cuttapaw R; border: near Philip Cloonenger's corner, John Kirkpatrick, & Leonard Killion; granted Jul. 21, 1774 to Barnet Lockerman.   Signed Isaac Lockerman. Witness John Allen & Sarah Lockerman. Rec. Oct. 1787. Book 3 p. 271; Book 14 p. 222

221. Aug. 8, 1787 George Eslinger & wife Fanny (Lincoln Co) to John Lowrey (same); for 113£ sold 200 ac on waters of Liles Cr; border: John Roak; part of grant Oct. 28, 1782 to Jacob Myars who sold to George Eslinger.   Signed Gerg Eslinger (german) & Fanny's mark. Witness David Ramsey & Robert Willes. Rec. Oct. 1787. Book 3 p. 273; Book 14 p. 223

222. Oct. 18, 1787 Matthias Cronister & wife Elisabeth (Lincoln Co) to Michael Buff (same); for 64£ NC money sold 300 ac on dividing ridge between Leonards fork and Indian Cr; granted Jan. 25, 1773 to Matthias Cronister.   Signed Marttew Konser (german) & Elisabeth's mark. Witness George Buff & Philip Cook. Rec. Oct. 1787. Book 3 p. 274; Book 14 p. 224

223. Oct. 2, 1787 Adam Koiser (Lincoln Co) to George Koiser (same); for 10£ NC money sold 150 ac on both sides of Beaverdam Cr waters of S fork of Cuttapaw Cr; border: Jacob Carpenter, Peter Carpenter, & a meadow.   Signed Hann Adam Keiser(?) (german). Signed . Martin Fritay (german) & John Crouse. Rec. Oct. 1787. Book 3 p. 275; Book 14 p. 225

224. Oct. 2, 1787 George Koiser (Lincoln Co) to Adam Koiser (same); for 10£ sold 148 ac on both sides of Beaverdam Cr; border: Jacob Carpenter, Peter Carpenter, a Mirey Spring dividing line, George Koiser, & Christian Carpenter; part of grant Apr. 10, 1761 to his father Laurence Koiser.   Signed Georg Krijer (german). Witness Martin Fritay (german) & John Crouse. Rec. Oct. 1787. Book 3 p. 276; Book 14 p. 226

225. Jun. 7, 1786 Robert Campbell (Lincoln Co) to William Berry (same); for 20£ sold 123 ac on waters of Little Cataba Cr; border: near a mirey branch; part of grant Nov. 5, 1764 to Thomas Campbell desc.   Signed Robert Campbel. Witness John McClure, James Campbell, & Jonn Gullick. Rec. Oct. 1787. Book 3 p. 278; Book 14 p. 227

226. Apr. 29, 1786 Robert Campbell (Lincoln Co) to William Berry (same); for 20£ sold (1) 20 ac on waters of Little Cataba Cr; border: his old line; part of grant Nov. 5, 1774 to Thomas Campbell desc; and (2) 180 ac on waters of Little Cataba Cr; border: near Brison, Gingles, & the long meadow; granted Nov. 25, 1771 to Thomas Campbell desc.   Signed Robert Campbell. Witness Jonn Gullick & John Wallace. Rec. Oct. 1787. Book 3 p. 279; Book 14 p. 228

227. Feb. 7, 1786 John Carpenter & wife Elisabeth (Lincoln Co) to John Miller (same); for 45£ sold 225 ac; border: Robert Ramsey and Pearsor; granted Feb. 25, 1775 (or 1075) to John Carpenter.   Signed John Carpenter & Elisabeth's mark. Witness David Ramsey & Petter Mosteller. Rec. Oct. 1787. Book 3 p. 280; Book 14 p. 229

228. Jan. 11, 1787 Michael Rudisealy (Lincoln Co) to Philip Rudisealy (same); for 10£ NC money sold 200 ac about 2 miles from his brother Philip Rudiseally; granted in 1754 to Michael Rudisealy.   Signed Mihel Rudisili (german). Witness Lemuel Saunders & Henry Rudisealy. Rec. Oct. 1787. Book 3 p. 280; Book 14 p. 229

229. Dec. 28, 1785 Frederick Shull sr & wife Sarah (Burke Co) to Peter Planck (Lincoln Co); for 200£ sterling sold 450 ac on Lyles Cr; border: Isaac Lowrance, Simon Jonas, Philip Sifala's conditional line, & Adam Cook; includes improvement where he lives.   Signed Friderih Sholl (german) & Sarah's mark. Witness Jno Perkins, Ephraim Perkins, & Isaac Lowrance. Rec. Oct. 1787. Book 3 p. 283; Book 14 p. 232

229A. Dec. 29, 1785 Frederick Shull sr & wife Sarah (Burke Co) to Peter Planck (Lincoln Co); [this is the release for #229]; granted Mar. 14, 1780 by Gov. Richard Caswell to Frederick Shull sr. Book 3 p. 284; Book 14 p. 232

January Court 1788
230. Apr. 2, 1787 Peter Mull esq (Burke Co) to John Shell (Lincoln Co); for 100£ NC money sold 33.75 ac on N side of Henrys fork of S fork of Catawba R; border: a ridge, "the" Mill Cr, & SW corner of mill survey; part of grant (#37) Dec. 10, 1778 to Peter Mull.   Signed Peter Mull. Witness Peter Peterson & Jacob Yont (german). Rec. Jan. 1788. Book 3p. 287; Book 14 p. 235

231. Jan. 5, 1788 Peter Mull esq (Burke Co) to John Yunt (Lincoln Co); for 20£ NC money sold 65 ac on S side of Henrys R and both sides of a Spring Br; border: said Mull's old survey, a hollow, & a ridge; granted (#855) Nov. 9, 1784 to [omitted].   Signed Peter Moll. Witness John Shell & John Yont (german). Rec. Jan. 1788. Book 3 p. 288; Book 14 p. 236

232. Dec. 18, 1787 Rosannah Reddick (Burke Co) to Archibald Little (Lincoln Co); for 12£ sold 100 ac on S side of Cuttabaw R; border: Wm Hega, Dry Br, Johnstones Cr, John Thomas, & William Little; granted Sept. 25, 1754 to Jno

Large who sold to James Armour who sold Aug. 25, 1755 to Dennis Dyer who sold Mar. 3, 1767 to Leonard Dozer who sold "Sr" 10, 1766 (sic) to Jno Stroud. Signed Rosannah Reddick's mark. Witness John Reed & John Reed sr. Rec. Jan. 1788. Book 3 p. 289; Book 14 p. 237

233. Jan. 14, 1787 Henry Sumrow (Lincoln Co) to Michael Sumrow (same); for 10£ NC money sold 263 ac; border: Jacob Carpinter's corner on waters of Clarks Cr, "the" old tract, Andrew Heady (Heddick--lined out), & Headick; granted Apr. 29, 1768 to Peter Summa and another grant Apr. 28, 1768 to Peter Summa and sold by Peter Summey (sic) to Henry Sumrow. Signed Henry Summerow. Witness Robt Blackburn, Wm Maclean, & John McGaughey. Rec. Jan. 1788. Book 3 p. 291; Book 14 p. 238

234. Jan. 5, 1788 Peter Mull esq (Burke Co) to John Yunt, yoeman (Lincoln Co); for 20£ NC money sold 100 ac on both sides of Henrys R & both sides of Shoal Cr; border: "beginning" corner of both of said Mull's old surveys, his lower survey, & N side of a ridge; "reference to a deed #856". Signed Peter Moll. Witness John Shell & Jacob Yund (german). Rec. Jan. 1788. Book 3 p. 292; Book 14 p. 239

235. Feb. 6, 1786 William Jenkins (York Co, SC) to John Wallace (Lincoln Co); for $50 sold 200 ac on a branch of Kings Cr. Signed William Jenkins. Witness John Russel & Marah Smith "ackd before" Jo Dickson. Rec. Jan. 1788. Book 3 p. 293; Book 14 p. 240

236. Dec. 28, 1787 Henry Thomson (Ga) to Robert Knox (Lincoln Co); for 120£ NC money sold 151 ac on W side of Catawba R & N side of Mountain Cr; border: Robert McKisick, "the" old line, & Samuel Thomson; part of land sold Jan. 5 & 6, 1765 by Abraham Collett to Henry Thomson sr who willed it May 22, 1777 to William Thomson who sold Feb. 5, 1783 to Henry Thomson. Signed Henry Thompson. Witness Jno Nelson, James Johnston, & Thomas Erwin. Rec. Jan. 1788. Book 3p. 294; Book 14 p. 241

237. Oct. 2, 1786 Thomas Little, planter (Lincoln Co) to John Reed (same); for 150£ NC money sold 220 ac on S fork of Mountain Cr; border: McCorkle's corner; part of grant Oct. 17, 1782 to Thomas Little (see Burke Co records). Signed Thomas Little. Witness Fras McCrokel & Robert Carithers. Rec. Jan. 1788. Book 3 p. 296; Book 14 p. 242

238. Aug. 16, 1785 James Wyatt (Spartanburg Co, SC) to George Lamkin (Lincoln Co); for 40£ sold 100 ac on E side of S fork of Cuttabaw R; part of of 392 ac grant to James Wyatt; includes Daniel Wyatt's improvement. Signed James Wyatt. Witness George Lamkin, Jean Dunlap, & Jinkey Jinkins. Rec. Jan. 1788. Book 3 p. 297; Book 14 p. 243

239. Dec. 6, 1787 Samuel Rankin (Lincoln Co) to William Rankin (same); for 20£ sold 65 ac; border: Saml Rankin's corner, Chanleys Cr, & "the" old survey; part of tract where Samuel Rankin lives.   Signed Samuel Rankin. Witness Richard Rankin & David Rankin. Rec. Jan. 1788. Book 3 p. 298; Book 14 p. 243

240. Jan. 5, 1788 Peter Moll esq (Burke Co) to John Yunt (Lincoln Co); for 20£ NC money sold 202.5 ac on both sides of Henrys fork of S fork of Catawba R; border: a ridge and John Shell; lower end of 500 ac granted (#37) Dec. 10, 1778 to John Butt who sold to Peter Mull.   Signed Peter Moll. Signed John Shell & John Yund (german). Rec. Jan. 1788. Book 3 p. 299; Book 14 p. 244

241. Jul. 28, 1787 John Sutton (Lincoln Co) to Abraham Earhart; for 150£ NC money paid in "open market" sold a Negro girl Cloey about 18 years old now in possession of said Earhart.   Signed John Sutton. Witness James Martin & Samvol (sic) Sutton. Rec. Jan. 1788. Book 3 p. 300; Book 14 p. 245

242. Jan. 5, 1788 Peter Mull esq (Burke Co) to John Yunt (Lincoln Co); for 20£ NC money sold 265 ac on N side of Henrys fork of S fork of Cutawba R; border: John Butts' "beginning" corner; being N side "of the fork of a tract" granted (#558) Oct. 11, 1783 to Peter Mull.   Signed Peter Moll. Witness John Shell & Jacob Yund (german). Rec. Jan. 1788. Book 3 p. 301; Book 14 p. 246

243. Oct. 25, 1787 John Tagert (Davidson Co "on" Cumberland [Tenn]) to Robert Wier (Lincoln Co); for 100£ NC money sold 640 ac on dividing ridge between waters of Indian Cr & Muddy fork of Buffaloe Cr and on both sides of waggon road from Moses Moore's to Broad R; border: waters of head branches of Indian Cr; granted Dec. 11, 1779 to John Tagert.   Signed John Tagert. Witness Joseph Robinson, R Martin, & Jacob Zimerdman (german) [Jacob Carpinter written in book]. Rec. Jan. 1788. Book 3 p. 302; Book 14 p. 247

244. Apr. 19, 1787 James Bryson (Lincoln Co) to Daniel McKisick (same); for 127£ sold 250 ac on head "drafts" of Keeners Cr and both sides of great road from Beaty's ford across W end of Little Mountain to Bellinger's Mill; border: Samuel Bryson; part of 525 ac granted Nov. 16, 1764 to James Thompson who sold Jan. 27, 1774 to William Bryson who sold Mar. 5 "last" to James Bryson.   Signed James Bryson. Witness James Martin & Valentine Little. Rec. Jan. 1788. Book 3 p. 304; Book 14 p. 248

245. Jun. 7, 1786 Robert Campbell (Lincoln Co) to John McClure (same); for 56£ sold 157 ac on waters of Little Cataba Cr; part of grant Nov. 16, 1764 to Thomas Campbell desc.   Signed Robert Campbell. Witness Jonn Gullick & Wm Berry. Rec. Jan. 1788. Book 3 p. 305; Book 14 p. 250

246. Nov. 17, 1785 George Leonard Saylor (Lincoln Co) to George Goodwin (same); for 6£ sold 149 ac on both sides of Sniders Cr; border: Joseph Saylor's place and Henry Slinker's place; granted to George L Saylor.   Signed Lenhard

Saihers (german). Witness Lemuel Saunders & Peter Snider. Rec. Jan. 1788. Book 3 p. 306; Book 14 p. 251

247. Nov. 3, 1777 William Patterson, planter (Rowan Co) to John Gray (York Co, Pa); for 100£ NC money sold 400 ac in Rowan formerly Mecklenburg Co on both sides of Welshes Cr; border: near Warluck; includes said Patterson's improvement; granted Apr. 28, 1768 to William Patterson and recorded in Sec. Office Book 13.   Signed William Patterson's mark. Witness Henry Hildebrand & Robt Blackburn. Rec. Jan. 1788. Book 3 p. 307; Book 14 p. 252

248. Jan. 1, 1787 John Bradburn esq (Burke Co) to Joseph Horton (Lincoln Co); for 150£ sold 640 ac on both sides of fork of a road from the Limestone hills to Hill's iron works & to Charlestown and from head of Catawba R to Sherrill's ford & to Salisburry; granted Oct. 28, 1783 to William McMullen who sold to John Bradburn; in Lincoln formerly Burke Co; border: Horse ford Cr.   Signed Jno Bradburn. Witness William Sherrill, John Reed, & Thomas Farley. Rec. Jan. 1788. Book 3 p. 309; Book 14 p. 253

249. Nov. 19,1787 James Lockhart (Lincoln Co) to Henry Cline (same); for 225£ NC money sold [ac omitted] on both sides of Lockharts Cr; border: Mills' old line and a branch; granted Nov. 15, 1762 to Nicholas Welsh who sold Mar. 30, 1774 to James Lockhart.   Signed James Lockhart. Witness Robt Blackburn & Wm Blackburn. Rec. Jan. 1788. Book 3 p. 311; Book 14 p. 255

250. Nov. 26, 1787 Thomas Harthorn (Ga) to John Will (Lincoln Co); for 100£ sold 200 ac on waters of Cobourns Cr; border: Armstrong, William Cathy, John Ramsey, & Bracher.   Signed Thomas Harton (sic). Witness Conrod Wills, John Walker, & James Freeman. Rec. Jan. 1788. Book 3 p. 312; Book 14 p. 256

251. Oct. 8, 1787 Polser Tarter (Lincoln Co) to Cunrade Gilbert (same); for 60£ NC money sold 200 ac on waters of Michaels Cr; border: Michael Rudisel, George Rush, & McKnitt Alexander.   Signed Palser Tete(?) (german) & Marey's mark. Witness Jno Fulenwider & Wm Tankersly. Rec. Jan. 1788. Book 3 p. 313; Book 14 p. 257

252. Oct. 9, 1787 John Smith (Lincoln Co) to John Basehore (same); for 40£ sold [ac omitted] on S side of Costners Br that runs into S fork of Cuttawba R; border: Dudderow's corner; granted Apr. 28, 1768 to Wooly Carpenter.   Signed John Smith. Witness Jacob Costner & Jno Fulenwider. Rec. Jan. 1788. Book 3 p. 314; Book 14 p. 258

253. Mar. 9, 1787 Barbara Trafelstate (Lincoln Ceo) to William Slone (same); for 10£ NC money sold 122 ac on branch of S fork of Lyles Cr; border: on N by William Slone, E & S by "esay", Barbara Trafelstate's SW corner, & Pope old corner; part of 320 ac granted to Barbara Trafelstate.   Signed Barbara

Trafelstate's mark. Witness John Sulors & Peter Trufelstate. Rec. Jan. 1788. Book 3 p. 315; Book 14 p. 258

254. Oct. 5, 1787 Solomon Saylor (Lincoln Co) to John Parc (same); for 60£ NC money sold 180 ac on both sides of Sniders Cr; border: George Snider's corner, Christopher Gyes corner, & Christofel Goies corner.   Signed Solomon Saylor's mark. Witness Lemuel Saunders & George Goodwin. Rec. Jan. 1788. Book 3 p. 316; Book 14 p. 260

255. Sept. 28, 1787 William Wittenburg (Lincoln Co) to George Smith jr (same); for 50£ NC money sold 161 ac on Moyers Br of Lyles Cr; border: Jacob Moyer's corner, Bernard Sigman, William Wittenberg, Henry Pope, & George Deal; sold Jun. 30, 1786 by John Foreman & wife Margaret to William Wittenburg & registered in Lincoln Co Book 14 p. 64 [sic p. 63] Aug. 1, 1786 by John Wilson, registr.   Signed William Wittenburg's mark. Witness John McGaughey, _?_ Sigman (german), & Gorg _?_berger (german). Rec. Jan. 1788. Book 3 p. 318; Book 14 p. 261

256. Oct. 30, 1787 George Dellinger (Lincoln Co) to Michael Dellinger (same); for 30£ sold 200 ac on N side of Dellingers Cr on Hag Br; border: Henry Dellinger on N side, Rhine, Peter Felker, & an old line; granted Oct. 9, 1783 to Nicholas Friday who sold Aug. 10, 1784 to George Dellinger.   Signed George Dellinger's mark. Witness Jno Fulenwider. Rec. Jan. 1788. Book 3 p. 319; Book 14 p. 263

257. Jan. 9, 1788 Isaac White (Lincoln Co) to George Sellers (Rowan Co); for 140£ sold 300 ac on waters of Long Cr where Nicholas Wisenant formerly lived; border: Hegar; granted Oct. 13, 1765 to Adam Wisenant and sold for 60£ Jan. 24, 1775 by Nicholas Wisenant to Christian Carpinter who sold Mar. 20, 1779 to Isaac White.   Signed Isaac & Jane White. Witness Joh Kreyser(?) [J. Kizer written in book] (german) & Lowretz Benson(?) (german). Rec. Jan. 1788. Book 3 p. 320; Book 14 p. 264

258. Mar. 4, 1786 Philip Null (Lincoln Co) to Palser Tarter (same); for 20£ NC money sold 200 ac on waters of Michaels Cr; border: Michael Rudisale, Michael Summy, his own land, & McKnitt Alexander.   Signed Philip Null & Margaret's mark.   Witness David Ramsey & Joseph Kennedy. Rec. Jan. 1788. Book 3 p. 321; Book 14 p. 265

259. Apr. 2, 1787 Peter Mull esq (Burke Co) to Peter Peterson (Lincoln Co); for 26£ NC money sold 185 ac on S side of Henrys fork of S fork of Catawba R; border: a ridge, SE & SW corner of an old survey, & John Butt's corner; part of 450 ac grant (#588) Oct. 11, 1783 to Peter Mull.   Signed Peter Moll. Witness John Shell & Jacob Yund. Rec. Jan. 1788. Book 3 p. 323; Book 14 p. 267

260. Sept. 6, 1771 Alexander Erwin (Rowan Co) to Jacob Nicholas (same); for 60£ sold 250 ac in Tryon Co on S side of Catauba R; border: John Hill; part of

1,000 ac grant Sept. 30, 1749 to John Killion who sold Jan. 1 & 2, 1754 to Jacob Brown who sold Jul. 14 & 15, 1757 to Wm Cathey who sold Aug. 19 & 20, 1763 to James Erwin desc and by heirship to his sold Alexander Erwin.   Signed Alexander Erwin. Witness Robert Luckie, Joseph Erwin, & Thos Johnson. Wit. oath (Salisbury) Mar. 12, 1772 by Joseph Erwin. Rec. [omitted]. Book 3 p. 324; Book 14 p. 268

[Note the original copy of Book 14 ends in the middle of this deed but Book 3 indicates the following three deeds were once in Book 14.]

261. Dec. 16, 1769 Daniel Warlick & wife Barbara (Tryon Co) to Philip Warlick (same); for 50£ sold 400 ac on both sides of Potts Cr; border: Frederick Wise's pasture, Sherrill's corner, & a meadow; part of 1,000 ac grant Sept. 3, 1753 to Daniel Warlick.   Signed Daniel Warlick & Barbara's mark. Witness Welkeed (sic). Rec. Jan. 1770 (sic). Book 3 p. 325; Book 14 p. 270

262. Apr. 5, 1776 Nicholas Clay (Tryon Co) to Hugh Montgomery, merchant (Salisbury, NC); for 150£ sold (1) 456 ac in Tryon formerly Mecklenburg Co on SW side of S fork of Catawba R; includes an improvement; sold Jan. 6 & 7, 1769 by John Potts & wife Mary to Nicholas Clay; and (2) 100 ac on S side of Potts Cr; border: said Clay, corner of "the" school house land, Stotler, Warlock, & "his" other survey; sold Sept. 20, 1772 by John Potts to Nicholas Clay (see Tryon Co Book 7).   Signed Nichlos Clah (german). Witness John Blake & Alex Brown. Wit. oath Jul. 9, 1797 by John Blake to Spruce Macay. Book 3 p. 327; Book 14 p. 372(sic)

263. Apr. 5, 1776 Peter Stetler (Tryon Co) to Hugh Montgomery (Salisbury, NC); for 100£ sold 400 ac in Tryon Co on both sides of Potts Cr on S side of S fork of Catawba R; border: Potts and near Overwinter; granted Apr. 28, 1768 to Peter Stetler (see Secretary's Book #13).   Signed Peter Ralller(?) (german). Witness John Blake & Alex Brown. Wit. oath Jul. 9, 1797 by John Blake to Spruce Macay. Book 3 p. 328; Book 14 p. 273

Book 3 and Book 15
April Session 1788
264. Mar. 1, 1778 Daniel Russel & wife Jemima (Burke Co) to John Waggoner (same); for 150£ sold 200 ac in Burke formerly Mecklenburg Co on S side of Cuttabaw R and both sides of Little Cr; border: Thomas Little and Archabald Little; granted Apr. 25, 1767 to Thomas Beaty who sold to David Robertson who sold to Aug. 16, 1776 to Daniel Russel.   Signed Daniel Russel & Jemima's mark. Witness Temperance Bradshaw, Ruth Bradshaw, & Rebekah Bradshaw. Rec. Apr. 1788. Book 3 p. 330; Book 15 p. 1

265. Mar. 3, 1787 Thomas Waggoner (Lincoln Co) to Edmond Waggoner (same); for 50£ NC money sold 100 ac in Lincoln formerly Burke Co on W side of Catawba R between Beaverdam Cr and Little Cr; border: Jno Waggoner, Reuben

Petties line, & a branch; granted Mar. 14, 1780 to Thomas Waggoner.   Signed Thos Wagoner. Witness John Allen, Thos Wheeler, & John Waggoner. Rec. Apr. 1788. Book 3p. 332; Book 15 p. 2 [Note: pages 3 & 4 missing from Book 15]

266. Apr. 3, 1788 Joseph Dickson (Lincoln Co) to James Dickson (same); for 5£ sold 300 ac between Cuttabaw R and South fork; border: "the" creek; part of land "I" bought of Thomas Polk esq and part of 200 ac granted from the state.   Signed Jo Dickson. Witness John Dickson & Eliva Dickson. Rec. Apr. 1788. Book 3 p. 333; Book 15 p. 4

267. Oct. 14, 1785 Thomas Robinson, Martha Morgan, & Elisabeth Cartright (Rutherford Co) to Nicholas Haviner (Lincoln Co); for 150£ NC money sold 300 ac on N side of Indian Cr; part of grant Apr. 10, 1752 to Evin Lewis in Anson now Lincoln Co and transfered to several person until Thomas Robinson, Martha Morgan, & Elisbath Cartright "became legally vest" with the property.   Signed Thomas Robinson, Martha Morgan, & Elisabeth Cartright. Witness Jacob Han & James Camp. Rec. Apr. 1788. Book 3 p. 335; Book 15 p. 6

268. Aug. 11, 1787 Philip Null & wife Margaret (Lincoln Co) to George Launce (same); for 200£ NC money sold 170 ac on both sides of Potts Cr; part of grant Sept 3, 1753 to Thomas Potts and Samuel Beason who sold to Joseph Milecan (or Millican) who willed it to his daughter Mary wife of William Diarment desc and Mary sold it Sept. 20, 1784 to Joseph Hoof who sold Sept. 30, 1784 to Joseph Nicewhanger who sold Feb. 8, 1786 to Philip Null.   Signed Philip Null & Margaret's mark. Witness Jacob Cotner & Robt Blackburn. Rec. Apr. 1788. Book 3 p.336; Book 15 p. 8

269. Aug. 11, 1787 Philip Null & wife Margaret (Lincoln Co) to George Launce (same); for 200£ NC money sold 250 ac on both sides of Potts Cr; border: Potts' old line; part of grant Sept. 3, 1753 to Thomas Potts and Samuel Beason who sold to Joseph Millican who willed it to daughter Catherine wife of Jonathan Jones (Potts--lined out) who sold Mar. 24, 1785 to Philip Null.   Signed Philip Null and Margaret's mark. Witness Jacob Cottner & Robt Blackburn. Rec. Apr. 1788. Book 3 p. 338; Book 15 p. 9

270. Feb. 20, 1788 Peter Shrum (or Srum) (Lincoln Co) to Nicholas Schrum (same); for 25£ NC money sold 360 ac; border: Christian Carpenter jr's old line. Signed Peter Shrum's mark. Witness Jacob Srum (german) & William Tankersley. Rec. Apr. 1788. Book 3 p. 339; Book 15 p. 11

271. Sept. 29, 1774 John Mull & wife Mary (Mecklenburg Co) to Benedick Hawn (same); for 30£ sold 73 ac in Mecklenburg Co on S side of S fork of Cuttabaw R; border: said Mull's old "beginning" corner; part of tract where John Mull lives. Signed John & Mary Mull's marks. Witness John Fisher & Josuer Gas (or Gape). Rec. Apr. 1788. Book 3 p. 340; Book 15 p. 13

Lincoln County, NC Deed book 3

272. Feb. 27, 1788 Adam Eaker (Lincoln Co) to William Whittenberg (same); for 20£ sold 50 ac on waters of Lyles Cr; border: his own land, a large spring, & Eaker's old corner; part of grant Oct. 11, 1783 to Adam Eaker.   Signed Adam & Mary Eaker's marks. Witness David Ramsey & Brent Sigman (german). Rec. Apr. 1788. Book 3 p. 342; Book 15 p. 14(renumbered p. 12)

273. Dec. 21, 1787 Charles Williams (Lincoln Co) to William Abernathy (same); for 20£ sold [ac omitted] on both sides of Doctors Br of Killions Cr; part of a grant to Jacob Forney, David Crites, & Paul Whisenhunt.   Signed Charles Williams. Witness Jos Abernathy "by order" Nathan Abernathy. Rec. Apr. 1788. Book 3 p. 343; Book 15 p. 15

274. Apr. 2, 1787 George Goodwin (Lincoln Co) to Hanray Hover (same); for 50£ sold 155 ac on both sides of Kislers Cr; border: mouth of a small branch and Limbery; part of grant by the king to John Coon who sold to George Gooden. Signed George Goodwin & Bebekah's mark. Witness Llias Meyers (german), Henry Baker, & Llias Meyer "uner" (Elias Myers written in book) (german). Rec. Apr. 1788. Book 3 p. 344; Book 15 p. 16

275. Apr. 7, 1788 Jacob Phifer (Lincoln Co) to Martin Speegle (same); for 25£ NC money sold 265 ac; border: Lutes' line on E side of N fork of Long Br, Alexander, George Hepner, James Wilson, & Danl McKisick; granted Mar. 14, 1780 to Jacob Weaver who sold Aug. 16, 1784 to Jacob Phifer.   Signed Jacob Phifer's mark. Witness Danl McKisick. Rec. Apr. 1788. Book 3 p. 345; Book 15 p. 18

276. Apr. 6, 1788 Frederic Hafner (Lincoln Co) to Adam Bolick (same); for 50£ NC money sold 100 ac on waters of Moyers Br of Lyles Cr; border: Jacob Moyer's old line, Roerk, Galbraith Falls' old line, & Benfield; granted (#1009) Aug. 7, 1787 to Frederic Hafner.   Signed Frirdrich Hafner (german). Witness Battrim Coles, Adam Bolik, & George Islinger (german). Rec. Apr. 1788. Book 3 p. 346; Book 15 p. 19

277. Sept. 28, 1787 James Hillhouse (Lincoln Co) to John Hufman (same); for 60£ sold 114 ac on waters of big Long Cr; border: Hufman, Roads' line, Massey, & Hoyle.   Signed James Hillhouse. Witness Joseph Massey & Holan Massey. Rec. Apr. 1788. Book 3 p. 348; Book 15 p. 21

278. Mar. 7, 1788 Joseph Henry esq (Lincoln Co) to Spruce Macay esq (Salisbury); for 150£ NC money sold a Negro names Squire.   Signed Joseph Henry. Witness Ad Osborn. Rec. Apr. 1788. Book 3 p. 349; Book 15 p. 22
279. Mar. 15, 1788 Joseph Dickson, commissioner in trust for Lincolnton, (Lincoln Co) to Martin Friday (same); for 40s NC money sold [ac omitted] lot 13 in SW of Lincolnton; lot is 6 by 14 rods.   Signed Jo Dickson. Witness John Dickson. Rec. Apr. 1788. Book 3 p. 349; Book 15 p. 23

280. Aug. 2, 1787 Henry Reynolds & wife Elisabeth (Lincoln Co) to Philip Anthony (same); for 50£ NC money sold 200 ac on N side of Indian Cr; border: Thomas Reynolds' old line "formerly"; granted Nov. 16, 1764 to Thomas Reynolds who sold Nov. 19, 1774 to Henry Reynolds.   Signed Henry Reynolds & Elisabeth's mark. Witness Jacob Cotner & Robt Blackburn. Rec. Apr. 1788. Book 3 p. 350; Book 15 p. 24

281. Aug. 2, 1786 Henry Reynolds & wife Elisabeth (Lincoln Co) to Philip Anthony (same); for 50£ NC money sold 300 ac on Lick fork of Indian Cr about 2.5 miles W of where John Reynolds lives; includes Waldings improvement; granted May 4, 1769 to David McKee who sold Apr. 8, 1778 to Richard McKee who sold to Henry Reynolds.   Signed Henry Reynolds & Elisabeth's mark. Witness Jacob Cotner & Robert Blackburn. Rec. Apr. 1788. Book 3 p. 352; Book 15 p. 26

282. Apr. 5, 1788 George Eslinger (Lincoln Co) to Jacob Bolick (same); for 100£ NC money sold 200 ac on Snow Cr; border: a meadow, a branch, & Perkins' mill Road; includes improvement made by Michael Hafner; granted (#1028) Aug. 7, 1787 to George Eslinger.   Signed Georg Eslinger (german). Witness Nathan Armitage, Johan Adam Colely (german), & John Rovek. Rec. Apr. 1788. Book 3 p. 353; Book 15 p. 27

283. Nov. 24, 1787 Peter Johnston (Lincoln Co) to Henry Shell (same); for 100£ NC money sold 380 ac on both sides of Clarks Cr; border: Peter Ichar, Fry, & Mill's land; granted May 18, 1771 to Peter Johnston.   Signed Peter Johnson. Witness David Miller, Rudolph Conrod, & John Shell. Rec. Apr. 1788. Book 3 p. 354; Book 15 p. 29

284. Apr. 7, 1788 John Gullick (Lincoln Co) to Jonathan Gullick (same); for 5£ NC money sold 200 ac on S side of S fork of Cuttabaw R on a creek formerly called Third Cr now Little Cuttabaw Cr; includes an Indian field; granted Feb. 3, 1754 to Robert Patterson and sold by sheriff to Nathaniel Alexander who sold Jan. 11, 1766 to John Gullick.   Signed John Gullick. Witness John Walloce, Robert Campbell, & John Gullick (sic). Rec. Apr. 1788. Book 3 p. 355; Book 15 p. 30

285. Apr. 9, 1788 John Porter & John Moore to Robert Weer; for 100£ NC money sold a Negro wench Rachel and a child Luce.   Signed John Porter & John Moore. Witness Jos Henry. Rec. Apr. 1788. Book 3 p. 357; Book 15 p. 32

286. Jan. 15, 1788 James Freeman (Lincoln Co) to Joel Doss (same); for 1,000£ sold 390 ac on W side of Cuttabaw R; border: near his other upper corner; includes surveys made by Thos Robison; granted Nov. 16, 1764 to Andrew Hazelip. Signed James Freeman. Witness Jo Dickson & Anthony Hinkle. Rec. Apr. 1788. Book 3 p. 357; Book 15 p. 32

287. Jun. 8, 1787 Absalom Bonham (Lincoln Co) to Abraham Havener (same); for 10£ sold 60 ac on waters of S fork of Cuttabaw R; border: Christian Horse, Palmer, & William Waddel; part of 160 ac grant to Absalom Bonham.   Signed Absalom Bonham. Witness David Ramsey & John Carpender. Rec. Apr. 1788. Book 3 p. 358; Book 15 p. 33

288. Apr. 10, 1788 Absalom Bonham (Lincoln Co) to Joseph Henry esq (same); for 27£ NC money sold [ac omitted] lot 13 in SW quarter of Lincolnton; lot is 6 by 14 rods; sold Jul. 20, 1786 by Joseph Dickson esq, proprietor in trust for commissrs. of Lincolnton, to Absalom Bonham.   Signed Absalom Bonham. Witness Robt McCasland, John Long, & Jno Wilson. Rec. Apr. 1788. Book 3 p. 359; Book 15 p. 34

289. Aug. 2, 1787 Henry Reynolds & wife Elizabeth (Lincoln Co) to Philip Anthony (same); for 500£ NC money sold 500 ac on both sides of Indian Cr; part of 600 ac grant Aug. 30, 1753 to Thomas Reynolds and transfered to "sundry persons" until Henry Reynolds became legally vested in the property.   Signed Henry Reynolds & Elizabeth's mark. Witness Jacob Cotner & Robert Blackburn. Rec. Apr. 1788. Book 3 p. 361; Book 15 p. 36

July Court 1788
290. Jan. 10, 1788 Joseph Dickson esq, proprietor in trust for commissioners for Lincolnton, (Lincoln Co) to Christian Renhart and Andrew Heddick, trustees for Societies of Dutch Presbyterians [Christian Renhart] and Dutch Lutherians [Andrew Heddick] of Lincolnton & the vicinity; for 10s sold 2 ac 16 square poles to build any house of public worship in the future on the land, a school house for both Dutch & English, & a burrial place for the dead of said societies; house of worship is already built and societies want to incorporate and vest land to their trustees and successors; land is in SE square of Lincolnton where Dutch meeting house stands; border: 30 ft from SE corner of Absalom Bonham's lot #13, S end of lots 13, 14, 15, & 16, & a branch; lot is 24 by 14 poles.   Signed Jo Dickson, Christian Renhart, & Andreioh Hudig (german). Witness W. Waightstile Avery & Jos Henry. Rec. Jul. 1788. Book 3 p. 362; Book 15 p. 37

291. Dec. 5, 1787 Joseph Henry (Lincoln Co) to William Maclean (same); for 125£ sold 500 ac on Indian Cr a S branch of S fork of Cuttabaw R about 3 miles above Thomas Reynolds; includes an old Indian Camp; sold Dec. 10, 1783 by executors of Francis Beatey desc to Joseph Henry.   Signed Jos Henry. Witness Ad Osborn & Thos Polk. Rec. Jul. 1788. Book 3 p. 364; Book 15 p. 41

292. Jun. 20, 1788 Rudolph Conrad (Lincoln Co) to Andrew Stockinger (same); for 15£ NC money sold 140 ac on both sides of northern branh of Pinch Gut Cr waters of Clarks Cr; border: John Smire, Conrad Tips, Frederick Marckles, Whittenberg, & a conditional line; granted Aug. 7, 1787 to Rudolph Conrad. Signed Rudolph Conrad. Witness David Allison & Henrich Collinger (german). Rec. Jul. 1788. Book 3 p. 365; Book 15 p. 42.

293. Jun. 21, 1788 David Witherspoon (Lincoln Co) to Basil Dawsey (same); for 20£ NC money sold 3 head of horned cattle: a red cow about 8 years old, a spotted 2 year old heifer, & a red yearling heifer, all his bedding & household furniture, flax and cotton now growing on my "plantation", 15 bushels of corn now growing on said "plantation" when grain is fit for pulling and enough corn fodder to winter two of the cattle.   Signed David Wespoon (sic). Witness Joseph Steel. Rec. Jul. 1788. Book 3 p. 367; Book 15 p. 44

294. Oct. 14, 1782 John Baird (Tryon Co) to Samuel Gordon (same); for 15£ sold 200 ac in Tryon Co on branches of Little Cuttabaw Cr and both sides of a path from said Baird's to widdow Smith's; border: hickory & oak marked "RB"; granted Mar. 2, 1775 to John Baird.   Signed John & Frances Baird. Witness James Baird & Robert Shanon. Rec. Jul. 1788. Book 3 p. 367; Book 15 p. 44

295. Feb. 15, 1787 John Hancel (Mceklinberg Co) to John Cooper (Burke Co) for 60£ NC money sold 150 ac on S fork of Mountain Cr; border: Wm Armstrong, John Saillor, a branch, "centre of the whole tract", & Philip Saillor; part of 300 ac granted Oct. 8, 1782 to John Saillor.   Signed John Hancel. Witness William Caldwell & John Sutton. Rec. Jul. 1788. Book 3 p. 369; Book 15 p. 46

296. Apr. 8, 1788 Margaret Beatty, William Beatty, & Francis McCorkle, executors of Thomas Beatty desc, to Isaac Cooper; for 100£ paid to Thomas Beatty sold 200 ac; part of 660 ac granted to John & Thomas Beatty who sold this part of John Conlay who sold to John Reed who sold 200 ac to Samuel Hunter & sold for 100£ paid in four "Gales" to Isaac Cooper and Samuel Hunter gave a bond of 400£ to Isaac Cooper on Sept. 14, 1782 to make a good title in 6 months; Samuel Hunter died intestate and Thomas Beatty was Samuel Hunter's administrator; Thomas Beatty was to made a good title because it appeared John Reed hadn't really sold 200 ac total to Samuel Hunter and now John Reed has made a deed to Isaac Cooper for 200 ac; grantees of this deed agree to keep John Reed "emnyfyed" for said deed.   Signed Margaret & William Beatty [Fracis McCorkle doesn't sign]. Witness Frs Cunningham & Davd. Chirry. Rec. Jul. 1788. Book 3 p. 370; Book 15 p. 47

297. Jul. 5, 1788 James Collins sr (Lincoln Co) to Alexander McIntire (same); for 50£ NC money sold 100 ac on W side of Buffaloe Cr; border: N line of an old tract; part of 300 ac granted Mar. 2, 1775 to James Collins.   Signed James Collins. Witness James McAfee, William Fowler, & ABm Collins. Rec. Jul. 1788. Book 3 p. 371; Book 15 p. 48

298. Jul. 7, 1788 Philip Burns (Lincoln Co) to John Benfield (saem); for 150£ NC money sold 350 ac on a branch of Elk Cr waters of Cuttabaw R; border: George Smith and "new lines"; granted Jun. 25, 1765 to George Smith who sold to Conrod Burns and conveyed to his oldest son Philip Burns, executor of Conrad Burns'

estate.   Signed Philip Burns' mark. Witness David Ramsey & Jacob Marten. Rec. Jul. 1788. Book 3 p. 372; Book 15 p. 50

299. Nov. 28, 1785 Field Bradshaw (Lincoln Co) to son Jonas Bradshaw (same); for love & affection gave a Negro girl Agness 13 years old.   Signed Field Bradshaw. Witness John Haskins & Benjamin Ratlist. Rec. Jul. 1788. Book 3 p. 373; Book 15 p. 51

300. Apr. 8, 1788 John Reed to Isaac Cooper; for 100£ NC money sold 200 ac; border: Abraham Wamuck's corner.   Signed John Reed. Witness Frs Cunningham & Davd. Chirry. Rec. Jul. 1788. Book 3 p. 374; Book 14 p. 51 [Note: deed #296 above not mentioned in this deed.]

301. Jul. 9, 1788 Peter Coone (Lincoln Co) to Peter Blonck (same); for 45£ NC money sold 232 ac on a branch of Ingen (sic) Cr; border: Money, Philip Null, & Henry Houser; granted Sept. 24, 1785 to Peter Coone.   Signed Peter Coon. Witness Fredk Aderholdt. Rec. Jul. 1788. Book 3 p. 375; Book 15 p. 53

302. Dec. 14, 1785 Joseph Henry, sheriff (Lincoln Co) to Drury Logan (same); for 132£ sold 300 ac on both sides of Indian Cr; border: Thomas Randle on S side of Indian Cr; includes half of the old place Moses Moore formerly lived on; sold due to writ Oct. 11, 1785 from Lincoln Co Pleas & Quarter Sessions Court to levy 130£ and 3£ 11s 3p cost from Moses Moore due to suit of Henry Hollman; money to be returned to court 1st Monday of Jan. "next" and sale authorized by act of Assembly on Oct. 25, 1764.   Signed Jos Henry. Witness Ad Osborn & Wm Sharpe. Rec. Jul. 1788. Book 3 p. 376; Book 15 p. 54

303. Ju. 5, 1788 James Collins sr (Lincoln Co) to Jacob Collins (same); for 50£ sold 50 ac on E side of Buffaloe Cr; border: Beaverdam Br; part of 300 ac granted Mar. 2, 1775 to James Collins.   Signed James Collins' mark. Witness Thomas McAfee, Alexander Mentier, & Jonathan Willson. Rec. Jul. 1788. Book 3 p. 378; Book 15 p. 56

304. Aug. 17, 1787 Daniel Bullinger & wife Barbary (Lincoln Co) to Anthony Hollman (same); for 300£ NC money sold 250 ac on S side of Howards Cr; part of grant May 17, 1754 to Francis McElwean and part of two other tracts granted to Samuel Howard and transfered to "various persons" until Daniel & Barbary Bullinger became vested in the title.   Signed Daniel Bullinger (german) & Barbary's mark. Witness Henry Hollman & Robt Blackburn. Rec. Jul. 1788. Book 3 p. 379; Book 15 p. 57

305. Apr. 8, 1788 Samuel Young (Rowan Co) to Samuel Caldwell (Lincoln Co); for 320£ sold 350 ac on S side of Cuttabaw R; border: mouth of Beaverdam Br; "plantation" where Wm Caldwell lives; part of a tract taken from James Carter esq by writ from Wilmington Supreme Court (New Hanover, Bladen, Onslow, Duplin, Anson, & Cumberland Cos) in 32nd year of reign of King George II

Lincoln County, NC Deed book 3

[1758] due to suit brought by John Brandon and sold Jan. 6 & 7, 1763 by sheriff John Haimer to Thomas McKnight who sold to Samuel Young.   Signed Saml Young. Witness Robt Alexander & Alex Nelson. Rec. Jul. 1788. Book 3 p. 380; Book 15 p. 58

306. Aug. 7, 1787 John & Philip Bullinger (Lincoln Co) to Anthony Hollman (same); for 200£ NC money sold 250 ac on N side of Howards Cr; border: "the" old line; part of grant May 17, 1754 to Francis McElwean and two other tracts granted to Samuel Howard and since transfered to "sundry different persons" until John & Philip Bullinger became vested in the title.   Signed Johoann Bollinger (german) & Filib Bollinger (german). Witness Reuben McClenachan & Robt Blackburn. Rec. Jul. 1788. Book 3 p. 382; Book 15 p. 60

307. Dec. 17, 1779 Jacob Baker (Lincoln Co) to Field Bradshaw (Mecklenburg Co); for 250£ sold 25 ac on S side of Catawba R; border: Abraham Scott and Coborns Cr; part of grant Sept. 13, 1759 to John Killion who sold to Richd Earhart and "by sundry conveyances" to Jacob Baker.   Signed Jacob Baker. Witness Vincent Cox & John Brown Skrimshire. Rec. Jul. 1788. Book 3 p. 384; Book 15 p. 62

308. Apr. 7, 1788 Peter Iker (Lincoln Co) to Laurence Iker (same); for 1£ sold 175 ac on waters of Clarks Cr; part of 500 ac willed to Peter Iker by his father Peter Iker (sic); border: Peter Iker, old corners, & a branch.   Signed Peter Iker. Witness David Ramsey & Henrich Eiger (german). Rec. Jul. 1788. Book 3 p. 385; Book 15 p. 63

309. Apr. (blank), 1786 James Johnston (Lincoln Co) to Lewis Hill (same); for 25£ NC money sold 50 ac on S side of Cuttaba R; border: Nance, Dunkin's old line, & Scott.   Signed Joseph Johnston. Witness John Baldridge & Anthony Hinkle. Rec. Jul. 1788. Book 3 p. 386; Book 15 p. 65

310. Jun. 15, 1788 Joseph Dickson, commissioner in trust for Lincolnton, (Lincoln Co) to Henry Hoke (same); for 2£ sold [ac omitted] lot 1 in SE square of Lincolnton; lot is 6 by 12 rods.   Signed Jo Dickson. Witness Eliza Dickson. Rec. Jul. 1788. Book 3 p. 387; Book 15 p. 66

311. May 6, 1788 Henry Reynolds (Lincoln Co) to Henry Hoke (same); for 20£ NC money sold 220 ac on Horse Br of Buffaloe Br of Indian Cr; border: Christian Acres and Nicholas Welsh's corner; granted Aug. 7, 1787 to Henry Reynolds. Signed Henry Reynolds. Witness Samuel Carbenter (sic) & Catherine Carpenter. Rec. Jul. 1788. Book 3 p. 388; Book 15 p. 67

312. Jul. 5, 1788 James Collins sr (Lincoln Co) to Abraham Collins (same); for 100£ NC money sold 150 ac on E side of Buffaloe Cr waters of main Broad R; border: Beaverdam Br; part of 300 ac granted Mar. 2, 1775 to said James Collins.

Signed James Collins' mark. Witness James McAfee, Alexander McIntire, & Jonathan Wilson. Rec. Jul. 1788. Book 3 p. 389; Book 15 p. 68

313. May 3, 1788 William McEwin (Lincoln Co) to Robert Johnston (same); for 200£ sold 200 ac on both sides of Doctors Cr; border: William Moore, "said" Millican, Hogan, & Jno Moore; sold Apr. 27, 1784 by Robert Johnston to William McEwin.   Signed Wm McEwin. Witness Robert Johnston & Jo Dickson. Rec. Jul. 1788. Book 3 p. 390; Book 15 p. 70

314. Jul. 17, 1778 David Abernathy (Lincoln Co) to Abraham Earhart, Peter Forney, Turner Abernathy, & Abraham Forney; for 30£ NC money sold 45 ac; border: Abernathy's corner.   Signed David Abernathy. Witness Matthias Peterson, Amos Pugh, & William Maskall. Rec. Jul. 1788. Book 3 p. 392; Book 15 p. 72

315. Feb. 22, 1788 Jacob Coon & wife Catey (Rowan Co) to Henry Cope (Lincoln Co); for 40£ NC money sold 300 ac on head of Leonards fork of Indian Cr; border: upper part of Henry Wartman's land.   Signed Jacob Kuhn (german) & Catey's mark. Witness   Johamer Kneber(?) (german) & Benshemen Nerren. Rec. Jul. 1788. Book 3 p. 394; Book 15 p. 74

316. Jul. 9, 1788 Joseph Henry, sheriff (Lincoln Co) to Thomas Polk esq (Mecklenburg Co); for 40£ 1s sold 300 ac on both sides of Camp Cr; border: below Nichs Welsh; sold due to writ Jan. 15, 1788 from Lincoln Co Pleas & Quarter Sessions Court to levy 668£ 13s and 3£ 4s 1p cost from James Foster due to suit to Thos Polk esq; money to be returnd to court 1st Monday of Apr. "next" and sale authorized by act of Assembly on Oct. 25, 1764.   Signed Joseph Henry. Witness Ad Osborn & R Wood. Rec. Jul. 1788. Book 3 p. 395; Book 15 p. 75

317. Jul. 9, 1788 Joseph Henry, sheriff (Lincoln Co) to Thomas Polk esq (Mecklenburg Co); for 25£ sold 300 ac on N fork of Indian Cr; border: a ridge on NE side of "the" branch; includes Welch's hunting camps; sold due to writ Jan. 15, 1788 from Lincoln Co Pleas & Quarter Sessions Court to levy 668£ 13s and 3£ 4s 1p cost from James Foster due to suit of Thos Polk esq; money to be returned to court 1st Monday of Apr. "next" and sale authorized by act of Assembly on Oct. 25, 1764.   Signed Joseph Henry. Witness Ad Osborn & R Wood.   Rec. Jul. 1788. Book 3 p. 397; Bok 15 p. 77

318. Jul. 9, 1788 Joseph Henry, sheriff (Lincoln Co) to Hugh Polock (Mecklenburg Co); for 30£ sold 450 ac on branches of Indian Cr a South branch of S fork of Cuttaba R; border: S corner of Thomas Reynolds and David Huddleston; sold due to wirt Jan. 15, 1788 from Lincoln Co Pleas & Quarter Sessions Court to levy 668£ 13s and 3£ rs 1p cost from James Foster due to suit of Thomas Polk esq; money to be returned 1st Monday of Apr. "next" and sale authorized by act of Assembly on Oct. 25, 1764.   Signed Joseph Henry. Witness Ad Osborn & R Wood. Rec. Jul. 1788. Book 3 p. 399; Book 15 p. 79

319. Jun. 2, 1788 Joseph Henry, sheriff (Lincoln Co) to Richard Vandike (same); for 19£ 3s 9p sold 100 ac on head of Wyatts branches of S fork of Cuttabaw R; border: McKnit & Wyatt; previously sold Oct. 6, 1786 by Stephen Senter to John Peter Baker; sold now due to writ Apr. 15, 1787 from Lincoln Co Pleas & Quarter Sessions Court to levy 15£ 11s 6p and 3£ 12s 3p cost from John Peter Baker due to suit of Richard Vandike; money to be returned to court 1st Monday of Jul. "next" and sale authorized by act of Assembly on Oct. 25, 1764.   Signed Jos Henry. Witness Jas Wilson, Sarah Wilson, & Jno Wilson. Rec. Jul. 1788. Book 3 p. 400; Book 15 p. 81

320. Apr. 5, 1788 George Eslinger (Lincoln Co) to John Roerh (same); for 150£ NC money sold 150 ac on waters of Lyles Cr; border: Balser Trait; granted (#975) Aug. 7, 1787 to George Eslinger.   Signed Georg Eslinger (german). Witness Nathan Armitage, Johanon Amledeg (german), & Jacob Hedeg(?) (german). Rec. Jul. 1788. Book 3 p. 402; Book 15 p. 83

321. Oct. 25, 1787 Lorance Yonts (Lincoln Co) to Peter Tinker (same); for 80£ NC money sold 200 ac on both sides of Indian Cr above the Scout Camps; border: Peter Moiars "third" corner & his last corner and an open line of former survey of which this is a part.   Signed Lorance & Elisabeth Yonts' marks. Witness Henrich Rummer (Henry Remer written in book) (german) & Herichen Ennib(?) (german). Rec. Jul. 1788. Book 3 p. 403; Book 15 p. 85

322. May 12, 1788 Philip Null & wife Margret (Lincoln Co) to Andrew Lorets (same); for 120£ NC money sold 125 ac on waters of Howards Cr; border: Abraham Beaker, widdow Bollinger, Stottler, & on Millstone Br; part of grant Mar. 28, 1757 to Thomas Potts who willed it to son Jonathan Potts who sold to John Firtress who sold in Mar. 1787 to Philip Null. Signed Philip Null & Margret's mark. Witness John Moore & Henry Hoke. Rec. Jul. 1788. Book 3 p. 405; Book 15 p. 86

323. Apr. 9, 1788 Peter Iker (Lincoln Co) to Henry Iker (same); for 1£ NC money sold 175 ac on waters of Clarks Cr; border: Lorance Iker; willed to Henry Iker (sic) by his father Peter Iker; part of 508 ac tract.   Signed Peter Iker. Witness David Ramsey & Lorance Eiher (german). Rec. Jul. 1788. Book 3 p. 406; Book 15 p. 87

324. Nov. (blank), 1782 Samuel Gordon (Lincoln Co) to James Huggins (same); for 50£ NC money sold 200 ac on branches of Little Cutaba Cr and both sides of path from Jacob Beard's to widdow Smith's; border: hickory & white oak marked "RB"; granted Mar. 2, 1775 to Samuel Gordon.   Signed Samuel Gordon. Witness Isaac Holland & Thos Campbell. Rec. Jul. 1788. Book 3 p. 407; Book 15 p. 89

October Court 1788

325. Feb. 13, 1788 Francis Cunningham (Lincoln Co) to his son John Cunningham (same); for love and affection gave 238 ac; border: "upper W corner" of 266 ac tract belonging to Francis Cunningham and Henry Partain; part of his deeded land on Beaverdam Br.   Signed Frs Cunningham. Witness Mary Cunningham & Elizabeth Cunningham. Rec. Oct. 1788. Book 3 p. 408; Book 15 p. 90

326. Sept. 11, 1788 Joseph Grissemore, tanner (Lincoln Co) to Conrod Tips (same); for 200£ NC money sold a bay horse branded on near buttock "H" and off buttock "D", a mare that said Grissemore is to get "from the Northward", a 3 year old steer of bridle colour, a 4 year old steer of bridle colour, a 2 year old steer of "whitish" colour, a one year old steer of bridle colour, a black cow, 100 bushels of Indian corn, 300 ac now occupied by William Sigman, & all his goods & chattels; deed void if Joseph Grissemore pays Conrod Tips 200£ and interest in 2 years 6 months from now.   Signed Johann Grisemor (german). Witness Wm Blackburn & Robt Blackburn. Rec. Oct. 1788. Book 3 p. 410; Book 15 p. 92

327. Jun. 24, 1788 William Hamby (Burke Co) to Malachi Fikes (Lincoln Co); for 30£ sold 100 ac on both sides of Battle Run of Mountain Cr on W side of Cuttaba R; border: Joh Painter and Charles Ward; granted Oct. 28, 1782 to [omitted]. Signed William Hamby's mark. Witness John Pittillo & Millington Pittillo. Rec. Oct. 1788. Book 3 p. 411; Book 15 p. 93

328. Mar. 14, 1786 Jacob Horse (Lincoln Co) to Anthony Horse (same); for 50£ NC money sold 110 ac on S side of S fork of Cuttaba R; border: a meadow and Havener's corner.   Signed Jacob Hors (german). Witness Conratd Natther (german) & Michael Buff. Rec. Oct. 1788. Book 3 p. 412; Book 15 p. 94

329. Oct. 10, 1788 Joseph Dickson, commissioner in trust for Lincolnton, (Lincoln Co) to Lewis Warlock (same); for 40s sold [ac omitted] lot 18 in NE square of Lincolnton "being a back lot"; lot is 6 by 14 poles.   Signed Jo Dickson. Witness Wm Sharpe & Ad Osborn.   Rec. Oct. 1788. Book 3 p. 413; Book 15 p. 96

330. Sept. 26, 1788 John Roark (Lincoln Co) to William Wittenburg (same); for 35£ sold 150 ac on waters of Lyles Cr; border: Palser Trit.   Signed John Roark's mark. Witness Thos Puntch & Jane Puntch. Rec. Oct. 1788. Book 3 p. 414; Book 15 p. 97

331. May 17, 1788 James Patterson, tanner & currier (Lincoln Co) to James McNair, weaver of Bullocks Cr (York Co, SC); for 200£ sold 450 ac on waters of Crowders Cr; border: Levan; all of two grants: (1) 300 ac on S side of N fork of said creek granted Nov. 16, 1764 by Gov. Dobbs to John Walker who sold Jan. 25, 1775 to James Patterson; includes said Walker's improvements and acknowledged in court Jan. 1775 & registered Mar. 17, 1775 in Lincoln Co; and (2) 150 ac on Crowders Cr & joins above tract granted Mar. 25, 1780 by Gov.

Caswell to James Patterson.   James Patterson. Witness James Wilson, Samuel Barret, & James Graham. Rec. Oct. 1788. Book 3 p. 415; Book 15 p. 98

332. Oct. 9, 1788 Philip Cansler (Lincoln Co) to Philip Devibach (same); for 30£ NC money sold 75 ac on N side of S fork of Cuttabaw R; border: Philip Cansler and Ramsey; granted (#356) Sept. 12, 1787 to Philip Cansler.   Signed Phillip Jantsler (german). Witness David Ramsey & Jhomon(?) Hin_?_ (german). Rec. Oct. 1788. Book 3 p. 416; Book 15 p. 100

333. Jan. 22, 1787 William Gant (Lincoln Co) to Benjamin Taillor (same); for 10£ NC money sold 100 ac on N fork of Mountain Cr waters of Cuttabaw R; border: Robert Biging Perkins, conditional line, & old original line; part of grant Mar. 14, 1789 to William Gant.   Signed William Gant. Witness Henry Loller, Littleton Pittillo, Ute Perkis, & Upshare Davis. Rec. Oct. 1788. Book 3 p. 418; Book 15 p. 101

334. Oct. 9, 1788 Peter Best (Lincoln Co) to Martin Hoyl (same); for 5£ sold 15 ac on E side of S fork of Stoney Run; border: Peter Hoyl; part of grant to Boston Best who sold to his son Peter Best.   Signed Peter Best. Witness John Moore & Nicholas Shrum. Rec. Oct. 1788. Book 3 p. 419; Book 15 p. 103

335. Sept. 10,1788 Thomas Waston (Ga) to Philip Wiseanand (Lincoln Co); for 80£ NC money sold 300 ac on W side of Cuttabaw R on both sides of Howards Cr; border: below Nicholas Friday and on a branch; includes "the" shoals; granted Apr. 29, 1768 to Teter Havener.   Signed Thos Wasdin. Witness _?_ (german) & Michael Buff.   Rec. Oct. 1788. Book 3 p. 420; Book 15 p. 104

336. Feb. 14, 1788 James Martin (Lincoln Co) to William Earwood, planter (same); for 40£ NC money sold 250 ac on waters of Mountain Cr; border: Samuel Bryson; granted Aug. 7, 1787 to James Martin. Signed James Martin. Witness James Bryson & John Bryson. Rec. Oct. 1788. Book 3 p. 421; Book 15 p. 106

337. Nov. 11, 1776 Peter Johnston (Mecklenburg Co) to Laurence Sterr (Tryon Co); for 42£ 4s sold 250 ac in Tryon Co on Hoysers Br of Middle Cr; border: Henry Slinkard, a field, Peter Crites, & Elias Moyer; granted May 14, 1772 to Peter Johnston.   Signed Peter Johnston. Witness Peter Crits(?) (german) & Elias Moyer (german). Rec. Oct. 1788. Book 3 p. 423; Book 15 p. 107

338. Oct. 12, 1786 James Holland to Robert Wire; for 20£ sold [ac omitted]; border: Barnett; granted Oct. 28,1782 to James Holland.   Signed Jas Holland. Witness Wm Johnson & David Miller. Rec. Oct. 1788. Book 3 p. 424; Book 15 p. 109

339. Mar. 14, 1786 Jacob Horse (Lincoln Co) to Francis Horse (same); for 200£ NC money sold 300 ac on S side of S fork of Cuttaba R.   Signed Jacob Hos

(german). Witness Conrath Natther (german) & Michael Buff. Rec. Oct. 1788. Book 3 p. 425; Book 15 p. 111

340. Jan. 27, 1787 Rudolph Conrud (Lincoln Co) to George Laurence (same); for 200£ sold 371 ac on N side of Pinch Gut Cr; border: his own line, George Lutes, Bollinger, Rodolph's Br, Simon Horse, & Jacob Lutes; granted Mar. 15, 1780 to Rudolph Conrud.   Signed Rudolph Conrud. Witness Jas Wilson & Robt Blackburn. Rec. Oct. 1788. Book 3 p. 427; Book 15 p. 113

341. Mar. 21, 1786 Jacob Horse (Lincoln Co) to John Horse (same); for 100£ NC money sold 300 ac on both sides of Leoanhards [sic] fork of Indian Cr; border: Samuel Hayerd; granted Apr. 16, 1765 to Wm Ramsey who sold to Jacob Horse. Signed Jacob Hors (german). Witness Conrath Nertther (german) & Michael Buff. Rec. Oct. 1788. Book 3 p. 428; Book 15 p. 114

342. Aug. 3, 1788 Robert McCissick & wife Margaret (Lincoln Co) to Robert Knox (same); for 115£ NC money sold 143 ac on W side of Cuttabaw R and N side of Mountain Cr; border: Saplin; part of tract sold Aug. 1, 1781 by Henry Thomson to Robert McCissick and sold Jan. 5 & 6, 1765 by Abraham Collett to Henry Thomson.   Signed Robert McCusick & Margaret's mark. Witness Samuel Thompson. Thos Bell, & Thon McCusick. Rec. Oct. 1788. Book 3 p. 429; Book 15 p. 115

343. Jul. 8, 1788 Jacob Costner jr (Lincoln Co) to Michael Costner (same); for 10£ NC money sold 268 ac; border: Nicholas Fryday and John Smith; includes part of two tracts joining S fork of Cuttaba R; being property of "their" father Jacob Costner desc and now sold by Jacob Costner jr, son & administrator of Jacob Costner's estate.   Signed Jacob Costner. Witness David Ramsey, Lorentz _?_ (german), & Wirey Rudisell. Rec. Oct. 1788. Book 3 p. 431; Book 15 p. 118

344. Jan. 7, 1788 Martin Colter sr, taylor (Lincoln Co) to George Wilfong, yoeman (same); for 50£ 2s 6p NC money sold 25 ac 10 poles on N side of S fork of Cuttaba R; border: said Wilfong; part of 520 ac granted (#51) Apr. 6, 1765 to Martin Colter sr.   Signed Mardin Colter (german). Witness John Wilfong & Jacob Sutelmire. Rec. Oct. 1788. Book 3 p. 432; Book 15 p. 119

345. Aug. 22, 1788 Jacob Yorty, yoeman (Burk Co, Ga) to Peter Baker, yoeman (Lincoln Co); for 140£ NC money sold 182 ac on both sides of Jacobs R; border: Henry Ashabranner on E; granted (#958) Aug. 7, 1787 to Jacob Yorty.   Signed Jacob Yortey "hant" (german). Signed Deniel Lundson & Thomas Wasdin. Rec. Oct. 1788. Book 3 p. 433; Book 15 p. 120

346. Aug. 4, 1788 Olia & Alexander Johnston, executors of Samuel Johnston desc, (Richmond Co, Ga) to Charles Williams (Lincoln Co); for 60£, paid to Samuel Johnston desc for which Samuel Johnston gave Charles Williams a bond of 300£ to made a deed for 300 ac, sold (1) 150 ac on both sides of Rominger s Br;

border: Wisenunt; and (2) 150 ac on same branch near "the" Dutch meeting house; both tracts were granted to George Rominger who sold to Samuel Johnston. Signed Alexr Johnston & Olley "her" mark (sic). Witness Thomas McGee, Joseph Beuker, & N Dougherty. Rec. Oct. 1788. Book 3 p. 435; Book 15 p. 122

347. Aug. 18, 1788 Henry Cline, blacksmith & wife Elisabeth (Lincoln Co) to Peter Finger (same); for 240£ NC money sold 250 ac on both sides of Lockharts Cr; border: Mills' old line by a branch; granted Nov. 15, 1762 to Nicholas Welsh who sold Mar. 15, 1774 to James Lockhart who sold Nov. 19, 1787 to Henry Cline.   Signed Henrich Klein (german) & Elisabeth's mark. Witness Johenn Fieynoer(?) (german) & Robt Blackburn. Rec. Oct. 1788. Book 3 p. 436; Book 15 p. 124

348. Jul. 14, 1788 Robert Knox & James Johnston, executors of Robert Ewart desc (late of Lincoln Co), to John Nelson; for 750£ NC money sold (1) 325 ac on S side of Cataba R; border: James Johnston on S and Alexander Baldrige on W; sold Jul. 14 & 15, 1753 by George Cathy jr to Charles McPeters who sold Jul. 13, 1762 to Robert Ewart; Robert Ewart's will dated Nov. 21, 1781 directed executors to sell his land not already devised and Robert Knox & James Johnston were appointed administrators; will was filed in Lincoln Co Pleas & Quarter Sessions Court; and (2) 70 ac on W side of Cuttaba R; border: above tract and James Johnston formerly Philip Alston's; granted Jul. 21, 1774 to Robert Ewart; Note: Robert Ewart died possessing "325 ac" and 70 ac are not mentioned in first part of deed where the will is discussed.   Signed Robert Knox & James Johnston. Witness Alex Nelson, Jas Reed, & Thos Bell. Rec. Oct. 1788. Book 3 p. 437; Book 15 p. 126

January Court 1789
349. May 30, 1787 Thomas Salter "Northern liberties", merchant (Philadelphia, Pa) to John Coxe, yoeman & brother "by the mother's side of Thomas Salter, (formerly of NJ and now of Lincoln Co); for love & affection and 5s sold 210 ac in Lincoln formerly Anson Co; border: an old marked corner and land "lately granted by" Thomas Salter to his nephew Isaiah Liming; being remainder of 410 (sic) ac grant Mar. 28, 1751 to Peter Harpell who sold Feb. 19 & 20, 1768 (in Mecklenburg Co) to Thomas Salter who sold May 25 "Inst by metes & bounds" Northermost part to newphew Isaiah Liming.   Signed Tho Salter. Witness Vallentine Mauny & R Whitehead. Rec. Jan. 1789. Book 3 p. 440; Book 14 p. 128

350. May 25, 1787 Thomas Salter "Northern liberties", merchant (Philadelphia, Pa) to Isaiah Liming, tanner (formerly of "upper freehold" Monmouth Co, NJ and now of Lincoln Co); for love & affection & for his living on premises & 5s sold 210 ac; part of 420 ac grant Mar. 28, 1751 to Peter Harpell in Anson now Lincoln Co on N fork of Indian Cr; grant bordered a black oak marked "PH" and had yearly rent of 4s per 100 ac; grant was sold Feb. 19 & 20, 1768 by Peter Harpell to Thomas Salter (registered in Mecklenburg Co).   Signed Tho Salter. Witness

Vallentine Mauney & R Whitehead. Rec. Jan. 1789. Book 3 p. 441; Book 15 p. 130

351. May 18, 1787 William Steret to John Henderson; for 20£ sold 100 ac on S fork of Cuttaba R above James Henderson's mill; part of 200 ac grant by the state to William Steret.   Signed William Steret. Witness John Gillespie, Jno patterson, & Jonn Gullick. Rec. Jan. 1789. Book 3 p. 443; Book 15 p. 132

352. Jan. 5, 1789 James Litten (Lincoln Co) to son-in-law Elias White (same); for love & affection gave [ac omitted]; joins "my" old survey on S side of Cuttaba R and both sides of a small creek that "falls in" below Sherrill's ford; border: James Clark, James Litten, & a branch; granted Oct. 28, 1782 by Gov. Alexr Martin (at Fairfield) to James Litten.   Signed James Litten. Witness James Holsclaw & John Cabe. Rec. Jan. 1789. Book 3 p. 444; Book 15 p. 133

353. Dec. 23, 1788 Michael Buff & wife Mary (Lincoln Co) to Peter Myar (same); for 60£ NC money sold 300 ac on dividing ridge between Leonard & Indian Creeks.   Signed Michaeal Buff & Mary's mark. Witness J_?_ Hoyy (german) & Jacob Saign. Rec. Jan. 1789. Book 3 p. 445; Book 15 p. 135

354. Oct. 8, 1788 William Sherrill (Burke Co) to Elisha & Moses Sherrill (Lincoln Co); for 140£ sold 103.5 ac on W side of of Catawba R; border: Adam Sherill's lower corner; sold Jul. 2, 1785 to William Sherrill by his father Wm Sherill sr & registered (in Lincoln Co) Aug. 9, 1785 in Book 13 p. 232 by Jno Wilson, regis. Signed William Sherrill. Witness Joshua White & Henry Hollman. Rec. Jan. 1789. Book 3 p. 446; Book 15 p. 136

355. Jan. 17, 1784 Martin Anthony & wife Catharine (Burke Co) to Jacob Hittle (same); for 100£ NC money sold 400 ac in Burke Co; border: John Killion, James Henning, Thomas Winkler, Daniel Bowman, Philip Hegar, & Winklers Br; formerly property of Conrad Winkler; includes "his" improvement; granted Oct. 29, 1782 to Martin Anthony.   Signed Martin Anthoni (german) & Ceirehwina(?) (german). Witness Jacob Kilian & Jibb(?) Kilion (german). Rec. Jan. 1789. Book 3 p. 447; Book 15 p. 137

356. Mar. 8, 1788 Henry Hollman (Lincoln Co) & Michael Keller (same), executors of Jacob Baker desc (Lincoln Co), to Devolt Honsicher (same); for 5£ NC money sold 150 ac on N side of Shoal Br on S side of Cuttawba R; border: said Baker desc's other survey; includes the powder Spring; granted (#157) Aug. 7, 1787 to said Jacob Baker.   Signed Henry Hollman & Mihael Keller (german). Witness Michoal Keller jr (german) & Nathan Armitage. Rec. Jan. 1789. Book 3 p. 449; Book 15 p. 139

357. Mar. 8, 1788 Henry Hollman & Michael Keller (Lincoln Co), executors of will of Jacob Baker desc (Lincoln Co), to Nathan Armitage, feltmaker (same); for 60£ NC money sold 50 ac on S side of Cuttawba R; border: formerly Christopher

Hainer and now Henry Hollman's corner; granted Oct. 11, 1783 to William Sherrill who sold Dec. 23, 1785 to Jacob Baker desc (see Lincoln Co Book 14 fol. 2; registered May 9, 1786 by Jno Wilson, regis).   Signed Henry Hollman & Michal Keller (german). Witness Michoal Keller jr (german) & Hefer(?) Keller (german). Rec. Jan. 1789. Book 3 p. 450; Book 15 p. 140

358. Nov. 26, 1788 John Polk, weaver ("Burke Lincoln" Co) to William Moore (Lincoln Co); for 100£ sold 200 ac on waters of Crowders Cr; border: Richard Venable's corner; granted Feb. 28, 1775 to John Polk.   Signed John Polk. Witness Samuel Taylor, J Thomson, & James Johnson. Rec. Jan. 1789. Book 3 p. 451; Book 15 p. 142

359. Dec. 5, 1788 Melchior Hafner, farmer (Lincoln Co) to son John Hafner (same); for love & affection gave 200 ac on SE side of Lyles Cr; border: Henry Pope, General Rutherford, Jacob Boleh, old "beginning" corner, & a cleared field. Signed Melchior Hafner's mark. Witness Nathan Armitage & Adam Darr (german). Rec. Jan. 1789. Book 3 p. 452; Book 15 p. 143

360. Oct. 30, 1788 Joshua Sherril (Lincoln Co) to James Holsclaw (same); for 106£ sold 106.75 ac on W side of Cuttaba R; border: Burchfields Cr; granted Nov. 1, 1784 to Joshua Sherrill.   Signed Joshua Sherrill. Witness Elias White & Elisha Sherrill. Rec. Jan. 1789. Book 3 p. 453; Book 15 p. 144

361. Mar. 21, 1788 David Heaker (Lincoln Co) to Simon Heaker (same); for 50£ NC money sold 110 ac on W side of Cuttaba R on E side of Killions Cr.   Signed David Heaker's mark. Witness John Beale & Jonathan Hodson. Rec. Jan. 1789. Book 3 p. 454; Book 15 p. 145

362. Mar. 21, 1788 John Beale (Lincoln Co) to David Heaker (same); for 50£ NC money sold 78 ac on W side of Cutaba R and E side of Killions Cr; border: corner of Beale's old survey, said Heaker, & waggon road from George Heaker's to Tool's ford.   Signed John Beale. Witness Simon Heaker & Jonathan Hodson. Rec. Jan. 1789. Book 3 p. 455; Book 15 p. 146

363. Jan. 1, 1789 Jacob Sebaugh (Lincoln Co) to Christian Sebaugh (same); for 300£ NC money sold 150 ac on S side of S fork of Cuttabaw R on Potts Cr; granted Aug. 30, 1758 to Thomas Potts who willed it to son John Potts who with wife Mary sold it Jan. 6 & 7, 1769 to Nicholas Clay.   Signed Jacob Sabouh (or Sebouh) (german). Witness John Gray & Michl Buff. Rec. Jan. 1789. Book 3 p.456; Book 15 p. 147

364. Dec. 30, 1788 James Armstrong (Granville Co, SC (sic)) to John Lower (Lincoln Co); for 50£ sold 250 ac on Shoal Br of Kittles Cr of S fork of Cataba R; border: Ramsey, Wm Armstrong jr, Laboon, & a "May pole" (or Maple); includes his own improvement.   Signed James Armstrong. Witness David Bullinger & Michl Buff. Rec. Jan. 1789. Book 3 p. 457; Book 15 p. 149

365. Oct. 9, 1788 Michael Williams & wife Barbara (Lincoln Co) to Michael Rudisail (same); for 150£ NC money sold 200 ac on N side of S fork of Cataba R; border: George Rush and Peter Mostiller; granted Apr. 9, 1770 to William Sims.   Signed Michael & Barbara Williams' marks. Witness Jno Fulenwider & Reason Holland. Rec. Jan. 1789. Book 3 p. 459; Book 15 p. 150

366. Oct. (blank), 1788 James Holland (Rutherford Co) to Elisabeth Ramsour, daughter of Jacob Ramsour desc (Lincoln Co); for 100£ NC money sold 200 ac on Long Br of Buffalow Cr; includes a meadow above Robert Wear's entry on said branch and E of Robert Wear's claim which is on Hicory Br.   Signed Jas Holland. Witness David Miller & Samuel Carbunder. Rec. Jan. 1789. Book 3 p. 460; Book 15 p. 151

367. Dec. 3, 1787 Henry Moss (Lincoln Co) to Aaron Forman (same); for 20£ sold 50 ac on both sides of a branch of Mountain Cr; border: John Snider's corner and Hollingsworth's old line; part of a grant "now in the Office" to Samuel Hollingsworth.   Signed Henry Moss. Witness James Bryson & Jacob Lollar. Rec. Jan. 1789. Book 3 p. 461; Book 15 p. 153

368. Oct. 14, 1788 Sarah Cumberland (late of Lincoln Co) to Andrew Grisel (Lincoln Co); for 50£ NC money sold 150 ac on a fork of Clarks Cr; border: James Lockhart, Alexr Lockhart, & John Boyd; includes her own improvement; granted Aug. 7, 1787 to Sarah Cumberland.   Signed Sarah Cumberland's mark. Witness Wm Blackburn, William Lockhart, & Robt Blackburn. Rec. Jan. 1789. Book 3 p. 462; Book 15 p. 154

369. Nov. 10, 1788 John Hiltebrand (Rutherford Co) to John Lingafeld (Lincoln Co); for 60£ sold 300 ac on both sides of Howards Cr between Nicholas Friday and Henry Hiltebrand; border: a gravelly hill and Friday's old & new surveys. Signed John Hiltebrand. Witness Henry Summerour & Michael Buff. Rec. Jan. 1789. Book 3 p. 463; Book 15 p. 156

370. Jan. 7, 1789 James Bryson (Lincoln Co) to Adam Killin (same); for 50£ NC money sold 166 ac on waters of Keeners Cr; border: Valentine Cline, Thomas Earwood, Wm Earwood, & near his own land; part of two tracts: (1) granted by the king and (2) granted by the state.   Signed James Bryson. Witness Daniel Hudson & David Ramsey. Rec. Jan. 1789. Book 3 p. 465; Book 15 p. 157

371. (blank), 1788 Adam Cloninger (Lincoln Co) to Michael Cloninger (same); for 50£ NC money sold 200 ac on both sides of Seagles Cr including the forks and his improvement; border: Thomas Beaty; granted Apr. 9, 1770 to Philip Cloninger who sold to Adam Cloninger.   Signed Adam Cloninger. Witness Peter Forney & Sulleudin Deowalt. Rec. Jan. 1789. Book 3 p. 466; Book 15 p. 159

372. Aug. 29, 1788 John Sutton (Lincoln Co) to William Harbison (same); for 165£ sold a Negro woman "and child named Cloe". Signed John Sutton. Witness William Harbson jr & Richd Beale. Rec. Jan. 1789. Book 3 p. 467; Book 15 p. 160

373. Aug. 29, 1788 Abraham Earhart (Lincoln Co) to John Sutton; for 150£ sold a Negro woman "and" child named Cloe; Note: Aug. 29, 1788 John Sutton assigns his right to William Harbison. Signed Abraham Earhart. Witness Wm Harbeson jr & Richd Beale. Rec. Jan. 1789. Book 3 p. 468; Book 15 p. 161

374. Dec. 29, 1788 Joseph Henry, sheriff (Lincoln Co) to David Ramsey (same); for [omitted] sold 300 ac on both sides of Kittle Shoal Cr; granted Nov. 17, 1764 to Henry Moyer who sold Mar. 10, 1765 to Peter Smith who sold Mar. 24, 1775 to Robert Ramsey; sold now due to writ Oct. 27, 1788 from Lincoln Co Pleas & Quarter Sessions Court to levy 113£ 14s 3p and 3£ 11s 11p cost from Robert Ramsey due to suit of David Ramsey; money to be returned to court 1st Monday of Jan. "next" and sale authorized by act of Assembly on Oct. 25, 1764. Signed Jos Henry. Witness Ad Osborn & Chrs Purviance. Rec. Jan. 1789. Book 3 p. 468; Book 15 p. 161

375. Jan. 12, 1788 Matthias Peterson (Lincoln Co) to Michael Cloninger (same); for 60£ sold 200 ac on S side of Cataba R and both sides of Seagles Cr; border: his own line; granted Oct. 17, 1772 to Philip Cloninger. Signed Matthias Peterson. Witness Abraham Earhart, Jonathan Hegar, & Eliad(?) Hegar (german). Rec. Jan. 1789. Book 3 p. 470; Book 15 p. 163

376. Oct. 25, 1788 Martin Rendleman (Lincoln Co) to William Bonner (Mecklenburg Co); for 90£ sold 250 ac on middle fork of Killions Cr; granted Mar. 24, 1754 to Leonard Killion. Signed Martin Rintelman (german). Witness Peter Forney & Aba Forney. Rec. Jan. 1789. Book 3 p. 471; Book 15 p. 164

377. Jan. 3, 1789 Ubrick Crowder (Lincoln Co) to Conrod Hoan (same); for 106£ 10s NC money sold 150 ac on both sides of Muddy Br waters of S fork of Cataba R; border: a new town land known as Ubricksburg and a branch; part of grant in 1764 to Ubrick Crowder. Signed Ubrick Crowder. Witness David Ramsey & Wm Temple Coles. Rec. Jan. 1789. Book 3 p. 472; Book 15 p. 165

378. Jan. 3, 1789 Joseph Dickson (Lincoln Co) to Abraham Devenport (same); for 100£ sold 200 ac on S side of S fork of Cataba R; border: John Gillespie's corner and near Hamilton. Signed Jo Dickson. Witness Eliza Dickson. Rec. Jan. 1789. Book 3 p. 473; Book 15 p. 167

379. Jan. 6, 1787 George Deal, farmer (Lincoln Co) to William Frizel; for 85£ sold 314 ac on Mulls Cr; border: Barnard Sigman, John Foreman, John Cowan, George Minges, Burges Philips, Peter Deal, & Jacob Moyar. Signed Gorg Diehl

(german). Witness Wilhelm Diehl (german) & Peter Justice. Rec. Jan. 1789. Book 3 p. 474; Book 15 p. 168

380. Jun. 14, 1788 Samuel Young to John Moore, Justice of Peace (Lincoln Co); Samuel Young says in 1754 he was deputy surveyor in North Carolina and, due to a warrant from Surveyor General, he surveyed 600 ac for Frederick Wise on Howards Cr on S side of S fork of Catabaw R; above land then known as Francis McElwain's, and Samuel Young now shows a red oak that was "beginning" corner, and a white oak he shows was the original second corner.   Signed Saml Young. Witness John Moore, JP. Rec. Jan. 1789. Book 3 p. 475; Book 15 p. 169

April Court 1789
381. Mar. 25, 1789 William Beatty (Lincoln Co) to James Little (same); for 5s sold 55 ac; border: Thomas Beatty, Davd. Cherry, & James Litle; granted Aug. 7, 1787 to William Beatty.   Signed William Beatty. Witness Alexander Reed & John Little. Rec. Apr. 1789. Book 3 p. 476; Book 15 p. 170

382. Apr. 9, 1789 James Henderson (Lincoln Co) to John Moore (same); for 60£ sold 300 ac near Hoyls Cr; border: Jno Moore on N side of Jacob Shutly, Abernathy, Alexr Moore, Boston Best, & Frohock; granted Oct. 28, 1782 to James Henderson.   Signed James Henderson. Witness James Little & John Dellinger. Rec. Apr. 1789. Book 3 p. 477; Book 15 p. 172

383. Jan. 2, 1789 John Wyatt (Lincoln Co) to Elijah Suddith (same); for 40£ NC money sold 173 ac on branches of Little Long Cr; border: Peter Carpenter, James Wyatt, Danl Gray, & his own line; granted Oct. 10, 1783 to Danl Wyatt.   Signed John Wyatt's mark. Witness Jacob Nein (or Nxin) (german) & Daniel Best. Rec. Apr. 1789. Book 3 p. 478; Book 15 p. 173

384. Feb. 10, 1789 Michael Potts & wife Catharine (Lincoln Co) to David Keebler (same); for 10£ NC money sold 100 ac on waters of Lick Run; border: said Potts' old line; granted Aug. 7, 1787 to Michael Potts.   Signed Michael Bots (or Botzn) (german) & Catriner Bots (german). Witness Robt Blackburn & D Gordon. Rec. Apr. 1789. Book 3 p. 479; Book 15 p. 174

385. Oct. 25, 1787 Philip Shifala & wife Mary Magdalen to Paul Sippe; for 500£ sold 554 ac on waters of Lyles Cr; border: Frederick Shull, Peter Yont, Griffith Edwards, Jacob Roseman, Simon Jones, & Jonas; granted Oct. 28, 1782 to Philip Shifala; Note: "this is a release, the lease has already been done & P Sipe lives on the land" ["lease" is mentiond but was evidently recorded in Book 3 p. 488 & Book 15 p. 184].   Signed Philip & Mary M. Shifala's marks. Witness Ephraim Perkins & Wilhelm Vollzoneht (german). Rec. Apr. 1789. Book 3 p. 480; Book 15 p. 176 [see also 385A below, after No. 389]

386. Jan. 1, 1788 Miles Abernathy (Lincoln Co) to John Will (same); for 20£ sold 33 ac on Dutchmans Cr; border: Jacob Sitz, Stofel, a branch, & John Wills.

Signed Milles & Sarah ann Abernathy. Witness John Abernathy, John Bynum, & Robt Abernathy. Rec. Apr. 1789. Book 3 p. 483; Book 15 p. 179

387. May 24, 1786 Thomas Espey, planter, & wife Martha (Lincoln Co) to John Sloan (same); for 250£ NC money sold 350 ac; border: James Ormond's survey on lower end, on S side of S fork of Cuttaba R, & on Long Cr; granted May 17, 1754 to "one" Meek who sold to John Hill who sold Feb. 4, 1771 to Thomas Espey.   Signed Thos Espay (sic) and Martha's mark. Witness John Carrith & James Espey. Rec. Apr. 1789. Book 3 p. 484; Book 15 p. 180

388. Oct. 18, 1788 John Altum (Lincoln Co) to Abraham McCurry (late of Rowan Co); for 120£ sold 200 ac in Lincoln formerly Tryon Co on N side of Broad R on a branch of Buffaloe Cr; border: James Sloan's survey; granted May 22, 1770 to John Taggert who sold Nov. 8, 1774 to Wm Graham who sold Apr. 8, 1775 to John Altum.   Signed John Altum's mark. Witness Thomas Parker sr & Thomas Parker jr. Rec. Apr. 1789. Book 3p. 486; Book 15 p. 182

389. Mar. 15, 1789 Robert Finley (Rutherford Co) to John Reed (Lincoln Co); a bond of 500£ NC money; on Jan. 7, 1772 John Reed & wife Martha made a deed for 300 ac to James Finley desc, and it wasn't good enough so John Reed was to make a new deed to Robert Finely, heir of James Finley desc; now Robert Finley is to pay damages that may arise due to John Reed making a deed and then bond is void.   Signed Robt Finley. Witness Jas Little & Margret Little. Rec. Apr. 1789. Book 3 p. 487; Book 15 p. 183

385A. Oct. 24, 1787 Philip Shifala & wife Mary (Burke Co) to Paul Sipe (Lincoln Co); for 5£ sterling sold 554 ac [this is the release for deed 385 in Book 3 p. 480 & Book 15 p. 176]. Book 3 p. 488; Book 15 p. 184

390. Oct. 31, 1788 Edward Cornwall (Rutherford Co) to George Galbraith, hammerman (Lincoln Co); for 35£ NC money sold 150 ac on Potts Cr; upper part of grant Oct. 9, 1783 by Gov. Alexr Martin to Edward Cornwall.   Signed Edward Cornwil. Witness Adam Carruth, Robt Mitchell, & Walter Carruth. Rec. Apr. 1789. Book 3 p. 489; Book 15 p. 186

391. Apr. 2, 1789 Isaac Hope (York Co, SC) to Andrew Turner (Lincoln Co); for 80£ sold 180 ac on Popular Br and Lick fork of Buffaloe Cr "with" Locust Ridge about 1.5 miles above Ben Shaw's survey and on path from Leon. Safaret's to James Kelly's; part of grant Nov. 17, 1764 to Frs Beatty.   Signed Isaac Hope. Witness Jno Bailey & Robert Allison. Rec. Apr. 1789. Book 3 p. 490; Book 15 p. 187

392. Feb. 21, 1786 George Ruminger sr (Lincoln Co) to George Ruminger jr (same); for 5s sold 150 ac; granted Dec. 21, 1763 and sold by Matthias Clous to Valentine Crots who sold to George Ruminger sr.   Signed George Ruminger sr's

mark. Witness Jos Abernathy & Elias Moyer (german). Rec. Apr. 1789. Book 3 p. 491; Book 15 p. 189

393. May 15, 1788 John Feagley (Lincoln Co) to Lodowick Bonner (same); for 30£ NC money sold 52 ac on waters of Henrys R of S fork of Cuttaba R; border: Jno Feagley and an old line; part of grant Apr. 6, 1765 to John Shell who sold to John Feagley.   Signed John Feagley's mark. Witness John Dellinger & Hugh Calhoon.   Rec. Apr. 1789. Book 3 p. 492; Book 15 p. 190

394. Apr. 14, 1787 Richard Lewis & wife Hannah (Rowan Co) to Jacob Fulbright (Lincoln Co); for 60£ NC money sold 199.5 ac on both sides of Lyles Cr and on W side of Cuttaba R; border: "the Petition line"; part of grant Apr. 4, 1761 by Earl Granville to Samuel Sherrill who sold Jul. 20, 1761 to Richard Lewis.   Signed Richard & Hannah Lewis' marks. Witness Henrey Hitt, Benjn Taylor, & Edward Williams. Rec. Apr. 1789. Book 3 p. 493; Book 15 p. 191

395. Aug. 4, 1784 Abraham Barrier & wife Elisabeth (Rowan Co) to Balsor Sigman (Lincoln Co); for 80£ sold 320 ac on a branch running into the three forks of Lyles Cr; being S or lower end of tract on said creek "taken up by" Abraham Barrier & Balsor Sigman.   Signed Abraham Bergh (or Bergner) (german) & Elisabeth's mark. Witness Meredeth Roper & Gorg Diehl (George Deal in book) (german). Rec. Apr. 1789. Book 3 p. 495; Book 15 p. 193

396. Apr. 3, 789 John Sloan (Lincoln Co) to Samuel Espey (same); for 100£ sold 100 ac; border: Robt Wier, Potts Cr, Muddy fork of Buffaloe Cr, the ford above "the Well field", a road to Sloan's Mill, & a black oak marked "IS"; part of grant Apr. 17, 1769 to Alexr Hoyl.   Signed John Sloan. Witness Walter Carruth & John Alexander. Rec. Apr. 1789. Book 3 p. 496; Book 15 p. 194

397. Apr. 4, 1789 Robert Ferguson (Lincoln Co) to James Ferguson (same); for 80£ sold 100 ac; border: Robert Ferguson and "his" old line.   Signed Robt Ferguson & Isabellah's mark. Witness John Barr, Moses Ferguson, & John Ferguson. Rec. Apr. 1789. Book 3 p. 497; Book 15 p. 195

398. Apr, 26, 1787 John Bohannen (Lincoln Co) to Joseph Dickson (same); for 150£ sold 157 ac between Cuttaba R, the South fork, & on branch of Moores Cr; border: Wm Newton and Joseph Dickson; sold Sept. 8, 1777 by Wm Sterrett to John Bohannen.   Signed John Behanan. Witness William Newton & Eben Buchanan. Rec. Apr. 1789. Book 3 p. 498; Book 15 p. 197

399. Jan. 16, 1789 James Rutledge (Lincoln Co) to John Will, planter (same); for 60£ sold 16.25 ac 16 poles on waters of Dutchmans Cr; border: near mouth of Walkers Spring Br on W side of creek, Stophel Lister, Abernathy, Jno Wills, Charles Rutledge, & an old field; part of two grants Jan. 25, 1773 and Nov. 1, 1784 to James Rutledge.   Signed James Rutledge. Witness Valendin Deowal(?)

(german) & Henor Dedelman(?) (german). Rec. Apr. 1789. Book 3 p. 499; Book 15 p. 199

400. Aug. 4, 1784 Abraham Barrier & wife Elisabeth (Rowan Co) to George Deal (Lincoln Co); for 70£ sold 270 ac on a branch that runs into the three forks of Lyles Cr; border: Bernard Stayway; being N or upper end of tract "taken up" by Abraham Barrier and Balsor Sigman see grant Mar. 14, 1780.   Signed Abraham Borgner (german) & Elisabeth's mark. Witness Bolsor Sigman & Merideth Roper. Rec. Apr. 1789. Book 3 p. 501; Book 15 p. 200

401. Mar. 16, 1789 John Reed & wife Martha (Lincoln Co) to Robert Finley (same); for 50£ sold 300 ac on S side of Cataba R; border: James Little & Cooper; part of 660 ac granted Sept. 24, 1754 to John & Thos Beatey who sold to John Connelly who sold to John Reed.   Signed John & Martha Reed. Witness James Little & Margret Little. Rec. Apr. 1789. Book 3 p. 502; Book 15 p. 201

July Court 1789

402. Feb. 16, 1784 John Huggins (Lincoln Co) to James Huggins (same); for 100£ sold 100 ac on both sides of Little Cuttaba Cr; border: vacant land; part of 300 ac "surveyed to" Hugh Berry and granted Apr. 25, 1767 to Hugh Berry.   Signed John Hugins. Witness Jerh Smith & William Huggins. Rec. Jul. 1789. Book 3 p. 503; Book 15 p. 203

403. Jun. 25, 1789 Henry Clark (Rutherford Co) to Peter Mosstitler (Lincoln Co); for 25£ NC money sold 100 ac on E side of S fork of Catabaw R and on both sides of Rudissells Cr; border: Rudissell.   Signed Henry Clark. Witness Daniel Gage & Benjmain Magness. Rec. Jul. 1789. Book 3 p. 504; Book 15 p. 205

404. Feb. 18, 1789 John Patrick (Georgia) to Thomas Huson jr (Lincoln Co); for 120£ "dollars" 8s sold 120 ac on W side of S fork of Catawbaw R above mouth of said fork; border: William Ratchford, Joseph Carrell, & Tyris Harris; includes his improvement.   Signed John Patrick. Witness Wm Maclean & Samuel Clowney. Rec. Jul. 1789. Book 3 p. 505; Book 15 p. 206

405. Jul. 6, 1789 Thomas Bell (Lincoln Co) to Lewis Hill (same); for 90£ sold 116 ac on W side of Cutaba R; border: Lewis Hill, Archd Little, & Graham; granted Jan. 25, 1773 to John Stroud who sold, with "appurtenances", to Thomas Heslip who sold to Thomas Bell.   Signed Thos Bell. Witness James Johnston, Betsey Ewart, & Jane Johnston. Rec. Jul. 1789. Book 3 p. 506; Book 15 p. 208

406. Jul. 7, 1789 David Ramsey (Lincoln Co) to Jonas Friday & Andrew Fryday (same); for 70£ NC money sold 300 ac on both sides of Kettle Shoal Cr; border: forks of said creek; land was formerly property def Robert Ramsey and was sold due to suit of David Ramsey by sheriff on Dec. 29, 1788 to David Ramsey. Signed David Ramsey. Witness Jos Henry, Jonn Gullick, & Jesse Robinson. Rec. Jul. 1789. Book 3 p. 507; Book 15 p. 209

407. May 4, 1789 Thomas Benteley (Lincoln Co) to wife Hannah Benteley; for love & affection gave all my goods & chattels, leases, debts, plate, jewels, working tools, & Negro man Saul.   Signed Thomas Benteley's mark. Witness Francis McNemr & Lemuel Saunders. Rec. Jul. 1789. Book 3 p. 508; Book 15 p. 210

408. Oct. 28, 1788 Joseph Lawrence (Rutherford Co) to Valentine Mauney (Lincoln Co); for 70£ sold 40 ac on waters of Indian Cr of Cuttaba R; border: Moses Moore and Thos Black; granted Feb. 28, 1775 to Moses Moore.   Signed Joseph Lowrance. Witness John Crouse, James Obryan, & Josh Roberts. Rec. Jul. 1789. Book 3 p. 509; Book 15 p. 211

409. May 27, 1789 Joseph Lawrence (Rutherford Co) to Peter Aker (Lincoln Co); for 23£ NC money sold 200 ac on waters of Indian Cr; border: "said" Moore's corner and Aker; granted Feb. 28, 1775 to Moses Moore.   Signed Joseph Lawrence "agent for Moses Moore". Witness Michael Eaker, Deny (or Dmy) Login, & Vallentine Mauny. Rec. Jul. 1789. Book 3 p. 511; Book 15 p. 213

410. Apr. 15, 1789 John Cunningham (Lincoln Co) to Francis Hartwell (same); for 195£ NC money sold 238 ac on W side of Great Cattaba R; border: upper W corner of 266 ac of Francis Cunningham and Henry Partain's line; part of grant from "the" governor to Reubin Simpson and sold by sheriff to Francis Cunningham who gave it to John Cuningham.   Signed Jno Cunningham. Witness Harbert Harwell & James Loftin. Rec. Jul. 1789. Book 3 p. 512; Book 15 p. 215

411. Mar. 25, 1788 Thomas Anderson jr (Lincoln Co) to John Clipard (same); for 30£ NC money sold [ac omitted]; border: widdow McCormack, crosses Missippe Br, & Michael Britt; granted Sept. 12, 1787 to Thomas Anderson jr.   Signed Thomas Anderson jr's mark. Witness Lemuel Saunders & Mary Saunders. Rec. Jul. 1789. Book 3 p. 513; Book 15 p. 217

412. Oct. 9, 1787 Adam Perkins (Lincoln Co) to Isaac Robinson (same); for 500£ sold 192 ac; border: Isaac Robinson and Cuttawba R; being part of where Adam Perkins lives and granted Oct. 28, 1782.   Signed Adam Perkins. Witness James Holsclaw & Richard Robinson. Rec. Jul. 1789. Book 3 p. 515; Book 15 p. 218

413. Jun. 8, 1789 Daniel McKisick, farmer (Lincoln Co) to John Campbell, shoemaker (same); for 15£ NC money sold [ac omitted] lot 15 in SE square of Lincolnton; lot is 6 by 14 rods.   Signed Danl McKisick. Witness Daniel Reider(?) (german) & Peter Edelman (german). Rec. Jul. 1789. Book 3 p. 516; Book 15 p. 220

414. Jan. 26, 1789 John Moyer, planter (Lincoln Co) to George Wilfong, yoeman (same); for 20£ NC money sold 150 ac on N side of S fork of Catawba R; border: Henry Whitener's N line and Abraham Moyer; part of 300 ac granted Apr. 22,

1763 to Peter Moll who sold Jan. 13, 1772 to John Moyer.   Signed John Moyer. Witness John Wilfong & Peter Willfong. Rec. Jul. 1789. Book 3 p. 517; Book 15 p. 221

415. Ju. 7, 1788 John Chittim (Lincoln Co) to Richard Fetherstone (same); for 500£ NC money sold (1) 300 ac on N side of S fork of Catawba R above place where Robert Leeper lives; granted Oct. 3, 1775 to Wm Patrick who sold to John Chittim; and (2) 300 ac on N side of S fork of Catawba R; border: his own land, "the" old survey, & above Wm Chittim; granted May 5, 1769 to John Chittim. Signed John Chittim. Witness Joseph Beaty, Robert Patrick, & Shadick Lefeey. Rec. Jul. 1789. Book 3 p. 518; Book 15 p. 223

416. Mar. 6, 1789 William Patrick (NC) to Thomas Huson (Lincoln Co); for 600£ NC money sold 500 ac on W side of Catawba R at mouth of South fork; border: McLean, John Patrick, Thomas Carrol, & Robert Leeper; granted Dec. 26, 1768 to William Patrick.   Signed Wm Pattrick. Witness Robert Patterson, Moses Ratchford, & John Faires. Rec. Jul. 1789. Book 3 p. 520; Book 15 p. 225

417. May 25, 1789 Hugh Torrence (Lincoln Co) to William Grover (same); for 200£ NC money sold 370 ac on branches of Crowders Cr and Little Catawba Cr; border: on NW side of Baird's Mountain near road from John Baird's to William Henry's, Nathaniel Auldridge, Job Robinson, & Torrence's line; granted Mar. 2, 1775 to Hugh Torrence.   Signed Hugh (or Huph) Torrans. Witness Wm Rice & John Massey. Rec. Jul. 1789. Book 3 p. 521; Bok 15 p. 227

418. Apr. 23, 1788 Esther Kennedy, executrix of Joseph Kennedy desc, (Charlotte, NC) to Leonard Fight, millright (Lincoln Co); for 500£ sold two adjoining tracts: (1) 200 ac on W side of Catawba R; border: Adair, a branch, & the river; and (2) 400 ac on W side of Mountain Island "above the described land"; border: Debruell (or Debrwll).   Signed Ester Kennedy. Witness Will Polk, Jam Martin, & Jo Kennedy. Rec. Jul. 1789. Book 3 p. 522; Book 15 p. 228

419. Dec. 31, 1787 Valentine Krots (Lincoln Co) to Henry Slinkard (same); for 52£ NC money sold 200 ac on both sides of Andersons Mill Cr of Catawba R; granted Jul. 21, 1774 to Jacob Hackelman who sold May 3, 1784 to Valentine Krots.   Signed Valentine Krots' mark. Witness Johann Slinker (german) & _?_ (german). Rec. Jul. 1789. Book 3 p. 524; Book 15 p. 230

420. Jun. 17, 1788 Joseph Beaty (Lincoln Co) to Richard Fetherston (same); for 60£ NC money sold (1) 70 ac on N side of S fork of Catawba R; border: John Armstrong & John Chittim; and (2) 90 ac on E side of S fork of Catawba R; border: John Chittim, John Armstrong, & Francis Armstrong; granted Oct. 28, 1782 to Joseph Beaty and Oct. 9, 1783 to Joseph Beaty.   Signed Joseph Beaty. Witness Jno Chittam, Robert Patrick, & Shadrick Lefery. Rec. Jul. 1789. Book 3 p. 525; Book 15 p. 233

421. Jul. 7, 1789 Ubrick Crowder (Lincoln Co) to Absalom Bonham (same); for 6£ NC money sold 144 square poles in each of 4 lots in a new town, Ubricksburgh, lately laid off on waters of Whiteners Cr of S fork of Catawba R: (1) lot 10 in NE square is 12 by 12 poles; (2) lot 11 in NW square is 12 by 12 poles; (3) lot 31 in SE square is 12 by 12 poles; and (4) lot 5 in NE square is 12 by 12 poles; part of grant Dec. 21, 1764 to Ubrick Crowder.   Signed Ubrick Crowder. Witness Saml Givens & David Ramsey. Rec. Jul. 1789. Book 3 p. 527; Book 15 p. 234

422. Nov. 19, 1787 Peter Peterson (Lincoln Co) to John Magors (same); for 41£ NC money sold 185 ac on S fork of Henrys fork of S fork of Catawba R; border: SE & SW corners of an old survey and John Butt; part of 450 ac grant (#588) Oct. 11, 1783 to Peter Mull.   Signed Peter Peterson. Witness Martin Couller & Jacob Gortner. Rec. Jul. 1789. Book 3 p. 528; Book 15 p. 236

October Court 1789
423. Aug. 29, 1788 John Perkins (Burk Co, Ga) to Jacob Gabriel (Lincoln Co); for 5s sterling sold 318.5 ac on both sides of Mountain Cr and W side of Catabaw R; border: an old tract; part of grant May 19, 1761 by Earl Granville to John Perkins, son of Richd Perkins.   Signed John Perkins. Witness Joseph Sherrill, Ephraim Perkins, & John Perkins. Rec. Oct. 1789. Book 3 p. 529; Book 15 p. 237

423A. Aug. 30, 1788 John Perkins (Burk Co, Ga) to Jacob Gabriel (Lincoln Co); for 200£ NC money sold 318.5 ac [this is the release for above deed #423]. Book 3 p. 530; Book 15 p. 239

424. Oct. 7, 1789 Joseph Dickson esq, commissioner in trust for Lincolnton, (Lincoln Co) to George Rush (same); for 40s sold [ac omitted] lot 14 in SW square of Lincolnton; lot is 6 by 14 rods.   Signed Jo Dickson. Witness John Carruth & Wm Sharpe. Rec. Oct. 1789. Book 3 p. 533; Book 15 p. 242

425. Aug. 6, 1789 John Schuyles (Green Co, NC [sic Tenn]) to Joseph Gladen (Lincoln Co); for 50£ NC money sold 125 ac on branch of Kings Cr; border: Jacob Connell's "third" corner; includes Jonathan Price's (or Rice's) improvement. Signed John Schuyles' mark. Witness Robert Wilson & Jno Wilson. Rec. Oct. 1789. Book 3 p. 534; Book 15 p. 243

426. Oct. 3, 1789 Joseph Crunkleton sr to Joseph Crunkleton jr; for 5s sterling sold 350 ac on S side of Mountain Cr; border: his old line; "granted" Dec. 13, 1770 by deed from Francis Beatey to Joseph Crunkleton sr "from" John Lyttle dy deed Jan. 4, 1771 and "from" Gov. Richard Caswell by grant Aug. 7, 1787. Signed Joseh Cronkton. Witness P(?) McEwin & Thos Wheeler. Rec. Oct. 1789. Book 3 p. 535; Book 15 p. 244

427. Oct. 3, 1789 Joseph Cronkleton sr to John Cronkleton jr; for 5s sterling sold 330.5 ac on N side of Mountain Cr; "granted" Dec. 13, 1770 by deed from Francis Beaty to Joseph Cronkleton sr, "from" John Lyttle by deed Jan. 4, 1771, & "from"

John Fleming by deed Sept. 1, 1772.   Signed Josph Cronkton. Witness P. McEwin & Thos Wheeler. Rec. Oct. 1789. Book 3 p. 536; Book 15 p. 246

428. May 2, 1789 Peter Moiar (Lincoln Co) to Simeon Lewis (same); for 35£ NC money sold 100 ac on both sides of Indian Cr about a mile above the Scout Camps; border: Peter Johnston's entry and an open line.   Signed Peter Mearr (german) & Mary's mark. Witness Forney Green Norman & John Vail. Rec. Oct. 1789. Book 3 p. 538; Book 15 p. 247

429. Mar. 10, 1788 Nathan Armitage (Lincoln Co) to Henry Hollman, planter (same); for 70£ NC money sold 50 ac on S side of Catawba R; border: said Hollman's upper corner of his survey; granted Oct. 11, 1783 to William Sherrill who sold Dec. 25, 1785 to Jacob Baker desc (reg. in Lincoln Co May 9, 1786 in Book 14 fol. 2 by Jno Wilson, regis.) and sold Mar. 8, 1788 by Henry Hollman & Michael Keller, executors of Jacob Baker desc, to Nathan Armitage.   Signed Nathan Armitage. Witness Michael Kellerr sr (german) & Michael Kellerr jr (german). Rec. Oct. 1789. Book 3 p. 539; Book 15 p. 249

430. Oct. 1, 1788 John Hiltebran, farmer (Rederford Co (sic)) to Daniel Ockerman (or Ackerman) (Lincoln Co); for 20£ NC money sold 100 ac on waters of Howards Cr; border: his own old corner; granted Aug. 7, 1787 to John Hiltebran.   Signed John Hiltebran. Witness Andrew Heess(?) (german) & Michael Buff. Rec. Oct. 1789. Book 3 p. 540; Book 15 p. 251

431. Oct. 3, 1789 Jacob Seitz (Lincoln Co) to Jacob Hinkle (same); for 20£ sold 100 ac on branches of Killions Cr; border: Jacob Seitz, Lifler, Ramsey's field; part of grant Sept. 24, 1754 to Thomas Aurick (or Ourick) who died & left only heir as Esther, wife of Lefler (or Lester) who together sold Mar. 22, 1783 to Jacob Seitz.   Signed Jacob Seitz. Witness George Seitz. Rec. Oct. 1789. Book 3 p. 541; Book 15 p. 252

432. May 24, 1779 George Pope (Burke Co) to Samuel Steel (same); for 1,100£ sold 320 ac on S side of (blank) Cr formerly known as Elk Cr; border: George Smith; part of grant Feb. 28, 1755 by Earl Granville to Boston Cline who sold Nov. 15, 1771 (or 1777) to George Pope.   Signed Georg Pope (german). Witness Joseph Steel & Jacob Müller (german). Rec. Oct. 1789. Book 3 p. 542; Book 15 p. 253

433. Sept. 28, 1789 John Sigman & wife Margaret (Lincoln Co) to Henry Cline (same); for 80£ NC money sold 103 ac on both sides of Clarks Cr; border: Jacob Carpenter, John Sigman, & an old line; granted Sept. 3, 1753 to Peter Broil who sold Jun. 3, 1758 to Derick Ramsour who sold Feb. 12, 1779 to John Sigman. Signed Johann Sigman (german) & Margaret's mark. Witness Henrich Hebuer (german) & Robt Blackburn. Rec. Oct. 1789. Book 3 p. 544; Book 15 p. 255

434. Jul. 7, 1789 John Sigman (Lincoln Co) to Henry Cline (or Hanray Clian) (same); for 30£ sold 100 ac on waters of Clearks Cr; border: Peter Lear and Jacob

Ramsour; part of grant Aug. 7, 1787 to John Sigman.   Signed Johann Sigman. Witness David Ramsey & Andreal Fütig (german). Rec. Oct. 1789. Book 3 p. 545; Book 15 p. 256 [Note: Book 3 ends on page 546 with this deed]

435. Aug. 4, 1789 Samuel Gerret (Lincoln Co) to Martin Speagel (same); for 5£ NC money sold 10 ac on waters of S fork of Catawba R; border: Speagel; part of tract Samuel Gerret lives on.   Signed Samuel Jarret (german). Witness David Ramsey & Jacob Wtezel(?) (german). Rec. Oct. 1789. Book 4 p. 1; Book 15 p. 258

436. Oct. 3, 1789 Henry Pope (Lincoln Co) and Conrod Adams (Lincoln Co, Va (sic)) to John Isenhour (Lincoln Co); for 30£ NC money sold 268 ac in Lincoln formerly Mecklenburg Co on branches of Lyles Cr; border: George Pope, Philip Adams, & Neal; granted (#88) Apr. 28, 1768 to Henry Pope and Philip Adams who sold to John Isenhour during lifetime of Philip Adams but Philip Adams died before a deed was made so Conrod Adams became heir to his father's real estate being "the one son".   Signed Henrich Popst(?) (german) & Conrad Adams' mark. Witness Polsar Sigman & John Wilfong. Rec. Oct. 1789. Book 4 p. 2; Book 15 p. 259

437. Sept. 30, 1789 Nicholas Friday & Nicholas Shrom (Lincoln Co) to Jacob Shrom (same); for 60£ NC money sold 250 ac on E side of S fork of Cuttawba R on Shoal Br "falling into the" high Shoals; border: Rhinehart, Dellinger, & a waggon road; granted Apr. 29, 1768 to Godfry Lype who sold to Friday & Shrom. Signed Nichlas Fryday & Nicholas Shrom's mark. Witness Jos Henry & Jacob Shutly (or Shöll) (german). Rec. Oct. 1789. Book 4 p. 4; Book 15 p. 261

January Court 1790
438. Oct. 26, 1789 David McCord (Lincoln Co) to Jonathan Greaves (same); for 300£ NC money sold 160 ac on Duharts Cr; border: John Moore.   Signed David McCord. Witness William Dickson. Rec. Jan. 1790. Book 4 p. 6; Book 15 p. 263

439. Nov. 19, 1785 Weiry Rudicell (Lincoln Co) to Peter Smith (same); for 100£ sold 128 ac in fork of Hoyls Cr; border: Hoyl's line and Limeberger; granted to Boston Best.   Signed Weiry Rudisell. Witness Alexander Moore. Rec. Jan. 1790. Book 4 p. 7; Book 15 p. 264

440. Nov. 19, 1785 Weiry Rudicell (Lincoln Co) to Peter Smith (same); for 3£ in fork of Hoyls Cr that runs into S fork of Cataba R; border: Hoyl's line, middle stream of Little Cr, & main stream of "the" creek; granted to Peter Hoyl.   Signed Weiry Rudisell. Witness Alexander Moore. Rec. Jan. 1790. Book 4 p. 9; Book 15 p. 266

441. Nov. 4, 1789 Michael Hoyl (Lincoln Co) to Michael Rign (same); for 10£ sold 48 ac on both sides of Long Cr; border: Hoyl and Mihel Rign; part of two

tracts belonging to Michl Hoyl.   Signed Mihel Heÿel (german). Witness Phillip Rhyne & Henry Jenkins. Rec. Jan. 1790. Book 4 p. 10; Book 15 p. 267

442. Dec. 26, 1789 Phillip Null (Lincoln Co) to Henry Fulinwider (Rowan Co); for 500£ NC money sold 260 ac on N side of S fork of Cataba R between David Ramsour and Andrew Heddeigh; granted Mar. 28, 1751 to Daniel Warlick. Signed Phillip Null. Witness Jno Fulenwider & Wm Temple Coles. Rec. Jan. 1790. Book 4 p. 12; Book 15 p. 268

443. Nov. 17, 1789 Alexander Johnson (Washington Co, Ga) to Robert Johnson jr (Lincoln Co); for 25£ NC money sold 96 ac on Doctors Cr on W side of Cataba R; border: Joseph Dickson and said Robt Johnson; granted to Wm Moore who sold to Robt Alexander who sold to Jas Milligan who sold to Robt Johnson who sold to Alexander Johnson.   Signed Alexander Johnson. Witness Robert Johnson & Andrew Johnson. Rec. Jan. 1790. Book 4 p. 13Book 15 p. 270

444. Jun. 26, 1778 William Moore to Thomas Polk (Mecklenburg Co); for 6,000£ NC money sold (1) 328 ac; border: Saml Coburn; sold Dec. 14, 1762 by Wm Cleghorn to William Moore;(2) 300 ac; border: Cabaeen's line; sold Sept. 14, 1762 by Wm Adaire to William Moore; (3) 102 ac; border: Carroll and Moore; sold Jul. 13, 1779 by Robert Abernathy to William Moore; and (4) 45 ac on waters of Dutchmans Cr and W side of Cataba R; border: Martin, Saml Kuykendal, & Bell; granted Feb. 7, 1773 to William Moore.   Signed William Moor. Witness Alex Eswin, Joseph Davies, & F. M. Gomery. Rec. Jan. 1790. Book 4 p. 15; Book 15 p. 272

445. Jan. 6, 1790 Joseph Dickson esq, commissioner in trust for Lincolnton, (Lincoln Co) to Arthur Graham (same); for 40s sold [ac omitted] lot 3 in NE of Lincolnton; lot is 6 by 12 rods.   Signed Jo Dickson. Witness Cary Hudgens & Isaiah Liming. Rec. Jan. 1790. Book 4 p. 17; Book 15 p. 273

446. Jan. 1, 1790 Joseph Dickson, commissioner in trust for Lincolnton, (Lincoln Co) to James Langsbee (Chester Co, SC); for 40s sold [ac omitted] lot 4 in NE square of Lincolnton; lot is 6 by 12 poles.   Signed Jo Dickson. Witness Jno Dickson. Rec. Jan. 1790. Book 4 p. 18; Book 15 p. 275

447. Jan. 6, 1790 Robert Luckey to Thomas Rhine; for 70£ NC money sold a Negro boy Jack 7 or 8 years old.   Signed Robt Luckey. Witness Joseph Dickson. Rec. Jan. 1790. Book 4 p. 19; Book 15 p. 276

448. Aug. 24, 1789 George Whitley, Margaret Whitley, Rebekah Oliphant, William Welsh, Nicholas Welsh, Thomas Welsh, Caleb Edmiston, & Thomas Martindell (first 2 of Lincoln Co & rest of 96 Dist, SC) to Henry Miller (Lincoln Co); for 314£ NC money sold 200 ac on both sides of Jacobs fork of S fork of Cataba R; granted by the king to John Welsh who died leaving the grantees as his heirs by will dated Jan. 5, 1769 with instructions to sell the land.   Signed George

& Margrett Whitley, Rebekah Oliphant's mark, William Welsh's mark, Nicholas Welsh's mark, Caleb Edmundson, Thomas Welsh's mark, & Thomas Martindell. Witness William Martindeal & John Miller. Rec. Jan. 1790. Book 4 p. 20; Book 15 p. 276

449. Jan. 5, 1790 Hanery Miller (Lincoln Co) to George Whitley (same); for 150£ NC money sold 100 ac on NW side of Jacobs R (fork--lined out); border: head of a hollow; part of 200 ac granted by the king to John Wealsh who willed it to son Nicholas Welsh and "others" of his children who sold to Henry Miller.   Signed Henrich Miller(?) (german). Witness David Ramsey & John Miller. Rec. Jan. 1790. Book 4 p. 22; Book 15 p. 279

450. Oct. 7, 1786 Henry Lollar (Lincoln Co) to Malachi Fyke (same); for 20£ sold 50 ac on both sides of Mountain Cr; border: mouth of Battle Run, Wm Osborn and foot of a hill; part of grant (#736) Oct. 11, 1783 to Richard Perkins.   Signed Henry Lollar. Witness Bengiman Tallor & Phinehas Creaton. Rec. Jan. 1790. Book 4 p. 23; Book 15 p. 280

451. Aug. 29, 1789 Thomas Carrel (York Co, SC) to William Maclean (Lincoln Co); for 3 "likely" young Negroes sold 478 ac on Little Cataba Cr on S side of Cataba R; border: Tyla Harris, Andrew Cathey, Henry Oneal, & Alexander Osborn.   Signed Thomas Carell. Witness Jno Leeper & Thomas Maclean. Rec. Jan. 1790. Book 4 p. 25; Book 15 p. 281

452. Dec. 30, 1789 Henry Howser (York Co, SC) to Christian Barr (Lincoln Co); for 100£ NC money sold 200 ac on branch of Howards Cr; border: Nathaniel Erwin, Waddle, & Alexander; includes Wm Thomson's improvement; granted Nov. 1, 1784 to Henry Howser.   Signed Henrich Hwyser(?) (german). Witness Fredk Adenhold. Rec. Jan. 1790. Book 4 p. 27; Book 15 p. 283

453. Dec. 1, 1788 George Goodwin (Lincoln Co) to John Parr (same); for 80£ sold 236 ac on waters of Killions Cr; border: Solomon Sailor, Slinker, & Abraham Earhart.   Signed George Goodwin. Witness Peter Forney & William Mayes. Rec. Jan. 1790. Book 4 p. 28; Book 15 p. 285

454. Oct. 13, 1788 Alexander Lockart, mason (Union Co, SC) to Henry Sumerour (Lincoln Co); for 40£ NC money sold 150 ac on E side of Clerks Cr; border: Welsh and an old tract; part of grant Dec. 23, 1768 to Alexander Lockhart. Signed Alexander Lockhart. Witness Edward Atkinson & William Lockhart "ackd before" John Moore. Rec. Jan. 1790. Book 4 p. 29; Book 15 p. 286

455. Oct. 20, 1788 William McClain (Lincoln Ceo) to Joseph Henry (same); for 200£ sold [ac omitted] on Indian Cr a S branch of S fork of Cataba R about 3 miles above Thomas Reynolds; includes "the Old Indian Camp".   Signed Wm Maclean. Witness J. Wilson & James Johnston. Rec. Jan. 1790. Book 4 p. 31; Book 15 p. 288

456. Jan. 6, 1790 Joseph Henry (Lincoln Co) to Ann Ramsour (same); for 300£ sold 500 ac on Indian Cr a S branch of S fork of Cataba R about 3 miles above Thomas Reynolds; includes "the Old Indian Camp"; granted Apr. 19, 1763 to Francis Beaty and sold by Robert Armstrong, Thomas Beaty, & James Beaty, executors of Francis Beaty, to Joseph Henry. Signed Jos Henry. Witness J. Wilson, James Johnston, & Jno Leeper. Rec. Jan. 1790. Book 4 p. 32; Book 15 p. 289

457. Dec. 30, 1789 Francis Cunningham (Lincoln Co) to William Fisher (same); for 50£ sold 63 ac on W side of Cataba R and waters of Beaverdam Cr; border: said Cunningham's E & W line, land granted to Reuben Simpson, & Robert Knox; granted in 1771 to Francis Cunningham. Signed Frs Cunningham. Witness John Barr & Johamer Collinger (german). Rec. Jan. 1790. Book 4 p. 34; Book 15 p. 291

458. Sept. 20, 1789 Philip Hains (Lincoln Co) to Leonard Hains (same); for 30£ sold 200 ac on Leonards Cr; border: Adam Wissenhunt, his own line, & Moore; includes a school house; granted Aug. 7, 1787 to Philip Hains. Signed J. Phillib Hen (german). Witness Vallentine Mauney, Isaiah Leming, & Saml Rose. Rec. Jan. 1790. Book 4 p. 35; Book 15 p. 292

459. Aug. 8, 1789 Peter Shoup (Lincoln Co) to Martin Coulter (same); for 40£ sold 150 ac on Stoney Cr a branch of Henrys fork a N fork of S fork of Cataba R; border: a hill on E side of the creek and a ridge; granted Jul. 10, 1788 to Peter Shoup. Signed Peter Shoup's mark. Witness John Wilfong & Jacob Summey. Rec. Jan. 1790. Book 4 p. 36; Book 15 p. 293

460. Nov. 4, 1789 John Woods (Lincoln Co) to Michael Rhyne (same); for 27£ NC money sold 134 ac on both sides of Long Cr; border: Peter Summey's lower line and Thomas Henry; granted Apr. 25, 1767 to John Sloan sr and sold by "said" John McElroy sr to John Woods. Signed John Woods. Witness Phillip Rhyne & Mihel Heyel (german). Rec. Jan. 1790. Book 4 p. 38; Book 15 p. 294

461. Jun. 21, 1789 Jacob Dellinger (Lincoln Co) to William Dellinger 9same); for 42£ sold (1) 400 ac; border: his own corner; granted Mar. 2, 1773 to Jacob Dellinger; and (2) 40 ac joining tract 1 and to "lye in a three square"; border: Jacob Dellinger; aprt of deed sold Feb. 1, 1786 from Henry Dellinger to Jacob Dellinger. Signed Jacob Dellinger's mark. Witness Lemuel Saunders, Robt Johnston, & Michel Engel. Rec. Jan. 1790. Book 4 p. 39; Book 15 p. 296

462. Jan. 2, 1790 Abraham Keenor sr (Lincoln Co) to Abraham Keenor jr (same); for 10£ NC money sold 78 ac on long branch of Sniders Cr; border: his other survey of 300 ac and Matthias Keelion; granted Aug. 7, 1787 to Abraham Keenor. Signed Abrahann Küher. Witness Lemuel Saunders & Mary Saunders. Rec. Jan. 1790. Book 4 p. 41; Book 15 p. 297

463. May 1, 1787 William Gant, planter (Lincoln Co) to Upsherre Davis (same); for 100£ NC money sold 100 ac on N fork of Mountain Cr waters of "Mountain" of Cuttaba R; border: Bigam Perkins and conditional line of William Gant & Benjn Taylor; part of grant Mar. 14, 1780 to William Gant formerly in Burke & now in Lincoln Co.   Signed William Gant. Witness Benjamin Tairler, Mollichier Fikes, & Melger Ward. Rec. Jan. 1790. Book 4 p. 43; Book 15 p. 299

464. Dec. 28, 1789 Abraham Keenor sr (Lincoln Co) to Jacob & John Keenor (same); for 100£ NC money sold 290 ac on waters of Sniders Cr; border: Matthias Keelion, Link, & his own old line; granted Aug. 7, 1787 to Abraham Keenor. Signed Abraham Kuhuer (german). Witness Lemuel Saunders & Larkin Johnson. Rec. Jan. 1790. Book 4 p. 45; Book 15 p. 301

465. Oct. 16, 1789 Henry Hoke (Lincoln Co) to Christian Rhinehart (same); for 32£ sold [ac omitted] lot 1 in SE square to Lincolnton; lot is 6 by 12 rods.   Signed Henry Hoke. Witness Andrew Turner & Joseph Morris. Rec. Jan. 1790. Book 4 p. 47; Book 15 p. 303

466. Nov. 4, 1789 Abraham Womack (Lincoln Co) to Abner Womack (same); for 5s sterling sold 160 ac on W side of Cuttaba R; granted by the king to John Beaty who sold to John Connelly who sold to John Reed who sold to Abraham Womack. Signed Abraham Womack. Witness Robert Caruthers & Jas Reed. Rec. Jan. 1790. Book 4 p. 48; Book 15 p. 304

April Court 1790
467. Jan. 8, 1790 Wm Hill esq (York Co, SC) to Doctr. John Allison (York Co, SC) & James Twaddell (Pa); for 3,000£ NC money sold (1) his third of Washington Furnace & Forge with 7,000 ac "held by several titles" now in possession of John Sloan and "in company with" John Sloan, Danl Burdeaux, & Joseph Atkison; and (2) his third of all tools, teams, & stock now in possession of John Sloan.   Signed Wm Hill. Witness Jno White, Shearad Thompson, & Lewis Thompson. Rec. Apr. 1790. Book 4 p. 50; Book 15 p. 305

468. Jan. 8, 1790 Wm Hill esq (York Co, SC) to Doctr. Jno Allison (York Co, SC) & James Twaddell (Pa); for 800£ NC money sold (1) his half of 140 ac of land & water in Lincoln Co & fishery & island in Cataba R; refer to deed in 1774 by Jabez Evans to Wm Hill; (2) his half of 300 ac on W side of Cataba R in Lincoln Co; see deed in 1774 by Jabez Evans to Wm Hill; and (3) his half of 250 ac on E side of Cataba R in Mecklenburg Co whereon is a grist mill; border: Mr. Greer & Mr. Cathey.   Signed Wm Hill. Witness Jno White, Shearod Thompson, & Lewis Thompson. Rec. Apr. 1790. Book 4 p. 51; Book 15 p. 306

469. Apr. 5, 1790 Martin Friday (Lincoln Co) to Andrew Friday (same); for 75£ NC money sold 300 ac on both sides of Kettle Shoal Cr; border: in forks of said creek; tract was formerly property of Robert Ramsey and sold Dec. 29, 1788 due

to suit of David Ramsey by sheriff to David Ramsey who sold Jul. 17, 1789 to Jonas & Andrew Friday who sold Apr. 2, 1790 to Martin Friday.   Signed Martin Ferttay (german). Witness Jos Henry & Jas Wilson. Rec. Apr. 1790. Book 4 p. 53; Book 15 p. 308

470. Apr. 1, 1789 Robert & Charles Abernathy (Lincoln Co) to Francis Summit (same); for 40£ sold [ac omitted] on waters of Leepers Cr; border: Charles Williams and Clobb.   Signed Robt & Charles Abernathy. Witness Jos Abernathy & Richard Nance. Rec. Apr. 1790. Book 4 p. 55; Book 15 p. 309

471. Dec. 28, 1789 Abraham Keenor sr (Lincoln Co) to John & Jacob Keener (same); for [omitted] sold 2 mares--a black branded on off shoulder "S7", a dark brown branded on near shoulder "   ", a black horse colt branded with "O" on off shoulder, a bright bay horse branded on off shoulder with "Ks", another bay branded on off shoulder "S7", all "the" cows & calves, a bull, a "Lume" & all slayes and all "belonging", all the plow irons & hoes, a pair stillyards, a lock chain, all sheep & all hogs I own, all beds & bed "cloaths", a frying pan, all metal pots, all pewter, all meat, corn & other grain, all money owing, saddles, bridles, axes, mattocks, "to contain" all moveables and all found of my estate.   Signed Abraham Kühner (german). Witness Lemuel Saunders, Sarah Saunders, & Mary Saunders. Rec. Apr. 1790. Book 4 p. 56; Book 15 p. 311

472. Jan. 6, 1790 John Potter (Granville Co, NC) to Lewis Potter (same); for 400£ sold 400 ac in Lincoln formerly Mecklenburg Co on Leonards fork of Indian Cr; border: Valentine Mauny and Howard.   Signed John Potter. Witness Jonathan Greaves, Henry Potter, & Eliza D. Greaves. Rec. Apr. 1790. Book 4 p. 57; Book 15 p. 311

473. Apr. 2, 1790 Jonas & Andrew Friday (Lincoln Co) to Martin Friday (same); for 70£ NC money sold 300 ac on both sides of Kittle Shoal Cr; border: in forks of said creek; formerly property of Robert Ramsey and sold Dec. 29, 1788 due to suit of David Ramsey by sheriff to David Ramsey who sold Jul. 17, 1789 to Jonas & Andrew Friday.   Signed Jonas & Andrew Friday. Witness Jos Henry & Jas Wilson. Rec. Apr. 1790. Book 4 p. 58; Book 15 p. 313

474. Dec. 3, 1787 Frederick Marckle & wife Ann Eve (Lincoln Co) to Godfrey Arends (same); for 55£ NC money sold 200 ac on both sides of Pinchgut Br waters of Clarks Cr; border: Rudolph Conrod and Whittenburg "or at present" John Warson; granted Apr. 28, 1768 to Frederick Marckle.   Signed Fridrik Merkle (german) & Ann Eve's mark. Witness Joseph Steel & John Drum. Rec. Apr. 1790. Book 4 p. 60; Book 15 p. 314

475. Feb. 26, 1790 James Collins sr (Lincoln Co) to wife Bithya Collins; for love and affection gave two adjoining tracts: (1) 100 ac where James Collins lives on W side of Buffalow Cr; border: "the" old line; part of 200 ac granted Oct. 13, 1765 by Gov. Wm Tryon to Alexr McIntire who sold Dec. 27, 1771 to James Collins

sr; and (2) 100 ac "runs up" McIntires Br; part of 400 ac granted Jan. 25, 1773 by Gov. Josiah Martin to James Collins sr.   Signed James Collins' mark. Witness Alexander McIntire & Michl Hogan. Rec. Apr. 1790. Book 4 p. 61; Book 15 p. 316

476. Mar. 19, 1790 John Springs to Adlai Osborn; for 50£ sold 400 ac in Lincoln formerly Burke Co; border: John Fisher, head branches of & both sides of Whiteners Cr that runs into S fork of Cataba R below Henry Whitener's house, on W side of Resaner's "or Ramsour's" road, John Hawn, Crawders road, Thomas Fisher, head of Camp Br, & forks of Ramsour's & Crowder's roads; granted (#281) Mar. 4, 1780 to [omitted].   Signed John Springs. Witness Jo Dickson. Rec. Apr. 1790. Book 4 p. 63; Book 15 p. 317

477. Apr. 3, 1790 William Green (Rutherford Co) & James McAfee, executor (Lincoln Co) to Joseph Green (Lincoln Co); for 100£ NC money sold 140 ac on Buffaloe Cr; border: mouth of Rushy Br, below an old ford on said creek, & below James McAfee; being part of tract where James McAfee lives; part of grant Apr. 21, 1764 to Joseph Green desc and "by heirship" to William Green.   Signed Wm Green & James McAfee. Witness R. Graham, James Collins, & Abm Collins. Rec. Apr. 1790. Book 4 p. 65; Book 15 p. 320

478. Sept. 8, 1789 John West (Lincoln Co) to John Bealk (same); for 50£ sold 80 ac on S side of Doctors Cr; border: William Moore, old School House Br, "his" corner, & "the fifth" line; part of 200 ac granted to John Bealy, schoolmaster, who sold to Edwd Hogan who sold to John Moore and "now" John Moore sells to Wm West who "made it over" to John West who "made it over" to John Bealk. Signed John West. Witness W. Rankin, Isaac West, & Charles Witt. Rec. Apr. 1790. Book 4 p. 67; Book 15 p. 321

479. Mar. 1, 1790 Stephen Senter (Lincoln Co) to Andrew Taylor (same); for 3£ NC money sold [ac omitted] in forks of Cataba R; border: Taylor and James Dickson.   Signed Stephen Senter. Witness James Dickson & Jean Taylor. Rec. Apr. 1790. Book 4 p. 68; Book 15 p. 322

480. Mar. 9, 1790 Alexander Martin esq and Adlai Osborn to John Springs, gentleman; for 50£ NC money sold 400 ac in Lincoln formerly Burke Co on head branches of & both sides of Whiteners Cr that runs into S fork of Cataba R below Henry Whitener's house; border: John Fisher, W side of Resoner's "or Ramsour's" road, John Hawn, Crowder's road, Thomas Fisher, head of Camp Br, & forks of Ramsour's & Crowder's roads; granted (#281) Mar. 4, 1780 to [omitted] & registered in Burke Co.   Signed Alex Martin & Ad Osborn. Witness Jo Dickson. Rec. Apr. 1790. Book 4 p. 70; Book 15 p. 324

481. Apr. 3, 1789 William Green (Rutherford Co) to James McAfee (Lincoln Co); for 100£ NC money sold 140 ac on N side of Buffaloe Cr; border: waggon ford and mouth of Rushy Br; part of grant Apr. 21, 1764 to Joseph Green desc.

Signed Wm Green. Witness James Collins, R. Graham, & Abm Collins. Rec. Apr. 1790. Book 4 p. 73; Book 15 p. 326

482. Dec. 31, 1787 Rudolph Conrod (Lincoln Co) to Godfrey Arends (same); for 55£ NC money sold 200 ac on both sides of Pinchgut Br waters of Clarks Cr; border: Frederick Whisnaunt and said Rudolph Conrod's old survey; granted Oct. 11, 1783 to Rudolph Conrod which grant is "expressed" to Conrod Rudolph but they are one in the same.   Signed Rudolph Conrad. Witness Joseph Steel & James Martin. Rec. Apr. 1790. Book 4 p. 74; Book 15 p. 328

483. Feb. 26, 1790 James Collins sr (Lincoln Co) to son Isaac Collins; for "good causes" gave (1) 150 ac with "grist tub" mill on McIntires Br of Buffaloe Cr; part of 400 ac grant Jan. 25, 1773 by Gov. Josiah Martin to James Collins sr; part of which [the grant] "called" 100 ac sold to William Suitor and "precisely" 100 ac James Collins gave to his wife Bithya Collins and remainder "200 or 150 ac as it may be" now goes to Isaac Collins; and (2) gave my blacksmith tools "so called", a riding horse & saddle, and 2 cows & calves.   Signed James Collins' mark. Witness Alexander McIntire & Michl Hogan. Rec. Apr. 1790. Book 4 p. 76; Book 15 p. 329

484. Oct. 5, 1789 Christian Carpendor (Lincoln Co) to Philip Tevepaugh (same); for 40£ sold 150 ac on waters of Buffaloe Cr; part of 250 ac granted Sept. 26, 1766 to Francis Beaty who sold to Christian Carpendor.   Signed Christian Carpendor's mark. Witness David Ramsey & Frederick Carpenter. Rec. Apr. 1790. Book 4 p. 77; Book 15 p. 331

485. Sept. 7, 1789 Michael Cloninger (Lincoln Co) to Philip Cloninger (same); for 50£ sold (1) 200 ac on both sides of Seegles Cr; border: Thomas Bently; includes the forks and his improvement; granted Apr. 9, 1770 to "said" Philip Cloninger who sold to Adam Cloninger who sold to Michael Cloninger; and (2) 200 ac on both sides of Shegels (sic) Cr; border: "his" line; granted Oct. 17, 1772 ato "said" Philip Cloninger who sold to Matthias Peterson who sold to Michael Cloninger.   Signed Michel Cloninger (german). Witness John Howell, Nicholas Hilderman (german), & Friter _?_ (german). Rec. Apr. 1790. Book 4 p. 79; Book 15 p. 332

486. Feb. 24, 1790 Andrew Wilson (Lincoln Co) to John Wilson (same); for 5£ NC money sold 38 ac on waters of S fork of Cataba R; border: Andrew Wilson, John Wilson's field, & an old line of John Wilson's own tract; part of grant Aug. 15, 1755 to his father Matthew Wilson who willed it to Andrew Wilson.   Signed Andrew Wilson. Witness David Ramsey & Jesse Robinson. Rec. Apr. 1790. Book 4 p. 81; Book 15 p. 344

487. Apr. 6, 1790 Conrod Adams (Lincoln Co) to Philip Guiger (same); for 11£ NC money sold 69 ac on head branches of Clarks Cr; border: Jacob Hittle and Conrod Adams; part of 640 ac granted (#17) Apr. 6, 1765 to Philip Adams who

died intestate and land went to "lawful heir" Conrod Adams.   Signed Conrod Adams' mark. Witness Henrh Miller (german) & Johan Killion (german). Rec. Apr. 1790. Book 4 p. 83; Book 15 p. 336

488. Apr. 8, 1790 Joseph Henry, sheriff (Lincoln Co) to Joseph Henry (sic) (same); for 12£ sold 72 square poles lot 4 in SE square of Lincolnton; lot is 6 by 12 poles; sold due to writ Jan. 15, 1790 from Lincoln Co Pleas & Quarter Sessions Court to levy 81£ 1s 5p and 5£ 11s cost from James Langsley due to suit of Philip Null; money to be returned to court 1st Monday of April "next" and sale authorized by act of Assembly on Oct. 25, 1764.   Signed J. Henry. Witness Ad Osborn & W. Avery. Rec. Apr. 1790. Book 4 p. 85; Book 15 p. 338

489. Apr. 9, 1790 Joseph Henry, sheriff (Lincoln Co) to Robert Craig (Burke Co); for 14£ 1s 6p sold 150 ac on Mountain Cr; border: Junt's line, Lolard, & Panther; granted (#245) Aug. 7, 1787 to Phinehas Creaton; sold due to writ Jul. 6, 1787 to levy 25£ and 2£ 11s 1p cost from Phinehas Creaton due to suit of Waightstile Avery esq; sale authorized by act of Assembly on Oct. 25, 1764.   Signed Jos Henry. Witness J. Wilson & James McEntire. Rec. Apr. 1790. Book 4 p. 87; Book 15 p. 340

July Court 1790
490. Nov. 11, 1789 Abraham Lefever & wife Elizabeth (Augusta Co, Va) to John Cressimore (Lincoln Co); for 50£ sold 350 ac; border: Pope & Fry; land was granted Apr. 28, 1768 to Sebastian Cline and was sold Apr. 6, 1769 by Sebastian Cline (then of Mecklenburg & now of Lincoln Co) to John Lefever (late of Berks Co, Pa), father of Abraham Lefever; John Lefever's will dated Oct. 28, 1778 (registered in Berks Co, Pa) divided his land in Pennsylvania but failed to do anything about above tract; Abraham Lefever is eldest son and is declaired heir-at-law.   Signed Abraham & Elizabeth Lefever's marks. Witness John Jarrett, Michael Garber, & Henry Mowrey (or Monrey). Rec. Jul. 1790. Book 4 p. 89; Book 15 p. 342

491. Nov. 15, 1789 Abraham Scott (Lincoln Co) to Moses Hayes (same); for 5£ NC money sold 90 ac in (blank) fork of Cataba R; border: Fight formerly Cathy's line and Henry; formerly land of Francis Beaty and sold to Philip Alston who sold to James Johnston who sold to Abraham Scott.   Signed Abm Scott. Witness Abraham Scott (sic), W. Brooks, & Jno Dickson. Rec. Jul. 1790. Book 4 p. 91; Book 15 p. 344

492. Jul. 9, 1790 Joseph Dickson, esq commissioner in trust for Lincolnton, (Lincoln Co) to Charles Scholl, sadler (same); for 40s NC money sold [ac omitted] lot 5 in NE square of Lincolnton; lot is 6 by 12 poles.   Signed Jo Dickson. Witness Waightstile Avery, R. Wood, & Wm Sharpe. Rec. Jul. 1790. Book 4 p. 93; Book 15 p. 346

493. Apr. 3, 1790 Martin Friday (Lincoln Co) to David Zimmerman, hatter (Lincolnton, NC); for 25£ NC money sold [ac omitted] lot 13 in SW square of Lincolnton; lot is 6 by 14 rods; lot was sold by Col. Joseph Dickson, commissioner in trust for Lincolnton, to Martin Friday.   Signed Martin Fridey (german). Witness Daniel Strider(?) (german). Rec. Jul. 1790. Book 4 p. [not in grantor or grantee indexes]; Book 15 p. 347

494. Jun. 10, 1790 Henry Whitenar sr (Lincoln Co) to son Henry Whitenar jr (same); for love and affection and 1£ 10s NC money sold 392 ac on both sides of Henry R (fork--lined out) of S fork of Cataba R; border: George Wilfong, a ditch, & Jacobs R; part of two grants to Henry Whitener sr: (1) 1,000 ac Sept. 29, 1750 and (2) 300 ac Apr. 19, 1763.   Signed Henrich Writner (german). Witness David Ramsey & Daniel Whitener. Rec. Jul. 1790. Book 4 p. 95; Book 15 p. 348

495. Jan. 14, 1789 Ulrick Crowder (Wilkes Co, Ga) to Jacob Miller (Lincoln Co); for 15£ NC money sold 28 ac on Muddy Br of Whiteners Cr waters of S fork of Cataba R; border: Miller's own line; part of grant in 1764 to Ulrick Crowder. Signed Ubrick Crowder. Witness David Ramsey & Wm Temple Coles. Rec. Jul. 1790. Book 4 p. 97; Book 15 p. 350

496. Apr. 2, 1790 James Bryson (Lincoln Co) to Thomas Earwood (same); for 50£ sold 17 ac; border: Killian, Thos Earwood, & William Earwood.   Signed James Bryson. Witness Fras McCorkle & Adam Killion. Rec. Jul. 1790. Book 4 p. 98; Book 15 p. 351

497. Mar. 19, 1789 Robert Luckey (Mecklenburg Co) to Walter Beatey (same); for 125£ sold 125 ac on waters of Cataba R; border: James Luckey.   Signed Robt Luckey. Witness Thos Frohock & David Kennedy. Rec. Jul. 1790. Book 4 p. 99; Book 15 p. 352

498. Jun. 21, 1790 Joseph Henry, sheriff (Lincoln Co) to Thomas McGee (same); for 33£ sold 125 ac on waters of Cataba R; border: James Luckey; sold due to writ Jan. 10, 1790 from Lincoln Co Pleas & Quarter Sessions Court to levy 84£ 3s and 12£ 12s cost from Robert Luckey due to suit of Thomas McGee; money to be returned to court 1st Monday of April "next" and sale authorized by act of Assembly on Oct. 25, 1764.   Signed Jos Henry. Witness W. Avery, J. Dickson, & Jo Dickson. Rec. Jul. 1790. Book 4 p. 101; Book 15 p. 354

499. Feb. 3, 1790 William Killen (Lincoln Co) to John Titerbeam (same); for 10£ sold 281 ac on W side of Buffaloe Cr; border: Robt Wair, his own land on Long Br of Buffaloe Cr, George Wisenhunt, & Ramsour; granted Aug. 7, 1787 to William Killen.   Signed William Killen. Witness Vallentine Mauny & Jhermer Köhn (?) (german). Rec. Jul. 1790. Book 4 p. 103; Book 15 p. 356

500. Mar. 3, 1790 William Killen (Lincoln Co) to John Titerbeam (same); for 200£ sold 200 ac on both sides of Buffaloe Cr of Broad R above land formerly

property of James Kelly; border: a hill below a "round" bottom on W side of the creek; granted Dec. 16, 1769 to David McCree who sold Jul. 2, 1771 to John Carson who sold in Jun. 1784 to William Killen.   Signed William Killen. Witness Vallentine Mauny & Johannes Böhn (or Höhn) (german). Rec. Jul. 1790. Book 4 p. 105; Book 15 p. 357

501. Jul. 12, 1785 Robert Carruth, blacksmith (Lincoln Co) to John Sloan (same); for 40£ sold 100 ac; border: his own line; granted Mar. 3, 1779 to Robert Carruth. Signed Robert Carruth. Witness James Sloan & Robt Ligget. Rec. Jul. 1790. Book 4 p. 107; Book 15 p. 359

502. Jul. 12, 1785 Robert Carruth, blacksmith (Lincoln Co) to John Sloan (same); for 140£ sold 200 ac on Muddy fork of Buffaloe Cr; border: new lines; granted Oct. 13, 1765 to Francis Beaty who willed it to Wallace Beaty who sold May 25, 1776 to Robert Carruth.   Signed Robrt Carruth. Witness James Sloan & Robt Ligget. Rec. Jul. 1790. Book 4 p. 108; Book 15 p. 360

503. Jun. 11, 1790 Henry Whitener (Lincoln Co) to John Mull (same); for love and affection & 1£ 10s sold 240 ac on both sides of Jacobs R; border: "second corner of second tract" belonging to same survey and "a maddow" swamp; part of 640 ac granted Mar. 28, 1751 to Henry Whitener.   Signed Henrich Weitner (german). Witness David Ramsey & Jesse Robinson. Rec. Jul. 1790. Book 4 p. 110; Book 15 p. 361

504. Jun. 11, 1790 Henry Whitener (Lincoln Co) to Henry Sumrow (same); for love and affection & 1£ 10 sold 200 ac on both sides of Jacobs R; border: "second corner of first tract", a "meadow" swamp, & John Mull; middle part of 640 ac grant Mar. 28, 1751 to Henry Whitener.   Signed Henrich Weitner. Witness David Ramsey & Jesse Robinson. Rec. Jul. 1790. Book 4 p. 111; Book 15 p. 363

505. Jul. 3, 1789 William Allen (Lincoln Co) to James Loftin (same); for 130£ sold 210 ac on W side of Cataba R; border: Thomas Gillelen; granted Mar. 15, 1780 to William Allen.   Signed William Allin. Witness Samuel Harwell & Rolley Harwell. Rec. Jul. 1790. Book 4 p. 113; Book 15 p. 364

506. Jul. 6, 1790 Francis Horse (Lincoln Co) to Anthony Horse (same); for 30£ NC money sold 45 ac on waters of S fork of Cataba R; border: division line between "him" and Francis Horse (sic); part of 400 ac sold (by deed) to Saml Wilson sr who sold Apr. 25, 1755 to John Parker who sold Apr. 9, 1756 to Saml Wilson jr who sold Jan. 5, 1770 to Jacob Horse.   Signed Frantz Hors (german). Witness David Ramsey & Michael Quikel (german). Rec. Jul. 1790. Book 4 p. 114; Book 15 p. 365

507. Jul. 6, 1790 Robert Abernathy to Alexander Nelson; for 20£ sold 70 ac; border: Alexr Nelson's N line, Robt Abernathy, Mountain Br & its head spring, & head spring of Cainey Br; granted in Nov. 1784 to said Robt Abernathy.   Signed

Robt Abernathy. Witness Jn Nelson & John Abernathy. Rec. Jul. 1790. Book 4 p. 115; Book 15 p. 367

508. Aug. 6, 1788 Vincent Cox (Lincoln Co) to Alexander Nelson (same); for 80£ sold 100 ac on W side of Cataba R; border: Kennedy's corner, Cox, & Bonner; part of grant Oct. 26, 1767 to Samuel Coborn and sold to George West who sold Jul. 21, 1776 to Vincent Cox.   Signed Vincent Cox. Witness Robt Abernathy, Joseph Moreland, & Ambros Cobb. Rec. Jul. 1790. Book 4 p. 117; Book 15 p. 369

509. May 1, 1790 James Baird & wife Mary (Lincoln Co) to Nathan Ford (same); for 280£ NC money sold (1) 150 ac on SW side of S fork of Cuttaba R "next below" Hugh Berry & John Armstrong near "the" waggon ford; includes improvement made by Wm McDowel & Abram Crain Jones; granted Apr. 21, 1764 to Francis Beatey and sold by Francis Beatey & wife Martha to Adam Crain Jones and sold Mar. 4, 1767 by Adam Crain Jones & wife Mary to John Beard and sold Jul. 25, 1774 by John Beard & wife Frances to James Baird; and (2) [ac omitted] on S side of S fork of Cataba R; includes said Baird's improvements; border: below Armstrong's ford, "the" road, & Patterson.   Signed James Baird & Mary's mark. Witness Js Holland, Robt Patterson, & Jacob Stow. Rec. Jul. 1790. Book 4 p. 119; Book 15 p. 370

510. May 10, 1786 John Hill, planter (Lincoln Co) to John Sloan (same); for 100£ NC money sold 200 ac on both sides of Espey's Mill fork of Long Cr; border: Peter Phink, Orman, & Espey; granted Feb. 28, 1795 to John Hill.   Signed John Hill. Witness John Carruth & Joseph Gladen. Rec. Jul. 1790. Book 4 p. 121; Book 15 p. 372

511. May 1, 1788 Michael Rudisell (Lincoln Co) to Jacob Rudisell (same); for 20£ NC money sold 200 ac on S side of Cataba R on Leepers Cr; border: a division line; part of grant Sept. 24, 1754 to Martin Talinger who sold to Michael Rudisell. Signed Michel Rudihil (german). Witness Henry Rudisealy (sic) & Michel Heyel (or Hoyl) (german). Rec. Jul. 1790. Book 4 p. 122; Book 15 p. 374

512. Dec. 10, 1788 Robert Abernathy (Lincoln Co) to Charles Williams sr (same); for 300£ NC money sold 250 ac on S side of Cataba R; border: Philip Earhart; part of 1,000 ac granted Sept. 30, 1749 to John Killion who sold Jan. 1 & 2, 1754 to Jacob Brown who sold Jul. 20, 1757 to John Hill who sold to Alexr Hemphill who sold Oct. 7, 1774 to Benjamin Armstrong and "to" Robert Abernathy. Signed Robt Abernathy. Witness James Johnston, John Bynum, & Jones Abernathy. Rec. Jul. 1790. Book 4 p. 124; Book 15 p. 375

513. Jun. 3, 1788 John Shufert (Lincoln Co) to George Shufert (same); for 50£ NC money sold 300 ac on both sides of Potts Cr; sold Sept. 19, 1787 by Joseph Henry, sheriff, to John Shufert.   Signed Johanis Sufderlt(?) (german). Witness

Linnhert Lerman(?) (german) & Jacob Summey. Rec. Jul. 1790. Book 4 p. 126; Book 15 p. 377

514. Jun. 3, 1788 John Shufert (Lincoln Co) to David Shufert (same); for 50£ NC money sold 527 ac on S side of S fork of Cataba R; border: near Rockey ford; part of tract sold Sept. 19 & 20, 1755 by John Clark to George Shufert who willed it to his son John Shufert.   Signed Johanes Sufferlt (german). Witness Linnhert Lerman(?) (german) & Jacob Summey. Rec. Jul. 1790. Book 4 p. 128; Book 15 p. 379

515. Jun. 3, 1788 John Shufert (Lincoln Co) to David Shufert (same); for 50£ NC money sold 443 ac on S side of S fork of Cataba R; part of tract sold Sept. 19 & 20, 1755 by John Clark to George Shufert who willed it to his son John Shufert. Signed Johanns Sufderlt (german). Witness Leinhert Lernner(?) (german) & Jacob Summey. Rec. Jul. 1790. Book 4 p. 130; Book 15 p. 381

516. Jan. 1, 1810 Alexander Macomb (or McComb), merchant & wife Jane (New York, NY) to William DuBourg, president of St. Mary's College (Baltimore, MD); Alexander owes William $2,193.11 U. S. money and has a bond "dated today" of $4,386.22 to insure payment with interest on Jan. 1, 1811; to insure payment and for $1 sold five tracts granted by Gov. Samuel Ashe to Lewis Beard: (1) grant #850--6,800 ac on waters of Kings Cr and Clarks fork waters of Broad R and on waters of Crowders Cr waters of Cataba R; border: Samuel Blackwood, widow Graham, John Falls, Arthur Patterson jr, John Dickson, James Hair, Andrew Ferguson, John Wilson, Nathan Mendenhall, on N side of a road from John Oats's to Samuel Blackwood's, his own 1,107 ac tract, crosses Crowders Cr below the shoals, George Falls, Amos Spice, near Charleston Road, "fourth" corner of "his" 300 ac ac bought of Lindsey, Arthur Patterson's 50 ac survey, a black oak marked "LB", the South Carolina line, a small road, McCarter, Henry, & a path from John Oats's to "the" meeting house; (2) grant #852--4,292 ac on Hagins fork, Lyles Cr, Falling Cr, & Balls Cr; border: James Wilson, Matthew Wilson, William & James Caldwell, John & Barnard Snyder, Frederick Ward, David Ramsey, Archd Hamilton, Isaac Robinson, Patrick OBrian, Henry Bullinger, & crosses a waggon road from Sherrill's ford to Morganton; (3) grant #854--4,904 ac on waters of Jacobs R and head waters of Buffaloe and Indian Creeks; border: John Mull, John Orr sr, John Orr jr, Aver Wender(?), Samuel Carpenter, Jesse Kirkendall, Jean Hogshead, Henry McElroy, Ambrose Bonham, James Johnston, Thomas Robinson, Leonard Piles, William Harbeson, Hafner, Solomon Wietz, widow Pilgrim, David Ramsey, Nicholas Chapman, Michel Shell, two post oaks marked "LB", John Orrs Cr, Burke Co line, intersection of Lincoln, Burke, & Rutherford Cos., Rutherford Co line, George Dailey's improvement, Nathaniel Harris, George Sealey, & a road; (4) grant #858--1,910 ac on waters of S fork of Catawba R and waters of Clarks Cr; border: Francis Ring, Matthias & Tobias Peterson, Monsier (sic), Horton, George Sides, on both sides of a road from Lincolnton to Morganton, a white oak marked "LC", & Stoney Cr; & (5) grant #865--200 ac on waters of Indian Cr and Buffalloe Cr; border: Absalom Bonham, William Chambers, Jacob Bullinger, Benjamin Hall,

Nicholas Coons, Henry Hellebrand, Henry Dellinger, Nathan Harris, Jean (or Jane) Hogshead, his own survey, Henry McElroy, Hovis, & Kirkendall; if Alexander Macomb defaults on payment, then William DuBourg can sell the land. Signed Alex and Jane Macomb. Witness S. Ricker jr. Wit. oath (New York) Feb. 7, 1810 by Alex & Jane Macomb to S. Riker jr "Master in chancery". Second Wit. oath (New York) Apr. 5, 1810 by Samuel Riker jr to Ambrose Spencer, justice of Supreme Court of New York. Apr. 5, 1810 Jacob Radcliff, mayor of New York City, certifys Ambrose Spencer is a justice of New York Supreme Court. Rec. (Lincoln Co) Jul. 1810. Book 4 p. 132; Book "401.10" p. 185

517. Apr. (blank), 1810 Wm Scott, Thos McLean, Moses Ratchford, Matthew Armstrong, & John Dameron, commissioners appointed by order of Lincoln Co Pleas & Quarter Sessions Court Apr. 1810 to divide the real estate of John Leeper desc on the petition of Andrew Leeper and William Armstrong, in right of his wife Mary; land is divided as follows: (1) lot 1--82 ac to Andrew Leeper; border: John Neagle's corner and Martin; (2) lot 2--90 ac to William Armstrong, in right of his wife Mary; border: John Neagle, James & Nancy Leeper, an old line, Andrew Leeper, & Martin; (3) lot 3--90 ac to James Leeper; border: "the" fork at the cannoe landing, Armstrong, John Neagle, & mouth of a branch; (4) lot 4--97 ac to Esther Leper (sic); border: James Leeper's "beginning" corner, Nancy Leeper, "the" fork at mouth of "the" spring branch, & up the fork; (5) lot 5--114 ac to Nancy Leeper; border: John Leeper's corner, an old line, James Leeper, & Esther Leeper; & (6) lot 6--80 ac to John Leeper; border: mouth of a branch "the old corner", Nancy Leeper, Esther Leeper, & "the" fork at mouth of "the" spring branch; Also John Leeper pays Andrew Leeper $187 and Nancy Leeper pays James Leeper $40 & she pays William Armstrong, in right of his wife Mary, $80. Signed Wm Scott, Thos McLean, Moses Ratchford, Matthew Armstrong, & John Dameron. Witness (none). Rec. Jul. 1810. Book 4 p. 147; Book "401.10" p. 195

518. Jul. 17, 1807 Jonathan Williams (Mecklenburg Co) to Robert Brown (Lincoln Co); for $100 NC money sold 60 ac on S side of Long Br of Indian Cr; border: said Brown's old tract, James Carrell, Mauney, & Coon. Signed Jonathan Williams. Witness Nicholas Iler & John Crego. Wit. oath Jul. 1810 by Nicholas Iler. Book 4 p. 150; Book "401.10" p. 196

519. Jul. 14, 1810 George Wilfong (Lincoln Co) to Daniel Whitener (same); for $400 sold 233 ac on both sides of Mulls Cr waters of Henrys R; border: a divsion line of an old 118 ac tract, Taylor, Hawn, & Shell; part of grant from the State to Christopher Reider who sold to George Wilfong and part of "several tracts" granted to George Wilfong. Signed George Wellfong's mark. Witness John Yoder & John Wellfong. Wit. oath Jul. 1810 by John Yoder. Book 4 p. 151; Book "401.10" p. 197

520. Sept. 20, 1808 Robert Ramsey (Lincoln Co) to John Miller (same); for 5s sold 150 ac on waters of Buffaloe Cr; border: Saml Ramsey & Henry Fritts.

Signed Robert Ramsey's mark. Witness Lemuel Saunders & Saml Wilson. Wit. oath Jul. 1810 by Leml Saunders. Book 4 p. 153; Book "401.10" p. 198

521. Oct. 14, 1809 Samuel Ramsey (Lincoln Co) to John Miller (same); for $550 sold 280 ac on waters of Buffaloe and Indian Creeks; border: John Curronel and "second" corner of "the" old survey.   Signed Saml Ramsey. Witness Lemuel Saunders & Saml Wilson. Rec. Jul. 1810. Book 4 p. 154; Book "401.10" p. 199

522. Nov. 18, 1809 John Miller (Lincoln Co) to Joel Williams (same); for 5s sold 430 ac in two tracts on waters of Indian and Buffaloe Creeks: (1) [ac omitted]; border: "second" corner of "the" old survey; and (2) [ac omitted]; border: tract 1, "said" Ramsey, & Henry Frittz's corner.   Signed John Miller. Witness Lemuel Saunders & Jos Abernathy. Wit. oath Jul. 1810 by Lemuel Saunders. Book 4 p. 156; Book "401.10" 200

523. Jan. 17, 1805 Joshua & Mary Burnet (Burke Co) to William Magness (Lincoln Co); for $150 sold "our part" of Negroes willed to Mary Roberts, now wife of Joshua Burnet, by Walter Pollard--three Negroes: Bet, Moll, & Peat and their issue.   Signed Joshua Burnett & Mary's mark. Witness John Roberts & M. Roberts. Wit. oath Oct. 1810 by John Roberts. Book 4 p. 158; Book "401.10" p. 202

524. Jun. 9, 1807 Jacob Deal (Lincoln Co) to George Deal (same); for $172 sold 172 ac on waters of Clarks Cr; border: Conrad Mingo on W side of School House Br, crosses third branches, & "the" old line; part of 400 ac granted (#523) Oct. 28, 1782 to William Deal.   Signed Jacob Deal's mark. Witness John Yoder, William diel (sic), Bottfaud Boleh (german), & Michl Cline. Rec. Oct. 1810. Book 4 p. 159; Book "401.10" p. 202

525. Feb. 18, 1809 Jeremiah Benich, Adam Benich, Phebe Benich, Anthony Shittle, & Catharine Shittle, heirs of Philip Benich desc, (Lincoln Co) to Henry Benich (same); for $120 sold 272 ac on waters of Indian Cr; border: Tobias James's corner and Jeremiah Benich.   Signed marks of Jeremiah Benich, Adam Benich, Phebe Benich, Anthony Shittl, & Catharine Shittle. Witness Saml Wilson, William Collins, & Saml Bigham. Wit. oath Oct. 1810 by Saml Wilson. Book 4 p. 160; Book "401.10" p. 203

526. Oct. 9, 1810 Jacob Dellinger (Lincoln Co) to Martin Goldman (Jefferson Co, Ky); for 7 silver dollars sold 7.5 ac; border: his own land.   Signed Jacob Dellinger's mark. Witness Adam Hoppes & Henry Link. Rec. Oct. 1810. Book 4 p. 162; Book "401.10" 203

Book 16
October Court 1790
527. Jan. 23, 1790 Vincent Wiatt (Lincoln Co) to Peter Rine (same); for 200£ sold 270 ac on both sides of Little Long Cr; border: Hovas and John Hoyle; granted

Oct. 26, 1767 to John Miers.   Signed Vincent Wyatt & Elisabeth's mark. Witness James Wethers & Jacob Rein (german). Rec. Oct. 1790. Book 16 p. 1

528. Jun. 4, 1788 William Bradshaw (Lincoln Co) to Alexander Nelson (same); for 200£ sold 100 ac on W side of Cataba R; border: point of a ridge on said river below Wm Bradshaw's clear land; includes a great bent in said river and "some" improvements; part of 140 ac granted May 15, 1772 to Francis Beatty and sold Jul. 24, 1775 by Hugh Beatty & Robert Armstrong, executors for Francis Beatty desc, to Benjamin Cochran who sold Apr. 24, 1776 to John Henderson who sold Dec. 24, 1778 to William Bradshaw.   Signed William Bradshaw. Witness John Turkefill (or Turlufill), David Alexander, Smith Alexander. Rec. Oct. 1790. Book 16 p. 1

529. Mar. 15, 1790 Francis Guthrie (Lincoln Co) to Daniel Collins (same); for 15£ NC money sold 40 ac on W side of Buffaloe Cr; border: said Guthrie's corner; part of tract on both sides of Buffaloe Cr sold Dec. 20, 1783 by Henry Carlock to Francis Guthrie.   Signed Francis Guthrie. Witness John Endsley & James Kid. Rec. Oct. 1790. Book 16 p. 3

530. Aug. 16, 1790 John Boreland (Lincoln Co) to Elisabeth Fulbright (same); for 30£ NC money sold 200 ac; border: "last" corner of "said" old tract and "old Shutting" line; part of grant Dec. 22, 1768 to John Boreland.   Signed John Borland. Witness Henry Stemy & Robt Blackburn. Rec. Oct. 1790. Book 16 p. 4

531. Oct. 5, 1790 James McCallon, planter (Lincoln Co) to Daniel Collins, planter (same); for 100£ NC money sold 150 ac on W side of Buffaloe Cr "although in his deed it says N side of Buffaloe"; border: George Davis, "his" beginning corner, & line conveyed to him by John Sanders in 1782 and formerly property of Thomas Welsh "bearing date" May 22, 1772.   Signed James McCallon. Witness John Endsley & Joseph McReynolds. Rec. Oct. 1790. Book 16 p. 5

532. Sept. 28, 1786 Reuben Simpson (Green Co [no state mentioned]) to Jemima Jones (Lincoln Co); for 50£ sold 140 ac on W side of Cataba R; border: Reuben Simpson; part of Reuben Simpson's "plantation"; granted by the governor to Reuben Simpson.   Signed Reuben Simpson. Witness James Holsclaw & Isaac Robinson. Rec. Oct. 1790. Book 16 p. 6

533. May 26, 1778 James Wilson jr, planter & wife Catharine (Burke Co) to Richard Johnston, farmer (same); for 50£ NC money sold 300 ac in Burke Co on Clarks Cr and Allens Br; border: Dunn's corner and James Wilson; granted Jan. 25, 1773 to James Wilson jr (see Secretary's Book #15 p. 207).   Signed James Wilson & Catharene Wilson. Witness Matthew Willson jr & Sarah Willson. Rec. Oct. 1790. Book 16 p. 7

534. Jul. 26, 1790 James Alexander (Spartanburg Co, SC) to James Cunningham (Lincoln Co); for 125£ NC money sold (1) 144 ac on S side of Cataba R; border:

Beatty, Wm Chronicle's old corner, Fight, said Cunningham, Barnett, & Hambright's old line; being three "sundry" tracts or two whole tracts and part of a third joning each other.   Signed Jas Alexander. Witness Jonn Gullick, Robt Paterson, & John Patterson. Rec. Oct. 1790. Book 16 p. 10

535. Dec. 29, 1789 David Elder (Lincoln Co) to John Titman (same); for 120£ NC money sold 225 ac on a branch of Duharts Cr; border: his own land on S side; part of which was granted to Nathaniel Henderson who sold to [omitted] and part was granted Oct. 9, 1783 to David Elder.   Signed David Elder. Witness Benjamin Newton & Jonn Gullick. Rec. Oct. 1790. Book 16 p. 11

536. Apr. 30, 1790 Paul Anthony (Burke Co) to John Smier (Lincoln Co); for 55£ NC money sold 210 ac on S branch of Clarks Cr; border: his own land, Crowder, & Neaves corner; granted Apr. 28, 1768 to Paul Anthony.   Signed Paulis Anthone. Witness Andrew Stothinger, Johanns Bess(?) (german), & Jacob Starr. Rec. Oct. 1790. Book 16 p. 12

537. Feb. 17, 1790 William Sims (Richmond Co, Ga) to Robert Ferguson (Lincoln Co); for 20£ sold 295.5 ac on waters of Crowders Cr; border: Robt Ferguson near a shoal, Chas McLean, & two branches of Crowders Cr; granted to William Sims. Signed William Sims. Witness Charles McLean, John Ferguson, & Ephraim McLean. Rec. Oct. 1790. Book 16 p. 13

538. Jun. 10, 1790 Henry Weitner (Lincoln Co) to son David Weitner (same); for love and affection and 1£ 10s NC money sold 480 ac; border: on E side of "the" river "nigh" mouth of a spring branch, a "Meadow" swamp, mouth of Muddy Br, & near Conrod Youder; part of three tracts granted (1) Sept. 29, 1750 to Henry Weitner, (2) Apr. 19, 1763 to Henry Weitner, & (3) Oct. 20, 1767 to Henry Weitner.   Signed Henrich Weitner. Witness David Ramsey & Henrich Weitner (sic) (german). Rec. Oct. 1790. Book 16 p. 15

539. Mar. (blank), 1788 Samuel Hughey (Burke Co) to Fendal Whitworth (Lincoln Co); for 100£ NC money sold 300 ac on waters of Littons Cr on W side of Cataba R; border: Willm Osburn & Jeremiah Davis' conditional line, crosses Cattail Br, & Wm Osburn & Abraham Robinson's conditional line; granted Mar. 14, 1780 to William Osborn.   Signed Saml Hughey. Witness John Carruth & Wm Magness. Rec. Oct. 1790. Book 16 p. 16

540. Feb. 16, 1790 William Sims (Ga) to Charles McLean (NC); for 5s NC money sold 4.5 ac on branches of Crowders Cr; border: his own line.   Signed William Sims. Witness Robt Ferguson & John Ferguson. Rec. Oct. 1790. Book 16 p. 17

541. Sept. 4, 1790 Christopher Ryder ((blank) Co, SC) to George Wilfong sr (Lincoln Co); for 25£ NC money sold 118 ac on S side of Mulls Cr and N side of Hope Cr; granted (#962) Aug. 7, 1787 to Christopher Ryder.   Signed Christopher Ryder's mark. Witness Peter Shoup & John Wilfong. Rec. Oct. 1790. Book 16 p. 18

542. Jul. 3, 1790 John & James Baird (Lincoln Co) to Adam Baird (same), all three are executors of John Baird desc; for 30£ NC money sold 83 ac formerly in Mecklenburg & now Lincoln Co on both sides of Little Catapa Cr; border: John Baird and Samuel Gingles; John Baird desc owned the land when he died and didn't mention it in his will but did direct to sell the rest of his estate; the will was proved in open court & filed in the clerk's office; so land was sold "at public vendue";   granted Oct. 26, 1767 to Benjamin Davidson who sold Jun. 22, 1768 to John Baird.   Signed James Baird & John Baird sr.   Witness Jno Barber, J. Wilson, & Job Robinson. Rec. Oct. 1790. Book 16 p. 20

543. Nov. 14, 1787 Hugh Robison (Rowan Co) to John Nixon (Lincoln Co); for 64£ sold 135 ac; border: on W side of N branch of Killions Cr, William Hager, & John Jewhart; includes Solomon Hoover's improvements on W side of Cataba R; granted Oct. 13, 1756 to Solomon Hoover.   Signed Hugh Robison. Witness William Nixon & Abner Womack. Rec. Oct. 1790. Book 16 p. 21

544. Jul. 4, 1788 Christian Carpenter, planter (Lincoln Co) to George Patterson, planter (same); for 160£ NC money sold 300 ac on both sides of Buffaloe Cr "near above" his father's survey; includes "the" High Sholas; granted Feb. 28, 1775 to Christian Carpenter.   Signed Christian Carpenter's mark. Witness Forney Green Norman & James McCallon. Rec. Oct. 1790. Book 16 p. 23

545. Aug. 18, 1790 John Moore (Lincoln Co) to Benjamin Smith (same); for 200£ sold 180 ac on Little Hoyls Cr "or" Beaverdam Cr; granted Aug. 30, 1753 to James Armstrong.   Signed John Moore. Witness Alexr Moore. Rec. Oct. 1790. Book 16 p. 24

546. Aug. 18, 1790 John Moore jr (Lincoln Co) to Benjamin Smith (same); for 200£ sold 250 ac; border: formerly Wm Smith's land on N side, Jacob Shutly, John Moore, & Abernathy; granted Oct. 28, 1782 to James Henderson.   Signed John Moore. Witness Alexr Moore. Rec. Oct. 1790. Book 16 p. 25

547. Jul. 28, 1790 Thomas Dickson (Lincoln Co) to John Dickson (same); for 5£ sold 100 ac; border: Massey, Gray, Wallace, & James Shannon.   Signed Thomas Dickson. Witness William Dickson. Rec. Oct. 1790. Book 16 p. 26

548. Jul. 20, 1789 Daniel McKisick (Lincoln Co) to John Hide (same); for 13£ NC money sold 100 ac on W side of Potts Cr and a branch of said creek; border: John Bradley's old survey and William Reed; includes John Hide's improvement; granted Aug. 7, 1787 to Daniel McKisick.   Signed Danl McKisick. Witness Joshua Wilson & William Hide. Rec. Oct. 1790. Book 16 p. 27

549. Aug. 16, 1790 John Borland (Lincoln Co) to Peter Fulbright (same); for 30£ sold 200 ac; border: Stemy's "beginning" corner and an old line; part of grant Dec.

22, 1768 to John Boreland.   Signed John Borland. Witness Henry Stemy & Robt Blackburn. Rec. Oct. 1790. Book 16 p. 28

550. Oct. 5, 1790 Henry Sumerour (Lincoln Co) to John Boyd (same); for 45£ NC money sold 150 ac on waters of Clerks Cr; border: Welsh and said Boyd's old line; part of grant Dec. 23, 1768 to Alexander Lockart who sold Oct. 30, 1788 to Henry Sumerour.   Signed Henry Summerour. Witness Adam Reeckinback, Robt Blackburn, & Wm Blackburn. Rec. Oct. 1790. Book 16 p. 30

551. Jul. 4, 1788 Christian Carpenter (Lincoln Co) to George Patterson (same); for 50£ sold 150 ac on middle fork of Buffalo Cr; border: John Carpenter and his own land.   Signed Christian Carpenter's mark. Witness Forney Green Norman & James McCallon. Rec. Oct. 1790. Book 16 p. 31

552. Sept. 4, 1789 John McCord (Lincoln Co) to Samuel Caldwell (same); for 120£ NC money sold 150 ac on E side of S fork of Cataba R; border: McKnight; part of grant to James Henderson who sold Sept. 1, 1777 to John McCord. Signed John McCord. Witness Jas Hanks & Joel Jetton. Rec. Oct. 1790. Book 16 p. 32

553. Jul. 14, 1787 Thomas McCormack (Lincoln Co) to William Nixon (same); for 30£ sold 100 ac; border: Yohard and Hoover; "dated" Mar. 25, 1780.   Signed Thomas McCormack's mark. Witness Jas Hill & Archibald Little. Rec. Oct. 1790. Book 16 p. 33

554. Apr. 30, 1790 Paul Anthony (Burke Co) to John Smier (Lincoln Co); for 50£ NC money sold 200 ac on both sides of a branch that runs into Clerks Cr below William Bost's; border: Bostian Cline, said Anthony, & a new line; granted Apr. 25, 1767 to Paul Anthony.   Signed Paulinh Antone (german). Witness Johannes Bost & Jacob Starr. Rec. Oct. 1790. Book 16 p. 35

555. May 7, 1790 John Shell (Burke Co) to Joseph Alexander (Lincoln Co); for 180£ sold 300 ac on Henrys fork of S fork of Cataba R; part of three tracts: (1) 33.75 ac on N side of Henrys fork and crosses Mill Cr; granted to John Butts who sold to Peter Mull who sold Apr. 2, 1787 to John Shell; (2) 25.5 ac W of tract 1 on W side of Mill Cr and crosses the creek; granted Oct. 11, 1783 to John Shell; & (3) 240.75 ac; border: tract 1, in forks of Mill Cr, & E line of tract 2.   Signed John Shell. Witness Joshua Perkins, Jno Bradburn, & Michael Grindstaff. Rec. Oct. 1790. Book 16 p. 36

556. Aug.12, 1790 Abraham Earhart (Lincoln Co) to Daniel Asbury (same); for 75£ NC money sold 150 ac on SW side of Andersons Cr; border: Abraham Earhart and an old line.   Signed Abraham Earhart. Witness Samuel Harwell & Jno Turbyfill. Rec. Oct. 1790. Book 16 p. 37

557. Oct. 13, 1789 William Chittim (Lincoln Co) to George Davenport (same); for 125£ NC money sold 200 ac on E side of S fork of Cataba R; border: Nicholas Leeper and James Chittim; granted Dec. 23, 1763 to William Chittim. Signed William Chittim. Witness William Davenport, John Chittim, & Richard Featherstone. Rec. Oct. 1790. Book 16 p.38

558. Jan. 31, 1789 William Nixon (Lincoln Co) to John Beale (same); for 130£ NC money sold 200 ac on W side of Cataba R. Signed William Nixon. Witness John Robinson & James Nixon. Rec. Oct. 1790. Book 16 p. 39

559. Apr. 3, 1789 John Fish (Lincoln Co) to Peter Dunkin (same); for 40£ sold 300 ac on S fork of Littens Cr waters of Cataba R; border: Jeremiah Davies' & Abraham Robinson's conditional line and Jeremiah Davies' & William Osborn's conditional line; granted Mar. 14, 1780 to Jeremiah Davies. Signed John & Mary Fish. Witness Thomas Bowers & Jno Bodine. Rec. Oct. 1790. Book 16 p. 40

560. Feb. 16, 1786 Thomas & Frank Winn (Lincoln Co) to Jacob Forney (Burke Co); for 150£ sold a Negro woman Lucy & Negro boy Joe. Signed Thomas & Frank Winn's marks. Witness Martin Rintelman & Moses Jenkins. Rec. Oct. 1790. Book 16 p. 41

561. Feb. 16, 1786 Thomas & Frank Winn (Lincoln Co) to Peter Forney (same); for 150£ sold a Negro girl Genn & Negro boy Ned. Signed Thomas & Frank Winn's marks. Witness Matthias Peterson, Martin Rintelman, & Moses Jenkins. Rec. Oct. 1790. Book 16 p. 42

562. Aug. 22, 1787 Thomas Smith (Rutherford Co) to Ben Smith (same); for 100£ sold a "likely" Negro girl Sall about 14 years old. Signed Thos Smith. Witness Joseph Burnett, Cloe Burn Burnet, & Mat Bilbo. Rec. Oct. 1790. Book 16 p. 42

January Session 1791
563. Sept. 6, 1790 Henry Wartiman & mother Elisabeth (Lincoln Co) to Michael Buff (same); for 60£ NC money sold 200 ac on head waters of Leoanhards (sic) fork of Indian Cr. Signed Henry Wartmin & Elisabeth's mark. Witness Jacob Bollinger & John Kennedy. Rec. Jan. 1791. Book 16 p. 43

564. Aug. 8, 1789 George Bayzour (Lincoln Co) to William Smith, blacksmith (same); for 100£ NC money sold 200 ac on Bakemans Br of S fork of Cataba R; border: Costner; granted Mar. 2, 1775 to George Bayzour. Signed George Bayzour's mark. Witness Samuel White & And Taylor. Rec. Jan. 1791. Book 16 p. 45

565. Apr. 4, 1790 John Cox & wife Margaret (Lincoln Co) to "his" son Morris Cox (same); for love and affection & 5s sold 158 ac on both sides of Lanords fork of Inden Cr; border: Aaron Cox and Isaac Limings; middle part of 420 ac granted

Mar. 28, 1751 to Peter Harpell who sold Feb. 19 & 20, 1768 to Thomas Salter who sold May 13, 1787 to John Cox.   Signed John & Margat Cox. Witness Moses Moore & Elisha Cox. Rec. Jan. 1791. Book 16 p. 47

566. Dec. 26, 1785 Thomas Lyttle, farmer (Lincoln Co) to William McCasland (same); for 100£ sold 250 ac on Halls Br of Mountain Cr of Cataba R; border: McCorkles Cr; granted May 15,1772 to Thomas Lyttle.   Signed Thomas Little & Susanna's mark. Witness Fras McCorkel & Wm Kerr. Rec. Jan. 1791. Book 16 p. 47

567. Nov. 12, 1790 Drury Logan (Lincoln Co) to Joshua Roberts (same); for 5£ NC money sold 155 ac on both sides of Inden (sic) Cr waters of S fork of Cataba R; border: Joshua Roberts, Valentine Mauney, & "second" corner of the old tract; part of grant in 1750 to Ritcherd Reynolds.   Signed Drury Logan. Witness David Ramsey & Valentine Mauny. Rec. Jan. 1791. Book 16 p. 48

568. Nov. 10, 1790 Drury Logan (Lincoln Co) to Valentine Mauny (same); for 140£ sold 150 ac on waters of Indian Cr of Cataba R; border: division line "made by Moses Moore unto" Thos Robinson and an old line; part of an old tract where Moses Moore formerly lived.   Signed Drury Login. Witness David Ramsey, Joshua Roberts, & Antony Mauny. Rec. Jan. 1791. Book 16 p. 49

569. Jan. 5,1790 Samuel Durmire, planter (Iredell Co) to Samuel Oxford sr, farmer (Lincoln Co); for 50£ NC money sold 200 ac on S side of Cataba R; border: David Bridges' upper line, mouth of a branch, & fork of the branch; granted (#264) Mar. 14, 1780 to Samuel Durmire (registered in Lincoln Co Apr. 1, 1786 in State Grants book #1 p. 194 by Jno Wilson regis.).   Signed Samuel Durmire's mark. Witness James Oxford, John Oxford, Jonathan Oxford. Rec. Jan. 1791. Book 16 p. 51

570. Apr. 4, 1790 Jacob Cox & wife Margaret (Lincoln Co) to "his" son Aaron Cox (same); for love and affection and 5s sold 158 ac on both sides of Leonards fork waters of Indian Cr; part of upper end of 420 ac granted Mar. 28, 1751 to Peter Harpell who sold Feb. 19 & 20, 1768 to Thomas Salter who sold May 13, 1787 to Jacob Cox.   Signed John & Margret Cox. Witness Moses Moore & Elisha Cox. Rec. Jan. 1791. Book 16 p. 52

571. Dec. 10, 1790 John Steamy (Lincoln Co) to John Leameans (same); for 30£ NC money sold 100 ac on waters of Potts Cr; border: "third" corner of old survey, Henry Hiltebrant, John Borland, & another old survey; part of grant Oct. 26, 1767 to John Steamy sr who died "ountested" and land went to his eldest son John Steamy.   Signed John Stamey. Witness Henry Carpenter & Jacob Troareback. Rec. Jan. 1791. Book 16 p. 54

572. Apug. 15, 1789 Henry Isenhart (Lincoln Co) to Peter Carpendor (same); for 100£ NC money sold 300 ac on S side of Beaverdam Cr waters of S fork of

Catawba R; border: Jacob Carpendor, Lawrence Koiser, & Christen Carpendor; granted Apr. 19, 1763 to Henry Isenhart.   Signed Henry Isenhart's mark. Witness Eliezer Givens & Christopher Carpenter. Rec. Jan. 1791. Book 16 p. 55

573. Dec. 7, 1790 Henry Whitener sr, planter, & wife Catherine (Lincoln Co) to Jesse Robinson (same); for 50£ NC money sold 520 (525--lined out) ac; border: mouth of a spring branch on E side of "the" river, Daniel Whitener, a Meadowy branch, his 300 ac tract, Jacob Miller, & "last" corner of "the" old survey; part of two grants to Henry Whitener (1) Apr. 15, 1763 and (2) Sept. 29, 1750.   Signed Henry Weitner (german) & Catharine Whitner. Witness Robt Blackburn & Henry Weitner jr (german). Rec. Jan. 1791. Book 16 p. 56

574. Jun. 28, 1777 Jacob Baker & wife Susanna (Tryon Co) to Christopher Nesinger (same); for 96£ NC money sold 486 ac; border: Abraham Keener, Dellinger, & a new line; granted Sept. 14, 1767 to Henry Jacobs and sold Oct. 4, 1769 by Henry Jacobs & wife Susanna to Michael Rudisel and sold May 14, 1770 by Michael Rudisel & wife Catharine to Jacob Baker.   Signed Jacob Beker (german) & Susanna's mark. Witness Jacob Seitz & George Seitz. Rec. Jan. 1791. Book 16 p. 57

575. Jun. 11, 1790 Henry Whitener (Lincoln Co) to daughter Mary Whitener (same); for love and affection and 1£ 10s NC money sold 200 ac on both sides of Jacobs R; border: the old survey; part of 640 ac granted Mar. 28, 1751 to Henry Whitener.   Signed Henrich Weitner (german). Witness Henrich Weitner (or Henry Whitener jr) (german) & Robt Blackburn. Rec. Jan. 1791. Book 16 p. 59

576. Dec. 31, 1790 Peter Hermon (Lincoln Co) to James Graham (same); for 150£ NC money sold (1) 100 ac in Lincoln formerly Tryon Co on both sides of N fork of Crowders Cr; and (1) 47 ac; border: tract 1; part of 300 ac granted Apr. 21, 1764 to Jonathan Newman who sold to Charles McLean who sold to Peter Hermon.   Signed Peter Herman. Witness James Wilson, Sarah Wilson, & J. Wilson. Rec. Jan. 1791. Book 16 p. 60

577. Jan. 3, 1791 John Barber (Lincoln Co) to Thomas White (same); for 80£ NC money sold (1) 100 ac on N side of S fork of Crowders Cr; border: Thomas Price and John Barber; granted (#365) Sept. 12, 1787 to John Barber; and 125 ac; border: "third" corner of tract 1, Thomas Price, old original survey, & William Henry; part of grant to Thomas Dixon who sold to William Henry who sold to John Barber.   Signed Jno Barber. Witness Abraham Enloe & J. Wilson. Rec. Jan. 1791. Book 16 p. 62

April Session 1791
578. Oct. 6, 1789 George Easlinger (Lincoln Co) to Henry Long Crayer (same); for 19£ NC money sold 40 ac on waters of Layleses Cr; border: Barnard Sigman and his own line; part of grant Aug. 7, 1787 to Frederick Havener.   Signed Gerg

Eslinger (german). Witness David Ramsey, William Edward, & Georg Ieker (or Deker) (german). Rec. Apr. 1791. Book 16 p. 63

579. Oct. 6, 1789 George Easlinger (Lincoln Co) to Henry Long Crayer (same); for 40£ sold 100 ac on waters of Lyles Cr; border: Peter Deal and Barnerd Sigman; part of grant Oct. 9, 1782 ato Jacob Miars. Signed Grg Eslinger (german). Witness David Ramsey, William Edwards, & Georg Deller (german). Rec. Apr. 1791. Book 16 p. 64

580. Jul. 28, 1789 Jemima Jones (Lincoln Co) to Henry Partin (same); for 40£ NC money sold 140 ac on W side of Cataba R; border: Reubin Simpson; part of 640 ac granted in 1783 to Reuben Simpson. Signed Jemima Jones' mark. Witness Harbert Harwell & Frs Cunningham. Rec. Apr. 1791. Book 16 p. 65

581. Jun. 20, 1788 Robert Campbell, planter (Morgan Dist, NC) to to Joseph Neel, planter (same); for 180£ NC money sold 300 ac on branch of Little Cataba Cr; border: an old waggon road, Robert Martin, & Brown; granted "date the latest" Mar. 2, 1775 to Thomas Campbell; part of two grants (sic) to Thomas Campbell who sold to Samuel Lofton who sold to Francis Adams who sold to Robert Campbell. Signed Robrt Campbell. Witness John Wallace, Jonn Gullick, & Margaret Gullick. Rec. Apr. 1791. Book 16 p. 66

582. Dec. 8, 1789 John Huggins (Lincoln Co) to Samuel Knight (same); for 200£ NC money sold 93 ac on Little Cataba Cr; border: his own line, Baird, & John Huggins jr; granted May 18, 1789 to John Huggins. Signed John Huggins. Witness Js Holland & Moses Ferguson. Rec. Apr. 1791. Book 16 p. 67

583. Sept. 16, 1789 Richard Vandike (Lincoln Co) to John Drake (same); for 40£ sold 100 ac on head of Wyatts Branches of S fork of Cataba R; border: McKnitt and Wyatt; sold Jun. 2, 1788 by Joseph Henry, sheriff, to Richard Vandike. Signed Richard Vandike. Witness Wm Vernor & John McCarver. Rec. Apr. 1791. Book 16 p. 69

584. Nov. 24, 1790 Jacob Rhodes (Robison Co, NC) to John Sloan (Lincoln Co); for 40£ sold [ac omitted] in "said" Bladen Co on NW side of Ten Mile Swamp and both sides of Ready Br; border: near mouth of a branch a litle above Reuben Royars, & John Cain; granted May 18, 1789 to Jacob Rhodes. Signed Jo Rhodes. Witness Jos McDowell & John Moore. Rec. Apr. 1791. Book 16 p. 70

585. Aug. 2, 1790 Bassel Dorsey (Lincoln Co) to William Sloan (same); for 40s sold 37.75 ac; border: Dorsey's corner of his 500 ac tract; part of grant Oct. 28, 1782 to Willm Crage. Signed Bassell Dorsey. Witness Matthew Wilson & Isaac Robinson. Rec. Apr. 1791. Book 16 p. 71

586. Oct. 29, 1790 Henry Miller & wife Sarah (Lincoln Co) to Jacob Gortner (same); for 90£ sold 177 ac on E side of S fork of Cataba R; border: James Wilson

on a hill and Matthew Wilson; granted May 4, 1769 to Jacob Wilthong who willed it to his daughter Sarah now wife of Henry Miller.   Signed Henrih Miller (german) & Sarah Miller (in English). Witness Danl McKisick & Jesse Robinson. Rec. Apr. 1791. Book 16 p. 72

587. Feb. 16, 1789 James Walker & wife Cathrine (Lincoln Co) to William Canady (same); for 50£ sold 275 ac on both sides of Balls Cr on W side of Cataba R; part of grant from Gov. Richard Caswell to James Walker.   Signed James & Catharine Walker. Witness Balsor Hale (or Hahl) (german) & John Thomas. Rec. Apr. 1791. Book 16 p. 72

588. Jan. 11, 1790 Joseph Porter (Mecklenburg Co) to Edward Melon (Lincoln Co); for 50£ NC money sold 200 ac on waters of Little Cattaba R; border: Robert Martin, James Craig, Wallace, Edward Melon, & Thomas Campbell; granted Dec. 6, 1771 to Robert Brown who sold Dec. 13, 1780 to William Balch who sold Aug. 12, 1782 to James Adams.   Signed Joseph Porter. Witness John Mellon & William Gilmor. Rec. Apr. 1791. Book 16 p. 73

589. Jan. 2, 1791 David Hecker (Lincoln Co) to John Edwards (same); for 50£ sold 78 ac on waters of Cataba R; border: John Beale's old suvey and a wagon road from Geo Hecker to Tool's ford.   Signed David Hecker's mark. Witness Peter Forney & John Beale. Rec. Apr. 1791. Book 16 p. 75

590. Jan. 29, 1790 John Bridges (Lincoln Co) to Palser Kail (same); for 229£ NC money sold 229 ac on waters of Balls Cr; border: W line of original grant and Elisha Bridges SW & SE corners; part of grant from Earl Granville to John Bridges. Signed John Bridges' mark. Witness Ephraim Perkins, Joseph Perkins, & Daniel Lorance. Rec. Apr. 1791. Book 16 p. 76

591. Jul. 28, 1790 Basil Dorsey (Lincoln Co) to Benjamin Dorsey (same); for 25£ NC money sold 175 ac; border: William Sloan; part of grant Oct. 28, 1782 to William Crage.   Signed Bassell Dorsey. Witness Matthew Willson & William Harlson (or Harbson). Rec. Apr. 1791. Book 16 p. 76

592. Dec. 6, 1790 Thos Wheeler, planter (Lincoln Co) to William Guin, planter (same); for 70£ sold 125 ac on W side of Cataba R; border: Jno Waggoner; granted Oct. 11, 1783 to Thos Wheeler.   Signed Thos Wheeler. Witness George Gwin & Theophilus Williford. Rec. Apr. 1791. Book 16 p. 78

593. Feb. 9, 1791 Jacob Bolick (Lincoln Co) to Jacob Starr (same); for 120£ sold 320 ac on both sides of Lyles Cr; border: Malcar Hafner, Genl. Rutherford's new corner, Barnet Sigman, & Palsor Sigman; granted Nov. 9, 1784 by Gov. Alexander Martin to Jacob Bolick.   Signed Jacob Boolih (german). Witness Joseph Steel & John Anthony. Rec. Apr. 1791. Book 16 p. 79

594. Dec. 12, 1790 William Sloan (Lincoln Co) to Benjamin Doresey (same); for 40s sold 5.5 ac & 33 poles on "a" branch.   Signed William Sloan. Witness Isaac Robinson & Matthew Wilson. Rec. Apr. 1791. Book 16 p. 80

595. Jul. 13, 1790 John Hawkins (Aberville Co, SC) to James Hawkins (Lincoln Co); for 5s sold 125 ac on W side of Cataba R; border: Matthew Hawkins and John Styles; part of grant from "the" governor to John Hawkins.   Signed John Hawkins' mark. Witness John Cunningham & Matthew Hawkins. Rec. Apr. 1791. Book 16 p. 81

596. Jan. 29, 1790 John Briges (Lincoln Co) to Elisha Briges (same); for 200£ NC money sold 200 ac on both sides of Balls Cr; border: W side of original survey at Palzer Kail's NW corner & his NE corner and John Briges; part of grant by Earl Granville to John Briges.   Signed John Briges' mark. Witness Ephraim Perkins, John Perkins, & Joseph Perkins. Rec. Apr. 1791. Book 16 p. 82

597. Aug. 25, 1790 John Kennedy, planter (Lincoln Co) to William Self, planter (same); for 70£ NC money sold 110 ac on both sides of Buffaloe Cr of Broad R; border: Christopher Carpenter on W side of the creek, Samuel Kehley on N side of the creek, a conditional line, & William Reynolds.   Signed John Kennedy. Witness Adam Cronester & Mathias Cronester. Rec. Apr. 1791. Book 16 p. 84

598. Apr. 8, 1789 Thomas Polk esq (Mecklenburg Co) to Tetrick Kootch, planter (Lincoln Co); for 50£ NC money sold 300 ac on both sides of Camp Cr below Nicholas Welsh; formerly property of James Forster and sold Jul. 9, 1788 by Joseph Henry, sheriff to Thomas Polk due to suit of Thomas Polk.   Signed Thos Polk. Witness Jo Dickson & Phillip Null. Rec. Apr. 1791. Book 16 p. 85

599. Apr. 16, 1790 John Kennedy (or Canady), planter (Lincoln Co) to Samuel Kehely, planter (same); for 55£ NC money sold 90 ac on E side of Buffaloe Cr of Broad R; border: Christopher Carpenter on E side of creek, Samuel Carpenter's "third" corner, a branch, William Reynolds, a ridge, & a conditional line; part of grant to Samuel Carpenter.   Signed Jno Kennedy. Signed Felix Landess & Adam Cronester. Rec. Apr. 1791. Book 16 p. 86

600. Feb. 9, 1791 Philip Rudisail, shoemaker (Lincoln Co) to Jacob & Michael Costner, planters (same); for 100£ NC money sold (1) 150 ac on N side of S fork of Cataba R; border: Philip Rudisail; includes "the" flat Rock; granted Nov. 16, 1764 to Philip Rudisail; and (2) 80 ac on N side of S fork of Cataba R; border: Friday, his own land, Fulenwider, & Dellinger; granted Nov. 1, 1784 to Philip Rudisail.   Signed Philip & Elizabeth Rudisail's marks. Witness Jno Fulenwider & William Edwards. Rec. Apr. 1791. Book 16 p. 87

601. Jan. 13, 1791 John Leeper (Lincoln Co) & Matthew Leeper (Green Co of "the ceded territory") to John Neagle (York Co, SC); for 200£ NC money sold 300 ac; border: Roaring Run, S fork of Cataba R, & mouth of Big Run Br.

Signed Jno & Matthew Leeper. Witness Wm Maclean & Thomas Maclean. Rec. Apr. 1791. Book 16 p. 88

602. Oct. 1, 1788 Wm Hamilton (Lincoln Co) to John Drake (same); for 25£ NC money sold 200 ac on a branch of Crowders Cr; border: Moses Henry, Foster, & John Henry; being all of a grant [no date or grantee mentioned].   Signed William Hamilton. Witness Mark Massey & John Massey. Rec. Apr. 1791. Book 16 p. 89

603. Jan. 10, 1791 William Coonce (Lincoln Co) to George Fry (same); for 70£ sold 200 ac on S side of Cane Br of Clarks Cr; part of 400 ac granted Oct. 11, 1783 by Gov. Alexander Martin to William Coonce.   Signed William Coonce's mark. Witness Joseph Steel & William Rathers. Rec. Apr. 1791. Book 16 p. 90

604. Mar. 14, 1791 Samuel Donnaway (Spartinburgh Co, SC) to John Heyel (Lincoln Co); for 100£ NC money sold 400 ac on Little Long Cr on N side; border: mouth of Rock Spring Br, James Wyatt, Peter Carpenter, Frederick Glance's entry, & Dodorow; granted Sept. 24, 1785 to Samuel Donnaway.   Signed Samuel Dunaway. Witness Peter Heyel & Andrew Heyel. Rec. Apr. 1791. Book 16 p. 91

605. Nov. 15, 1790 Benjamin Bradshaw (Lincoln Co) to Jeremiah Garner (same); for 80£ sold 100 ac; border: Coborns Cr, a new line, & Charles Williams.   Signed Benjamin Bradshaw's mark. Witness Robt Abernathy & Hugh Miller. Rec. Apr. 1791. Book 16 p. 92

606. Feb. 28, 1791 Charles Rutledge (Lincoln Co) to James Rutledge (same); for 35£ sold 35 ac on W side of Dutchmans Cr; border: John Wills and Charles Rutledge; part of tract where Charles Rutldge lives and granted to George Rutledge desc who willed it to Charles Rutledge.   Signed Charles Rutledge. Witness Joseph Rankin & Moses Williams. Rec. Apr. 1791. Book 16 p. 93

607. Nov. 11, 1789 Joseph Neel (Lincoln Co) to Jonas Clark (Mecklenburg Co); for 200£ NC money sold 300 ac on N fork of Mill Cr; border: Thomas Campbell; part of grant Sept. 26, 1766 to Richd Gullick who sold Aug. 7, 1770 to Joseph Neel and "contents" of two other grants to Joseph Neel the latest is dated Sept. 24, 1785.   Signed Joseph Neel. Witness John Clark, Robert Berry, & William McClure. Rec. Apr. 1791. Book 16 p. 95

608. Mar. 24, 1790 Henry James (Lincoln Co) to Catharine Cooper (York Co, SC); for 93£ sold (1) ac on Potts Br of Buffaloe Cr; border: Solomon Beeson and his own land; granted (#399) Nov. 10, 1784 to James Huggins; and (2) 100 ac on waters of Potts Cr; border: Cornwall and his own land; granted Oct. 9, 1783 to James Huggins who sold to Henry James.   Signed Henry James. Witness James Smith & Humphrey Parker. Rec. Apr. 1791. Book 16 p. 96

609. Jan. 16, 1783 John Horse (Burke Co) to John Hostlebarrier & Rodolph Conrod (both of Lincoln Co); a bond of 400£ in gold & silver; John Hostlebarrier and Rodolph Conrod are securities on a bond from John Horse to administrators of estate of Simon Horse desc for 7,527£ NC money and interest from Jan. 17, 1780 for John Horse's share as a child of Simon Horse; if John Hostlebarrier & Rodolph Conrod don't loose anything as securities, then this bond is void. Signed Johannes Horz (german). Witness Joseph Steel & Peter Iker. Rec. Apr. 1791. Book 16 p. 98

610. Oct. 28, 1791 John Sloan (Lincoln Co) to Adam Carruth (same); for 140£ NC money sold a Negro man Cain 25 years old.   Signed John Sloan. Witness [none]. Rec. Apr. 1791. Book 16 p. 99

611. Feb. 2, 1791 Cary (or Kerry) Hudgens (Lincoln Co) to William Cornelius (same) for 16£ NC money sold a feather bed & furniture, a cow & calf, a horse briddle & saddle, a pot, a Dutch oven, a flax wheel & cards, six Delf plates, a walnut plank table, an axe, & a small plow.   Signed Cary Hudgons. Witness Samuel Long & Abner Cornelius. Rec. Apr. 1791. Book 16 p. 100

612. Feb. 11, 1791 John Cougran (Lincoln Co); an oath that "by power of sating and delasing of the devil" he falsely wronged Samuel McMinn (Lincoln Co) by falsely claiming he bugered his own mare for which John Cougran had neither grounds nor "sircomstances".   Signed John Cohran (sic). Witness James Nixon, John Nixon, & William Blalk. Rec. Apr. 1791. Book 16 p. 100

July Court [1791]
613. Dec. 16, 1790 Isaac Lollar & wife Martha (Lincoln Co) to Martin Miller (Rowan Co); for 200£ NC money sold 200 ac on both sides of S fork of Mountain Cr; border: William Gant; granted Jan. 30, 1773 to Isaac Lollar.   Signed Isaac Lollar & Martha's mark. Witness Andrew Stockinger & Conrod Tippon. Rec. Jul. 1791. Book 16 p. 100

614. Jun. 18, 1791 Thos Beatty (Rowan Co) & Robert Armstrong (Lincoln Co), executors of Frans Beatty desc (Mecklenburg Co) to Benjn Nerren (Lincoln Co); for 100£ sold 400 ac on head waters of Indian Cr; includes a spring and two large meadows; granted (#260) Nov. 16, 1764 to Francis Beatty; executors appointed in Francis Beatty's will dated Jun. 23, 1773 recorded in Mecklenburg Co.   Signed Thos Beatey & Robert Armstrong. Witness Francis Armstrong & Wallace Beatey. Rec. Jul. 1791. Book 16 p. 102

615. Jul. 7, 1791 Martin & Mary Friday (Lincoln Co) to Philip Canseller (same); for 10£ NC money sold 100 ac; border: said Canseller's old tract on E side of S fork of Cataba R and a division line; part of grant Aug. 7, 1787 to Nicholas Friday who directed in his will for his executors to "make a deed" to said Canseller for said land and that is what is done now.   Signed Martin Feritay (german) & Mary's mark. Witness W. Alexander & Wm Tankesley. Rec. Jul. 1791. Book 16 p. 89

616. Jun. 30, 1790 Rodolph Conrod & John Husselbarer, executors of William Deal desc, (Lincoln Co) to Peter Philips (same); for 150£ NC money sold 400 ac on waters of Clarks Cr; border: Conrod Mingo on W side of School House Br, Deals Br, Barrings Br, Peter Grunt, Graff, Jacob Deal, N side of Sherill's Road, & crosses a road; granted Oct. 28, 1782 by Gov. Alexr Martin to George Deal desc. Signed Rodolph Conrod & John Hasselbarer's mark. Witness Joseph Steel & Is Holland "to Rodolph signing" and David Robinson. Rec. Jul. 1791. Book 16 p. 105

617. Dec. 16, 1790 Isaac Lollar & wife Martha (Lincoln Co) to Martin Miller (Rowan Co); for 200£ NC money sold 600 ac on both sides of S fork of Mountain Cr; border: Wm Gant, road from Ramsour's mill to Sherril's ford on Cataba R, Saml Hollingsworth, Isaac Lollar, Thos Welsh, & James Martin; granted Oct. 28, 1782 to Isaac Lollar. Signed Isaac Lollar & Martha's mark. Witness Andrew Stockinger & Conrod Tippon. Rec. Jul. 1791. Book 16 p. 106

618. Nov. 12, 1790 John Shell (Burke Co) to Henry Shell (Lincoln Co); for 200£ sold 250 ac in Lincoln formerly Burke Co on both sides of Hopps Cr a branch of S fork of Cataba R; granted Oct. 11, 1783 by Gov. Alexander Martin & John Shell. Signed John Shell. Witness Joseph Steel & John Barnfield. Rec. Jul. 1791. Book 16 p. 108

619. Feb. 8, 1791 William Tate (Orange Co) to Robert Abernathy, planter (Lincoln Co); for 220£ NC money sold 400 ac on S side of Cataba R; border: Reeds Cr. Signed Wm Tate. Witness Wm Beatty, Daniel Nance, Clemont Nance, & Isaac Bonds. Rec. Jul. 1791. Book 16 p. 109

620. May 28, 1791 James Withrow & wife Nancy (Lincoln Co) to John Dietz (same); for 212£ NC money sold 250 ac on W side of S fork of Cataba R; border: Anthony, James Wilson, Leganeer, Heselberger, & Robinson; granted Oct. 31, 1758 to James Wilson who sold Sept. 31, 1765 to James Witherow. Signed James & Nancy Withrow's marks. Witness Robt Blackburn & Ferderih Scimÿ. Rec. Jul. 1791. Book 16 p. 110

621. Apr. 2, 1791 Joseph Beason (Lincoln Co), son & heir of Solomon Beason desc, to Peter Harmon (same); for 100£ sold 150 ac on both sides of Solomons Cr; border: Solomon Beason's "beginning" corner and "the" old line; includes where said Harmon lives; granted to Solomon Beason. Signed Joseph Beason. Witness Joseph Gladen & John Carruth. Rec. Jul. 1791. Book 16 p. 113

622. Jul. 8, 1786 William Jones (Lincoln Co) to John Tucker (same); for 25£ NC money sold 200 ac on both sides of Buffaloe Cr; border: top of a hill on W side of the creek. Signed William Jones. Witness Samuel Tucker & John Carruth. Rec. Jul. 1791. Book 16 p. 114

623. Jul. 8, 1786 William Jones (Lincoln Co) to John Tucker (same); for 100£ NC money sold 200 ac on both sides of Buffaloe Cr; border: new lines. Signed William Jones. Witness Samuel Tucker & John Carruth. Rec. Jul. 1791. Book 16 p. 115

624. Sept. 10, 1789 John Houfman (Lincoln Co) to Jacob Roads (same); for 10£ sold 21 ac on waters of Long Cr; border: Houfman; part of grant Sept. 27, 1776 to John Houfman; "the grant" dated Jun. 15, 1774 to Daniel McCarty (sic). Signed John Hufman. Witness P. Holland & Stephen Sentor. Rec. Jul. 1791. Book 16 p. 117

625. Jul. 13, 1786 William Jones (Lincoln Co) to John Tucker (same); for 25£ NC money sold 100 ac on E side of Buffaloe Cr; border: a Stoney hill near a branch. Signed William Jones. Witness Samuel Tucker & John Carruth. Rec. Jul. 1791. Book 16 p. 118

626. Jul. 23, 1790 Phineas Creaton (Lincoln Co) to William Dunlop (York Co, SC); for 235£ NC money sold 300 ac on both sides of Buffaloe Cr; granted Dec. 23, 1768 to Wm Sims who sold to Peregreen Magness who sold Jan. 31, 1771 to John Carson by whose will Phineas Creaton became owner of it. Signed Phinehas Creaton & Mary's mark. Witness Wm Love, John Endsley, & Phillip Null. Rec. Jul. 1791. Book 16 p. 120

627. Sept. 24, 1789 Charles Rutledge (Lincoln Co) to Valentine Devault (same); for 6£ 6s sold 6 ac on NE side of Dutchmans Cr; border: said Devalt and said Charles Rutledge. Signed Charles Rutledge. Witness Johanes Will (german) & James Rutledge. Rec. Jul. 1791. Book 16 p. 121

628. Sept. 10, 1789 Jacob Roads (Lincoln Co) to John Houfman (same); for 10£ NC money sold 9 ac on both sides of Long Cr; border: Houfman; includes lower part of his mill dam; part of grant Sept. 20, 1766 to Jacob Roads. Signed Jechob Rotes (german). Witness Stephen Senter & Is Holland. Rec. Jul. 1791. Book 16 p. 122

629. Aug. 2, 1790 Jeremiah Smith (Greenville Co, SC) to William Price (Lincoln Co); for 50£ sold 93 ac on a small branch of Crowders Cr; border: Jno Henry, Alexr Denny, James Martin's entry, & Foster. Signed Jeremiah Smith. Witness Jno Barber, Thos White, & Isabel Barber. Rec. Jul. 1791. Book 16 p. 124

630. Apr. 9, 1791 Zachariah Downs (Lincoln Co) to Martin Speegle (same); for 110£ NC money sold 200 ac in Lincoln formerly Burke Co on both sides of Jacobs R a branch of S fork of Cataba R; border: John Miller's survey and a ridge on S side of river; granted Jul. 10, 1788 to Zachariah Downs. Signed Zachariah Downs. Witness Robt Blackburn & Daniel Hudson. Rec. Jul. 1791. Book 16 p. 125

631. Jul. 17, 1786 Edward Cornwell & wife Agnes (Lincoln Co) to Amos Speece (same); for 20£ sold 200 ac between waters of Crowders Cr & Kings Cr; border: Patterson; includes crossing of "roads" from Beeson's to Harmon's; granted Oct. 9, 1783 to Edward Cornwell. Signed Edward Cornwell. Witness Peter Haramon, John Harmon, & Arthur Patterson. Rec. Jul. 1791. Book 16 p. 127

632. (blank) Andrew Parker & wife Mary (Lincoln Co) to Amos Speece (same); for 15£ NC money sold 100 ac W of Kings Cr; border: George Patterson's entry "he" bought of Kimball on N side "higher up than his other entry" and said Kimball's corner; granted Oct. 9, 1783 to George Patterson who sold Jul. 13, 1785 to Andrew Parker. Signed Andrew Parker [Mary doesn't sign]. Witness Peter Harmon, Arthur Patterson, & John Harmon. Rec. Jul. 1791. Book 16 p. 128

633. Dec. 29, 1790 James Arrowood (Lincoln Co) to Thomas Parker (same); for 70£ NC money sold 125 ac on S side of Cataba R on waters of Killions Cr; border: Philip Earhart; granted Apr. 18, 1777 to Matthias Patterson and sold to Michael Engel who sold to Lemuel Saunders who sold to James Freeman who sold to Thomas Brion who sold to James Arrowood. Signed James Arrowood. Witness John Duncan & Absolom Duncan. Rec. Jul. 1791. Book 16 p. 129

634. Jan. 6, 1791 Elias Mayar sr (Lincoln Co) to John Duncan (same); for 100£ sold [ac omitted] on Long Br of Grays Cr; border: John Limberger on NE side. Signed Elias Mayar's mark. Witness Thomas Parker & Absalom Duncan. Rec. Jul. 1791. Book 16 p. 130

635. Jun. 2, 1789 John Sigman (Lincoln Co) to Andrew Heddick (same); for 10£ sold 100 ac on waters of Clearks (sic) Cr; border: near a waggon road from Lincoln Town to Island ford on Cataba R, Henry Cline, Rhinhart, & Jacob Ramsour; part of grant Aug. 7, 1787 to John Sigman. Signed Johanns Sigmann (german). Witness David Ramsey & Henrich Klin (german). Rec. Jul. 1791. Book 16 p. 131

636. Oct. 15, 1789 John Holland (Rutherford Co) to Robert Weer (Lincoln Co); for 40£ NC money sold 200 ac on both sides of Suck fork of Buffaloe Cr; border: William Booth; includes Samuel Julkins improvement; granted Nov. 1, 1784 to John Holland. Signed John Holland. Witness Saml McFadin & Jo Dickson. Rec. Jul. 1791. Book 16 p. 132

637. Jun. 27, 1791 John Baldridge (Lincoln Co) to William R. Sadler (same); for 50£ NC money sold 0.9 ac on E side of Killions Cr. Signed John Boldrige. Witness Peter Forney & Henry Sadler. Rec. Jul. 1791. Book 16 p. 134

638. Jul. 2, 1791 John Boldridge (Lincoln Co) to Henry Sadler (same); for 230£ NC money sold 112 ac; border: on N side of Killions Cr; includes a mill. Signed John Boldrige. Witness Peter Forney & William R Sadler. Rec. Jul. 1791. Book 16 p. 134

639. Jun. 8, 1790 Jeremiah Pickett (Caroline Co, Va) & Neal Little (Robinson Co, NC) to John Will (Lincoln Co); for 100£ NC money sold a Negro wench Sarah about 18 years old.   Signed Jeremiah Pickett & Neil Little. Witness Robt Abernathy, Joseph Rankin, & James Rutledge. Rec. Jul. 1791. Book 16 p. 135

640. May 13, 1791 in SC Alexander Nelson, merchant (Lincoln Co) to Joshua Hargreaves, merchant (Charleston, SC); for 5s sterling sold 100 ac on W side of Cataba R; border: Bonner; part of grant by "province of NC" to Samuel Coborn. Signed A Nelson. Witness Saml Mathis & John Nelson. Wit. oath May 16, 1791 by Samuel Mathias. Rec. Jul. 1791. Book 16 p. 136

640A. May 14, 1791 in SC Alexander Nelson, merchant (Lincoln Co) to Joshua Hargreaves, merchant (Charleston, SC); [this is the release for above deed] for 154£ 8s 11p sterling, which is amount of debt mentioned below, sold 100 ac where A Nelson lives; border: Canaday and Bonner; deed void if A Nelson pays debt of 154£ 8s 11p & interest; a bond given of 308£ 17s 10p.   Signed A Nelson. Witness Saml Mathis & John Nelson. Wit. oath May 16, 1791 by Samuel Mathis. Rec. Jul. 1791. Book 16 p. 137

641. May 13, 1791 in SC John Nelson (Lincoln Co) to Joshua Hargreaves (Charleston, SC); for 5s sterling sold 200 ac where John Nelson lives on S side of Cataba R; border: to E by said river, to NW by Alexander Baldridge, to S & W by said John Nelson; part of grant to George Cathy.   Signed Jn Nelson. Witness Saml Mathis & Alexr Nelson. Wit. oath May 16, 1791 by Samuel Mathis. Rec. Jul. 1791. Book 16 p. 140

641A. May 14, 1791 John Nelson (Lincoln Co) to Joshua Hargreaves (Charleston, SC); [release for above deed] John Nelson has a bond with John Hargreaves for 308£ 17s 10p sterling to pay 154£ 8s 11p sterling and interest; for that amount, John Nelson mortgages to Joshua Hargreaves his land [200 ac]; deed void if J Nelson pays the debt.   Signed John Nelson. Witness Samuel Mathis & Alexr Nelson. Wit. oath Mary 16, 1791 by Samuel Mathis. Rec. Jul. 1791. Book 16 p. 142

October Court 1791
642. Aug. 20, 1791 Elijah Lyon (Rowan Co) to James Johnston, Richard Johnston, John Johnston, & Matthew Johnston (Lincoln Co); for 100£ sold 200 ac on both sides of Henry Weidner's fork of S fork of Cataba R; border: above "the" Joiner's botom; granted Apr. 28, 1768 by Gov. Wm Tryon to Samuel Wilson who sold Sept. 1, 1772 to Jacob Anthony who sold in 1791 to Elijah Lyon.   Signed Elijah Lyon. Witness John Wilson & John Tate. Wit. oath Oct. 1791 by John Wilson. Book 16 p. 147

643. Oct. 3, 1791 John Wilfong to Henry Miller, tanner; for 6£ 15s NC money sold 45 ac on S side of Jacobs R; includes an old improvement; border: Henry Miller's line formerly Welsh's; granted (#393) May 18, 1789 to John Wilfong.

Signed John Wilfong. Witness George Whitley & Thomas Martintell. Wit. oath Oct. 1791 by John Wilfong esq. Book 16 p. 148

644. Oct. 5, 1791 Joseph Bulling (Rutherford Co) to George Seely (Burke Co); for "good causes & valuable consideration" sold 100 ac on waters of Indian Cr at mouth of Such Br.   Signed Joseph & Michel Bullin. Witness Robt Orr & John Crage. Wit. oath Oct. 1791 by Robert Orr. Book 16 p. 149

645. Aug. 9, 1777 William Fairis (Tryon Co) to Thomas Dickson (same); for 300£ NC money sold 240 ac in Tryon Co on W side of Kings Cr above McDowall or Aidenton's land; part of 600 ac grant Apr. 19, 1763 to Francis Beatty.   Signed William Faris. Witness Aaron Ryley & William Henry. Wit. oath Oct. 1791 William Henry. Book 16 p. 150

646. Apr. 14, 1790 Philip Hain, carpenter (Lincoln Co) to Francis Smith (same); for 30£ NC money sold 178 ac; border: Dover.   Signed Pillib Hen (or Philip Hain) (german). Witness Francis McNemar & Lydia McNemar. Wit. oath Oct. 1791 to Francis McNemar. Book 16 p. 152

647. Jan. 28, 1791 Jacob Sides (Lincoln Co) to Peter Edleman (same); for 114£ sold [ac omitted] on waters of Leepers Cr; border: John Edleman and Conrod Wills.   Signed Jacob Seits. Witness Gerg Abrm(?) Meÿer (german) & Henrich Heyss(?) (german). Rec. Oct. 1791. Book 16 p. 153

648. Apr. 10, 1790 Philip Hain, house carpenter (Lincoln Co) to Edward Smith (same); for 16£ NC money sold 100 ac on waters of Solomons Cr of Buffaloe Cr; border: Hain and Dover.   Signed Phillip Hein (or Philip Hain) (german). Witness Francis McNemar & Adw McMani (or MMerni) (german). Wit. oath Oct. 1791 by Francis McNemar. Book 16 p. 154

649. Aug. 6, 1789 John Dinwody (or Dunwiddy) & wife Frances (Lincoln Co) to Peter Carson, blacksmith (same); for 120£ sold 143 ac on W side of N fork of Crowders Cr; border: Alexander Gilliand and side of a hill; half of 286 ac grant Nov. 9, 1764 to Jacob Cobron on N fork of Crowders Cr.   Signed John & Frances Dinwodey. Witness Jas Falls & Jno Carson. Rec. Oct. 1791. Book 16 p. 155

650. Jul. 16, 1790 John Bell (Lincoln Co) to George Wilson (same); for 30£ NC money sold 100 ac on both sides of Long Br of Crowders Cr; granted Mar. 2, 1775 to John Bell.   Signed John Bell. Witness James Denny & James Falls. Wit. oath Oct. 1791 to James Falls. Book 16 p. 156

651. Sept. 22, 1790 Richard West (Lincoln Co) to Rodolph Conrod (same); for 100£ sold 250 ac on waters of Clarks Cr; granted (#723) Oct. 11, 1783 to Richard West.   Signed Richard West. Witness William Heinan & Thomas Puntch. Wit. oath Oct. 1791 by Thomas Puntch. Book 16 p. 157

652. Aug. 4, 1786 Albert Corpening, farmer & wife Barbary (Burke Co) to Margaret Baker, executrix, and Elias Baker & Beales Baker, executors of Charles Baker desc (Lincoln Co), planters; for 150£ NC money, paid by Charles Baker, sold 300 ac in Lincoln formerly Burke Co on E branch of Clarks Cr known as Anthony's mill Cr; border: Conrod Mingon, Jacob Deal, Paul Anthony, "others", Bolick, & Falls corner; granted Oct. 29, 1782 to Albert Corpening. Signed Albert Carpening & Barbary's mark. Witness John Sigman & Conrod Mingon. Wit. oath Oct. 1791 by John Sigman. Book 16 p. 158

653. Dec. 16, 1789 Charles Williams (Lincoln Co) to Charles Abernathy (same); for 5s sold 150 ac on both sides of George Rominger's Br; border: Wisenhunt and a new line. Signed Charles Williams. Witness Thomas McGee & Frederick Williams. Wit. oath Oct. 1791 by Frederick Williams. Book 16 p. 160

654. Jul. 10, 1778 Archibald Little, planter, & wife Sarah (Tryon Co) to Reuben Petty, planter (late of Rowan & now of Burke Co); for 50£ sold 300 ac in Tryon Co & Burke Co "occasioned" by line that divides the two counties on S side of Cataba R; border: John Beatty and crosses Beaverdam Cr; granted Apr. 25, 1767 to Archibald Little. Signed Archibald Little & Sarah's mark. Witness James Johnston & Thos Wheeler. Wit. oath Oct. 1791 by Thos Wheeler. Book 16 p. 161

655. Mar. 4, 1790 Catharine Smith (Lincoln Co) to William Bennet (same); for 20£ sold 150 ac on waters of big Long Cr; border: John Pinner and her own land; granted (#384) Oct. 13, 1783 to Catharine Smith. Signed Catharine Smith. Witness James Hillhouse & John Pack. Wit. oath Oct. 1791 by John Pack. Book 16 p. 162

656. Jan. 22, 1791 Daniel Smith (Lincoln Co) to Philip Killian (same); for 200£ NC money sold 200 ac on S side of Henrys fork of S fork of Cataba R; border: Johnston; part of 500 ac granted (#37) Dec. 10, 1778 to John Butt and part of 90 ac granted (#619) Oct. 11, 1783 to John Shell. Signed Daniel Smith. Witness Daniel Chester & Peter Frey (german). Wit. oath Oct. 1791 by Daniel Chester. Book 16 p. 163

657. Sept. 10, 1791 Robert Orr (Lincoln Co) to George Seelly (Burke Co); for "good causes & valuable consideration" sold 100 ac on S side of Jacobs R of S fork of Cataba R above Alex Andrews on both sides of Camp Cr; includes fork of said creek and his improvements; "surveyed" Mar. 28, 1780 for Robert Orr. Signed Robert & Ann Orr. Witness Deornel Wortmen & Thomas Higdon. Wit. oath Oct. 1791 by Robert Orr. Book 16 p. 165

658. Aug. 5, 1791 John Clipard (Lincoln Co) to Conrod Leer (same); for 50£ NC money sold 250 ac; border: widow McCormack, Michael Butts, "the" bottom, & "the" branch; granted Sept. 12, 1787 to Thomas Anderson who sold Mar. 20, 1788 to John Clippard. Signed Johannes Clippert (or John Clippard) (german).

Witness Lemuel Saunders & Sarah Saunders. Wit. oath Oct. 1791 to Lemuel Saunders. Book 16 p. 166

659. Oct. 9, 1790 Adam Carruth (Lincoln Co) to Samuel Love (Iredell Co); for 100£ sold 200 ac on both sides of Long Br of Indian Cr above Reynolds' mill; granted Dec. 16, 1769 to Adam Carruth.   Signed Adam Carruth. Witness John Carruth & James Ferguson. Wit. oath Oct. 1791 by Adam Carruth. Book 16 p. 168

660. Oct. 5, 1791 Joseph Dixon (sic), commissioner in trust for Lincolnton, (Lincoln Co) to Wallace Alexander; for 40s sold 72 square poles lot 3 in SE square of Lincolnton; border: NW corner of lot 2 in SE square; lot is 6 by 12 rods. Signed Jo Dickson. Witness Wm Maclean & R Wood. Wit. oath Oct. 1791 by Jo Dickson. Book 16 p. 169

661. Oct. 5, 1791 Joseph Dixon (sic), commissioner in trust for Lincolnton, (Lincoln Co) to Joseph Morris (same); for 40s sold 72 square rods lot 4 in NE square of Lincolnton; border: first cross street; lot is 6 by 12 rods.   Signed Jo Dickson. Witness Wm Sharpe & Ad Osborn. Wit. oath Oct. 1791 by Jo Dickson. Book 16 p. 170

662. Jul. 9, 1791 John Bradley (Lincoln Co) to Henry Neff (same); for 210£ NC money sold 300 ac; border: Daniel Warleck, "a" branch, Philip Anthony, Welshes Br, James Wilson, said Bradley's old line, & Henry Hiltebrand; granted Aug. 7, 1787 to John Bradley "but before" granted Apr. 6, 1765 to Francis Beatty and sold Oct. 5, 1774 by Thomas Beatty, Hugh Beatty, & Robert Armstrong, executors for Francis Beatty, to John Bradley.   Signed John Bradley's mark. Witness Anthony Hollman & Danl McKisick. Rec. Oct. 1791. Book 16 p. 171

663. Jul. 20, 1791 Robert Duncan (Orange Co) to Joseph Morris (Lincoln Co); for 43£ 10s sold 181 ac on S side of S fork of Cataba R; border: Horse, Abraham Havener, & Waddel; granted Dec. 8, 1787 to Peter Johnston who willed it to John Duncan and "inherited" by Robert Duncan.   Signed Robert Duncan. Witness Jno Moore & Jacob Dyer. Wit. oath Oct. 1791 by Jno Moore esq. Book 16 p. 173

664. Mar. 12, 1790 Michael Miller to Andrew Grisel (same); for 30£ sold 175 ac on both sides of Leopards Cr; border: John Keener and Michael Miller's old line; part of grant Nov. 16, 1764 to William Armstrong who sold Oct. 8, 1765 to Michael Miller.   Signed Michael Miller's mark. Witness Robt Blackburn & Wm Blackburn. Wit. oath Oct. 1791 by Michael Miller. Book 16 p. 174

665. Sept. 8, 1791 Rudolph Conrod (Lincoln Co) to John & Catharine Yoder, administrators of Conrod Yoder desc; for following 3 notes: 24£ 4s, 6£ 9s 1p, and 2£ 19s 4p sold [ac omitted] in Lincoln formerly Burke Co on waters of Clarks Cr; border: James Kenner, Jacob Weaver, Galbraith Falls, & Christopher Cline; granted in 1783 to Richard West and sold Sept. 22, 1790 to Rudolph Conrod; deed

void if notes and interest are paid on May 8, 1792. Signed Rudolph Conrd. Witness Alexr Erwin & Jo Dickson. Wit. oath Oct. 1791 by Jo Dickson. Book 16 p. 176

666. Jul. 28, 1791 Francis Cunningham (Lincoln Co) to Jonathan Long (same); for 35£ "hard money" sold 100 ac on W side of Cataba R; border: William Allen, John Haukins, & Francis Cunningham; granted Aug. 7, 1787 to Francis Cunningham. Signed Frs Cunningham. Witness Richard Fisher & Henry Partain. Wit. oat Oct. 1791 by Henry Partain. Book 16 p. 176

667. Jan. 1, 1791 John Reed & wife Martha (Lincoln Co) to James Reed (same); for 40£ sold 200 ac; border: Abernathy & John Reed. Signed John & Martha Reed. Witness Isaac Bond & A. Womack. Wit. oath Oct. 1791 by Isaac Bond. Book 16 p. 177

668. Oct. 5, 1791 Mordecai Nearns (Lincoln Co) to Michael Buff (same); for 45£ NC money sold 65 ac on both sides of Indian Cr; border: Benjamin Nearn & an old line; part of grant Dec. 22, 1768 to Daniel Hudson who sold Aug. 30, 1785 to Peter Myers who sold May 2, 1789 to Simeon Lewis who sold Oct. 9, 1790 to Mordecai Nearns. Signed Mordecai Nearns' mark. Witness Robt Blackburn & Timy Twings. Wit. oath Oct. 1791 by Mordecai Nearns. Book 16 p. 178

669. Oct. 9, 1790 Simeon Lewis (Lincoln Co) to Mordecai Nearns (same); for 40£ NC money sold 100 ac on both sides of Indian Cr about a mile above the Scout Camps; border: Peter Johnston's entry and an old survey; Simeon Lewis only warrants the part that is free of old survey that "interpases on upper part of it". Signed Simeon Lewis' mark. Witness Daniel Bentley & Pery Reynolds. Wit. oath Oct. 1791 by Daniel Bentley. Book 16 p. 180

670. Sept. 19, 1791 George Wilfong (Lincoln Co) to John Moyer (same); for 20£ NC money sold 150 ac on N side of S fork of Cataba R; border: Jesse Robinson's (formerly Henry Whitenar's) N line and Abraham Moyers; part of 200 ac granted Apr. 22, 1763 to Peter Mull who sold Jan. 13, 1772 to John Moyer who sold Jan. 26, 1789 to George Wilfong. Signed George Wilfong. Witness Coper(?) Sihell (german) & John Willfong. Wit. oath Oct. 1791 by George Wilfong. Book 16 p. 181

671. Sept.30, 1791 Powers Lamkin & wife Jean (Union Co, SC) to Ann Ramsour (Lincoln Co); for 50£ sold 200 ac; border: Andrew Wilson, an oak marked "AR", an old line, & crosses Bits Br near the forks; part of 640 ac granted Apr. 19, 1763 to William Welch and by deed of gift from William Welch to Sarah, Ann, & Jean Mills and now Jean Mills is wife of Powers Lamkin; "part and the upper end and part of 600 ac". Signed Powers Lamkin & Jean's mark. Witness William Lockhart, Sarah Welden, & Samson Lamkin. Wit. oath Oct. 1791 by Samson Lamkin. Book 16 p. 182

Lincoln County, NC Deed Book 16

January Court 1792

672. Dec. 26, 1791 Jonas & Andrew Friday, farmers (Lincoln Co) to Martin Friday, planter (same); for 200£ NC money sold 150 ac on Piney old field Br on N side of S fork of Cataba R; border: "said" Friday's field and milk house; part of two grants (1) Sept. 24, 1754 and (2) Oct. 5, 1764 to Derick Ramsour who sold Apr. 23, 1770 to Nicholas Friday who sold to Martin Friday who sold Dec. 24, 1791 to Jonas & Andrew Friday.   Signed Jonas & Andrew Friday. Witness Jno Fulenwider & Michael Quikel. Rec. Jan. 1792. Book 16 p. 183

673. Jun. 16, 1790 James Palley (Lincoln Co) to Benjamin Hamsley (same); for 30£ NC money sold 155.5 ac on Muddy fork; border: his own land, Abraham Barnett, & James Palley.   Signed James Palley. Witness Adam Niel, William Ledford, & John Neil. Rec. Jan. 1792. Book 16 p. 184

674. Nov. 23, 1791 Joseph Dixon, commissioner in trust for Lincolnton, (Lincoln Co) to Joseph Henry (same); for 40s sold 84 square poles lot 24 in SE square of Lincolnton; border: NE corner of lot 23 in SE square; lot is 6 by 14 poles.   Signed Jo Dickson. Witness John Carruth. Rec. Jan. 1792. Book 16 p. 187

675. Nov. 23, 1791 Joseph Dixon, commissioner in trust for Lincolnton, (Lincoln Co) to Joseph Henry (same); for 40s sold 72 square poles "or perches" lot 12 in SE square of Lincolnton; border: faces main street and is last lot in first row in said square and NE corner of lot 11; lot is 6 by 12. Signed Jo Dickson. Witness John Carruth. Rec. Jan. 1792. Book 16 p. 188

676. (blank) 29, 1791 John Scott (Lincoln Co) to Samuel Caldwell (same); for 60£ NC money sold 112 ac on W side of Cataba R; border: Peter Fite and Saml Caldwell; part of grant Feb. 23, 1754 to William Barnett who sold Feb. 16, 1769 to William Chronicle desc who willed it to John Scott.   Signed John Scott. Witness James McKee & Jonn Gullick. Rec. Jan. 1792. Book 16 p. 189

677. Feb. 28, 1786 Valentine Warlock & wife Catharine (Lincoln Co) to Philip Null (same); for 400£ sold 260 ac on N side of S fork of Cataba R; border: David Ramsour & Andw Heddeigh; granted Mar. 28, 1751 to Daniel Warlock.   Signed Vallentin Worlich (german) & Catharine's mark. Witness George Rush & Philip Rudisill. Rec. Jan. 1792. Book 16 p. 190

678. Dec. 26, 1789 Henry Fullenwider (Rowan Co) to George Rish (Lincoln Co); for 500£ NC money sold 260 ac on N side of S fork of Cataba R; between David Ramsour & Andrew Heddeigh; granted Mar. 28, 1751 to Daniel Warlock. Signed Henry Follenwider. Witness Jno Fullenwider & Wm Temple Coles.   Rec. Jan. 1792. Book 16 p. 192

679. Dec. 9, 1791 George Rish (Lincoln Co) to Philip Null (same); for 400£ sold 260 ac on N side of S fork of Cataba R; between David Ramsour & Andrew Heddeigh; granted Mar. 28, 1751 to Daniel Warlock.   Signed George Rish.

Witness Christian Renhart & Georg Loretz (or Lorets) (german). Rec. Jan. 1792. Book 16 p. 193

680. Dec. 28, 1791 Philip Null (Lincoln Co) to Henry Hoke (same); for 450£ sold 260 ac on N side of S fork of Cataba R; between David Ramsour & Andrew Heddeigh; granted Mar. 28, 1751 to Daniel Warlock.   Signed Phillip Null. Witness W. Alexander & Saml Givens. Rec. Jan. 1792. Book 16 p. 194

681. Nov. 27, 1788 George Goodwin (Lincoln Co) to Henry Barlo Baker (same); for 30£ NC money sold 150 ac on both sides of Keenors Cr of Cataba R; border: mouth of Single Br of said creek, head of "a" branch, & a conditional line. Signed George Goodwin. Witness John Arwood & Thomas Anderson. Rec. Jan. 1792. Book 16 p. 195

682. Aug. 20, 1791 Henry Boner, laborer (York Co, Pa) to Michael Quiggle (Lincoln Co); for 20£ NC money sold 300 ac on N side of Ramsours Mill Cr above Renhart; granted Oct. 9, 1783 to Henry Boner. Signed Henrich Bohner (german). Witness Nicholas Betton & Jacob Chansman(?) (german). Rec. Jan. 1792. Book 16 p. 197

683. Sept. 28, 1791 Lemuel Saunders (Lincoln Co) to William Bishop (same); for 25£ NC money sold 125 ac on waters of Killion Cr; border: William Bishop and Thomas Parker; granted Apr. 18, 1771 to Matthias Petterson who sold Jan. 25, [omitted] to Michael Engle who sold Apr. 26, 1773 to Lemuel Saunders.   Signed Lemuel Saunders. Witness Beel Biship & Dicy Johnson. Rec. Jan. 1792. Book 16 p. 198

684. Jan. 2, 1792 Adam & Anney Wisenhunt, executors of Philip Wisenhunt desc, (Lincoln Co) to Peter Mosteller (same); for 65£ NC money sold 124 ac on both sides of Howards Cr; border: Adam Wisenhunt, an old survey, & John McGaughey; part of 300 ac granted Apr. 29, 1768 to Deter Havener who sold to Thomas Wasdon who sold Sept. 10, 1788 to Peter Wisenhunt.   Signed Adam & Anney Wisenhunt's marks. Witness David Ramsey & Georg Keyser (german). Rec. Jan. 1792. Book 16 p. 199

685. Sept. 8, 1791 John Campell, shoemaker (Lincoln Co) to Christian Renhart, tanner (same); for 18£ NC money sold [ac omitted] lot 15 in SE square of Lincolnton; lot is 6 by 14 rods; granted to Joseph Dickson, esq commissioner for Lincolnton, who sold Jul. 3, 1786 to Danl McKisick.   Signed John Campbell. Witness Andrew Turner & John Reinhart. Rec. Jan. 1792. Book 16 p. 201

686. Sept. 15, 1791 Peter Bullinger (Washington Co of "ceded territory") to John Hofner (Iredell Co); for 230£ sold 256 ac on Howards Cr a branch of S fork of Cataba R; border: Andrew Lorats, Holdman, & Philip Bullinger; part of two tracts devised to Peter Bullinger by the will of his father Henry Bullinger on both sides

of Howards Cr. Signed Peter Bullinger. Witness James Cross & David Bullinger. Rec. Jan. 1792. Book 16 p. 202

687. Nov. 15, 1791 Leonard Webb (Ga) to John Walker (Lincoln Co); for 200£ NC money sold 200 ac on Lick Br of Coburns Cr of Cataba R; border: Jacob Baker, John McCarthy, & John Baker; includes my improvement. Signed Leonard Webb's mark. Witness Jns Mills, Wm Luckey, & John Luckey. Rec. Jan. 1792. Book 16 p. 203

688. Dec. 21, 1791 Jacob Yoder (Lincoln Co) to David Yoder (same); for 50£ NC money sold 65 ac on both sides of Jacobs R a prong of S fork of Cataba R; border: John Yoder, David Yoder's old line, & Whitener; part of three surveys: (1) granted Mar. 28, 1751 to Henry Whitener who sold part Dec. 4, 1762 to Conrod Yoder, (2) granted Oct. 11, 1783 to Conrod Yoder, & (3) granted May 18, 1789 to Conrod Yoder and Conrod Yoder died intestate and Jacob is a son & heir and land was divided agreeable to an act of General Assembly for dividing land of intestates among the sons; the division was made Jan. 5, 1791. Signed Jacob Yoder (german). Witness John Yoder & Christian Hahn (german). Rec. Jan. 1792. Book 16 p. 204

689. Dec. 21, 1791 Jacob Yoder (Lincoln Co) to John Yoder (same); for 50£ sold 65 ac on both sides of Jacobs R a prong of S fork of Cataba R; border: widow Yoder; part of three grants: (1) granted Mar. 28, 1751 to Henry Whitener who sold part Dec. 4, 1762 to Conrad Yoder, (2) granted Oct. 11, 1783 to Conrad Yoder, & (3) granted May 18, 1789 to Conrad Yoder who died without a will and Jacob is a son; Conrad's land was divided Jan. 5, 1791 agreeable to an act of General Assembly for dividing desceased's land among his sons. Signed Jacob Yoder. Witness David Yoder (german) & Cheslean Hahn (german). Rec. Jan. 1792. Book 16 p. 206

690. Oct. 10, 1791 Ben Smith (Lincoln Co) to Jonathan Greaves (same); for 100£ sold a Negro wench Sal about 19 years old. Signed Ben Smith. Witness Alexander Moore. Rec. Jan. 1792. Book 16 p. 207

691. Oct. 10, 1791 Benjamin Smith (Lincoln Co) to Jonathan Greaves (same); for 200£ sold 180 ac on Little Hoyls Cr "or" Beaverdam Cr; border: a branch; granted Aug. 30, 1753 to James Armstrong. Signed Ben Smith. Witness Alexander Moore. Rec. Jan. 1792. Book 16 p. 208

692. Oct. 10, 1791 Ben Smith (Lincoln Co) to Jonathan Greaves (same); for 150£ sold 250 ac; border: land formerly of John Moore on NE & Jacob Shutley on "opposite" side and Abernathy. Signed Ben Smith. Witness Alexander Moore. Rec. Jan. 1792. Book 16 p. 209

693. Nov. 2, 1791 John Gross (Lincoln Co) to John Colter (same); for 200£ NC money sold 157.5 ac; border: Gasper Shell, George Wilfong, & Martin Colter;

part of 424 ac granted Apr. 28, 1768 to Peter Mull and regranted Oct. 11, 1783 to Peter Mull with addition of 76 ac and part was sold Jan. 20, 1786 by Peter Mull to John Gross.   Signed John Gross' mark. Witness John Wilfong. Rec. Jan. 1792. Book 16 p. 210

694. Dec. 10, 1791 John Collins (Liberty Co, NC (sic)) to Henry Harmon (Lincoln Co); for 100£ sterling sold 150 ac in Lincoln formerly Tryon Co on both sides of Besons Cr above Abraham Clark's entry.   Signed John Collins' mark. Witness Geo(?) Foster JP, Angus McDonald, & Joseph Collins. Rec. Jan. 1792. Book 16 p. 211

695. Dec. 24, 1791 Martin Friday & Michael Quiggle (Lincoln Co) to Jonas & Andrew Friday, farmers (same); for 300£ NC money sold 300 ac on Piney old field Br on N side of S fork of Cataba R; granted in two grants to Derick Ramsour (1) Sept. 24, 1754 and (2) Oct. 5, 1764 who sold Apr. 23, 1770 to Nicholas Friday sr who sold (a) Jun. 29, 1771 and (b) Mar. 11, 1777 to Martin Friday & Michael Quiggle.   Signed Martin Friday & Michael Qüiggle (german). Witness Jno Fulenwider. Rec. Jan. 1792. Book 16 p. 212

696. Dec. 26, 1791 Jonas & Andrew Friday (Lincoln Co) to Michael Quiggle (same); for 200£ NC money sold 150 ac on N side of S fork of Cataba R and on Piney old field Br; border: Martin Friday's field and Friday's mill house; part of two granted Sept. 24, 1754 and Oct. 5, 1764 both to Derick Ramsour who sold Apr. 23, 1770 to Nicholas Friday sr who sold to Michael Quiggle (sic) who sold Dec. 24, 1791 to Jonas & Andrew Friday. Signed Jonas & Anderew Friday. Witness Jno Fulenwider & Martin Friday. Rec. Jan. 1792. Book 16 p. 214

697. Sept. 5, 1789 Robert Carruth (Rutherford Co) and John Carruth (Lincoln Co) to James Hillhouse (Lincoln Co); for 50£ NC money sold 200 ac on E branch of Long Cr; border: Moore and McCarty; granted Dec. 22, 1768 to Henry Ferguson who sold Jan. 4, 1769 to Adam Carruth and now sold by Robert & John Carruth, executors of Adam Carruth's will.   Signed Robert & John Carruth. Witness John Sloan & Robert Campbell. Rec. Jan. 1792. Book 16 p. 215

698. Oct. 2, 1790 Wendle Weeant and Yost Weeant (upper Hanover township, Montgomery Co, Pa), executors of their father Wendle Weeant desc's will (of same place), to Jacob Roseman, yoeman (Lincoln Co, late of Rowan Co); for 100£ Pa money, paid to Wendle Weeant, & for 5s Pa money, paid Wendle & Yost Weeant, sold 415 ac in Lincoln, late Rowan, "Township"; border: Conrad Booby, Elk Cr, & on W side of Cataba R; granted Apr. 28, 1756 by Earl Granville to Conrad Mull and sold May 20, 1771 by Peter Mull to Wendle Weeant "alias Weddell Wyant", father of said desc (see Rowan Co deed Book 8 p. 141). Signed Wardel Wiand (german) & Ioht (or Joht) Wiand (german). Witness Jno Richards & Devball Hunsiker (or Devolt Hunsucker) (german). Rec. Jan. 1792. Book 16 p. 216

699. Dec. 2, 1791 John McKnitt Alexander (Mecklenburg Co) to William Massey (late of Lincoln Co, now of Spartanburg Co, SC); for 40£ NC money "or security" to be paid by note of hand Feb. 23, 1774 for 40£ payable Mar. 1, 1775 (sic) sold 200 ac on S side of S fork of Cataba R & both sides of Little Shoal Br waters of Long Cr; includes improvements William Massey formerly made & lived on; granted (#278) Sept. 26, 1766 by Gov. Wm Tryon to John McK Alexander. Signed J Mc Alexander. Witness James Morn, Joseph Carson, & Rahel (or Asahel) Boggs. Rec. Jan. 1792. Book 16 p. 218

700. May 30, 1791 John Horse (Lincoln Co) to Simon & George Horse (same); for 200£ sold 618 ac on E side of Clarks Cr and on both sides of Bullinger's Mill Cr & Horse Br that leads up in Abner's land; border: Bullinger on SE side of "said" branch, a field, near a school house, Joseph Steel, Fry, Peter Iker, Jacob Lutes, & Rodolph; granted Oct. 11, 1783 by Gov. Alex Martin to John, Simon, & George Horse.   Signed Johannes Hross (german). Witness Joseph Steel & John Boyd. Rec. Jan. 1792. Book 16 p. 219

701. Dec. 14, 1791 Philip Null (Lincoln Co) to Wallace Alexander (same); for 100£ sold 72 square "rods or poles" lot 1 in NE square of Lincolnton; border: town "central & vacant" lot on NW corner of lot 1 and on Main Street; lot is 6 by 12 poles.   Signed Phillip Null. Witness Johannes Fiegman (german) & Martin Feritay (german). Rec. Jan. 1792. Book 16 p. 221

702. Dec. 14, 1791 Philip Null (Lincoln Co) to Wallace Alexander (same); for 100£ sold 72 square rods lot 2 in NE square of Lincolnton; lot is 6 by 12 rods. Signed Phillip Null. Witness Johannes Fiegman (german) & Martin Feritay (german). Rec. Jan. 1792. Book 16 p. 222

703. May 21, 1789 Christian Sabough (Lincoln Co) to Nicholas Clay (same); for 300£ NC money sold 150 ac on S side of S fork of Cataba R on Potts Cr; granted Aug. 30, 1753 to Thomas Potts who willed it to son John Potts who with wife Mary sold Jan. 16 & 17, 1769 to Nicholas Clay (sic).   Signed Christian Sabough's mark. Witness Joseph Needwenger(?) (german), Jacob Leebeh(?) (german), & Michael Buff. Rec. Jan. 1792. Book 16 page 223

704. Dec. 1, 1791 John Cox (Lincoln Co) to Paul Cox (same); for 100£ sold 600 ac on N side of S fork of Cataba R on S branch of Fishers Cr; entered by & granted to Peter Harpill who sold to Thomas Salter and "sold & given" to John Cox to issue to certain persons, described in said deed, after his death.   Signed John Cox. Witness James Sulavan & Moses Moore. Rec. Jan. 1792. Book 16 p. 225

705. Dec. 29, 1791 Henry Hoke to Christian Rinehart; a bond of 200£; Henry Hoke on same day bought a tract on S fork of Cataba R between Andrew Heddick and David Ramsour "plantion" Henry Hoke bought from Peter Null; if Henry Hoke gives Christian Rinehart right to build a dam not more that 3 feet from bottom of the river & on Henry Hoke's land & across S fork of Cataba R, then

bond is void; waters are not to cover any land more than covered when river is at its "common" height, otherwise dam is to be removed at Henry Hoke's request. Signed Henry Hoke. Witness W. Alexander. Rec. Jan. 1792. Book 16 p. 226

706. Dec. 28, 1789 Jacob & John Keenor, farmers (Lincoln Co) to Abraham Keenor, farmer (same); a bond of 500£ NC money; Jacob & John Keenor to pay Abraham Keenor 250£ NC money "on demand" and give him "lawfull maintainance" of clothing and eatables "douring" his natural life and find him a horse and saddle to ride; then bond is void.   Signed Jacob & John Keenor's marks. Witness Lemuel Saunders & Larkin Johnson. Rec. Jan. 1792. Book 16 p. 226

April Court 1792
707. Dec. 31, 1791 James Wilson, executor, & Elisabeth Johnston, executrix of Richard Johnston desc, (Lincoln Co) to William Taylor (Burke Co); for 12£ sold 200 ac on waters of Cataba R; border: William McMullins; granted Oct. 28, 1782 to Richd Johnston desc. Signed Elisabeth's mark and James Wilson. Witness Matthew Wilson & Patt Collins. Rec. Apr. 1792. Book 16 p. 227
708. May 2, 1791 Joseph Alexander (Lincoln Co) to Daniel Smith (same); for 200£ sold 300 ac on Henrys fork of S fork of Cataba R; part of three tracts: (1) 33.75 ac on N side of Henrys fork and Mill Cr; granted to John Butt who sold to Peter Mull who sold Apr. 2, 1787 to John Shell; (2) 25.5 ac on W of tract 1 and on W side of Mill Cr; granted Oct. 11, 1783 to John Shell; & 240.75 ac; border: tract 1, fork of Mill Cr, & tract 2.   Signed Joseph Alexander. Witness David Chester & Absalom Wineson(?). Rec. Apr. 1792. Book 16 p. 288

709. Mar. 11, 1791 James Henry (Lincoln Co) to John Turbyfill (same); for 200£ sold 248 ac on W side of Cataba R; border: Francis Cunningham, Reubin Simpson, Beaverdam Br, John Hawkins, & Adam Perkins; granted in 1782 to James Henry.   Signed James Henry's mark. Witness Francis Harwell & Evin Sherrill. Rec. Apr. 1792. Book 16 p. 230

710. Feb. 9, 1791 George Ruminger (Lincoln Co) to Miles Abernathy (same); for 100£ sold 150 ac on both sides of Leepers Cr; sold by Matthias Clouse who sold to Valentine Crotts who sold to George Ruminger.   Signed George Ruminger's mark. border: Peter Forney & Jos Abernathy. Rec. Apr. 1792. Book 16 p. 231

711. Apr. 3, 1792 Robert Alexander (Lincoln Co) to Neal Connelly (same); for 30£ NC money sold 50 ac on waters of Indian Cr; border: "second" corner of said tract and an old line; part of grant Jun. 12, 1786 to John Moore and sold by sheriff to Robert Alexander.   Signed Robt Alexander. Witness Jos Henry & James Johnston. Rec. Apr. 1792. Book 16 p. 232

712. Mar. 31, 1792 Conrad Gilbert (Lincoln Co) to George Dellinger (same); for 5s sold 150 ac on waters of Leepers Cr; border: Jacob Hoyl's old corner and Reel's

old line; granted Aug. 7, 1787 to Conrad Gilbert.   Signed Conrad Gilbert's mark. Witness Jos Abernathy & Jasper Cleb (or Clob). Rec. Apr. 1792. Book 16 p. 233

713. Apr. 2, 1789 George Deal, yoeman (Lincoln Co) to George Isehaur, yoeman (same); for 10£ NC money sold 132 ac on both sides of three forks of Lisles Cr; border: John Isehaur's NW corner on W side of said creek and Barnett Stayway; granted (#971) Aug. 2, 1787 to George Deal. Signed George Deal's mark. Witness Valentine Isehaur & Johannes Rein (german). Rec. Apr. 1792. Book 16 p. 235

714. Apr. 4, 1792 David Ramsey (Burke Co) to Samuel Ramsey (Lincoln Co); for 30£ NC money sold 160 ac on waters of Buffalow and Indian Creeks; border: Michael Reap and John Kirkconnel.   Signed David Ramsey. Witness David Ramsey (sic) & William McCasland. Rec. Apr. 1792. Book 16 p. 236

715. Jan. 10, 1792 Jackson Harwell, planter (Lincoln Co) to John Lanbarger (Pa); for 80£ NC money sold 150 ac on W side of Cataba R; border: Barkley and Lockman; granted Aug. 7, 1787 to Samuel Fisher.   Signed Jackson Harwell. Witness Samuel Harwell & Peter Lengbarer (sic). Rec. Apr. 1792. Book 16 p. 237

716. Jan. 17, 1792 Frederick Shool (Burke Co) to Arthor Hershen (Lincoln Co); for 100£ NC money sold 400 ac "being the part" on E of William Sigman; border: an old tract.   Signed Frederick Shull's mark. Witness Joseph Steel & Peter Phillips. Rec. Apr. 1792. Book 16 p. 239

717. Dec. 22, 1791 Bostian Cline & wife Elisabeth (Lincoln Co) to Jacob Cline (same); for 100£ NC money sold 151 ac on both sides of Clarks Cr waters of S fork of Cataba R; border: John Cline's W corner "on the old survey", Michael Kline (sic), & Philip Huyerd's (or Heyerd) formerly Robert Simonton's line; "plantation" where Bostian & Elisabeth Cline live; part of 598 ac granted May 10, 1762 by Earl Granville to Bostian Cline.   Signed Bosion Klen (or Klea) (german) & Elyssebith [no last name]. Witness Michael Cline & John Willfong. Rec. Apr. 1792. Book 16 p. 240

718. Apr. 2, 1792 Robert Campbell (Lincoln Co) to James Gingles (same); for 60£ sold 200 ac on waters of Little Cataba Cr; border: John Scott; granted (#411) Nov. 25, 1771 to Thomas Campbell desc.   Signed Robt Campbell. Witness John Baird & Wm Ryndles. Rec. Apr. 1792. Book 16 p. 241

719. Mar. 31, 1792 Benjamin Dorsey (Lincoln Co) to James Baker (same); for 100£ NC money sold 175 ac; border: William Sloan; part of granted Oct. 28, 1782 to William Craig.   Signed Benjamin Dorsey. Witness Wm Harbson jr & David Falls. Rec. Apr. 1792. Book 16 p. 242

720. Dec. 22, 1791 Bostian Cline & wife Elisabeth (Lincoln Co) to Jacob Cline (same); for 50£ NC money sold 100 ac on waters of Clarks Cr; border: John Cline's SW corner, Bostian Cline, Samuel Killian, & John Killian; granted (#226)

Mar. 14, 1780 to Bostian Cline.   Signed Bostion Klen & Elisebeth. Witness Michael Cline & John Willfong. Rec. Apr. 1792. Book 16 p. 243

721. Feb. 9, 1792 John Perkins & wife Catherine to Jacob Sherrill jr; for 50£ NC money sold 200 ac on both sides of Browns Cr on SW side of Cataba R; border: corner of land surveyed for Samuel Brown and Perkins' old line; part of 600 ac granted Oct. 11, 1783 by Gov. Alexander Martin to John Perkins.   Signed Jno & Catherine Perkins. Witness Ephraim Perkins, Elisha Perkins, & John Perkins jr. Rec. Apr. 1792. Book 16 p. 245

722. Mar. 25, 1792 Michael Summy, yoeman (Lincoln Co) to Peter Mosteller, farmer (same); for 25£ NC money sold 50 ac on N side of S fork of Cataba R; border: Michael Williams and George Rush; granted May 18, 1789 to Michael Summy.   Signed Michal Summey's mark. Witness Christian Summey, Charles Inglefinger, & David Mostiller. Rec. Apr. 1792. Book 16 p. 246

723. Apr. 5, 1792 Christian Reinhard (Lincoln Co) to Arthur deBardeleben (same); for 5s NC money sold 72 square poles lot 1 in SE square of Lincolnton; border: "both" Main Streets; lot is 6 by 12 poles; sold for 7 years beginning Jan. 1, 1793, afterward Arthur deBardeleben agrees to leave all improvements that might be built on the lot and to return lot to Christian Reinhard.   Signed Christian Reinhart & Arthur deBardeleben. Witness John Reinhart & David Zimmerman (german). Rec. Apr. 1792. Book 16 p. 247

724. Mar. 31, 1792 Benjamin Dorsey (Lincoln Co) to James Baker (same); for 5£ sold 5.25 ac and 32 poles; border: a branch.   Signed Benjamin Dorsey. Witness Wm Harbeson jr & David Falls. Rec. Apr. 1792. Book 16 p. 248

725. Mar. 28, 1792 Elisabeth & James Abernathy (Lincoln Co) to Smith Abernathy (same); for 5s sold 135 ac on Cataba R; border: Elisabeth's mark and James Abernathy. Witness Jos Abernathy & Jon Rockett. Rec. Apr. 1792. Book 16 p. 250

726. Oct. 10, 1787 James Gingles (Lincoln Co) to John Baird jr (same); for 100£ sold 200 ac on both sides of middle fork of Crowders Cr; between Alexr McCalister and Robert Peterson; granted Apr. 22, 1763 to Saml Gingles desc. Signed James Gingles. Witness Wm Berry, John Berry, & Robert Bery (or Besy). Rec. Apr. 1792. Book 16 p. 251

727. Apr. 4, 1792 William Ramsey (Lincoln Co) to David Ramsey (same); for 10£ NC money sold 100 ac in Burke Co on both sides of Jacobs R; border: William Read.   Signed William Ramsey. Witness Richard Vandike & George Anderson. Rec. Apr. 1792. Book 16 p. 252

728. Jun. 16, 1790 Jacob Roseman (Lincoln Co) to Peter Plunk (same); Jacob owes Peter, by bond, 148£ NC money with condition to pay 74£ NC money with

interest on Jun. 16, 1791; for that bond and 5s sterling "Great Britain" money (paid by Peter to Jacob) sold 415 ac in Lincoln formerly "Roan" Co; border: Conrad Booley on W side of fork that runs into Elk Cr and W side of Cataba R; granted Apr. 28, 1756 by Earl Granville to Conrad Mull "transfered" to Peter Mull who sold May 20, 1771 to Windel Wyant and sold Oct. 2,1790 by Windel & Yost Weiant, executors of Windel Wyant desc, to Jacob Roseman; if bond paid, then deed is void.   Signed Jacob Roseman's mark. Witness John Willbrooks, Abraham Seib (or Abm Sipe) (german), & Yenil(?) Seib (german). Rec. Apr. 1792. Book 16 p. 253

729. Feb. 9, 1792 Elisha Perkins & wife Jane (Burke Co) to Jacob Sherril jr (Lincoln Co); for 5s sterling sold 144 ac on W side of Cataba R.   Signed Elisha & Jane Perkins. Witness John Perkins jr, John Perkins, & Ephraim Perkins. Rec. Apr. 1792. Book 16 p. 255

729A. Feb. 10, 1792 Elisha Perkins & wife Jane to Jacob Sherril jr; for 500£ sold 144 ac [this is release for same land in deed 718]; granted Jan. 7, 1761 by Earl Granville to Samuel Brown.   Signed Elisha & Jane Perkins. Witness John Perkins jr, John Perkins, & Ephraim Perkins. Rec. Apr. 1792. Book 16 p. 256

730. Nov. 21, 1791 Acquila Sherril & wife Lucresy (Green Co, NC) to John Perkins (Lincoln Co); for 5s sterling sold 400 ac on S side of Cataba R; border: Uriah Sherril, McCormack, Jacob Fulenwider, & John Perkins; includes "a meaders".   Signed Acquila & Lucresy Sherrill's marks. Witness Ephraim Perkins, John Perkins, & Thomas Bridges. Rec. Apr. 1792. Book 16 p.258

730A. Nov. 22, 1791 Acquila Sherril & wife Lucresy (Green Co, NC) to John Perkins (Lincoln Co); for 450£ sold 500 ac [this is release for land in deed 719]; granted Oct. 11, 1783 by Gov. Alexander Martin to Acquila Sherril.   Signed Acquila & Lucresy Sherrill's marks. Witness Ephraim Perkins, John Perkins, & Thomas Bridges. Rec. Apr. 1792. Book 16 p. 259

July Court 1792
731. Jun. 30, 1792 John McGaughey (Burke Co) to Joseph Paxton (Lincoln Co); for 50£ sold 115 ac on waters of Howards Cr; border: head of a branch, Johnson's old line, Nicholas Friday, Jacob Renhart, & Valentine Lowar; part of 500 ac granted Nov. 17, 1790 to John McGaughey.   Signed John McGaughey. Witness Waightstile Avery & James Gorder. Rec. Jul. 1792. Book 16 p. 262

732. Apr. 30, 1787 James Wilson (Lincoln Co) to Christopher Porter (same); for 100£ NC money sold 131 ac on both sides of Sims Spring Br of Crowders Cr "a little above" John Walker; part of grant Jul. 21, 1774 to John Wells who sold Feb. 2, 1780 to James Wilson.   Signed James Wilson. Witness Samuel Lindsey & James Wasson. Rec. Jul. 1792. Book 16 p. 263

733. Jul. 2, 1792 Francis & Wallace Beatey (Rutherford Co) to Peter Sides (Lincoln Co); for 50£ sold 200 ac on waters of Kuykendalls Cr; includes where Robt McCashland built a house; granted Apr. 25, 1767 to Robert McCashland. Signed Francis & Wallace Beatey. Witness Jno Shoore & W. Alexander. Rec. Jul. 1792. Book 16 p. 265

734. Apr. 11, 1792 Richard Reynolds, planter (Lincoln Co) to George Patterson (same); for 200£ NC money sold 250 ac on both sides of Indian Cr of S fork of Cataba R. Signed Richard Reyolds's mark. Witness Forney Green Norman & Danl Collins. Rec. Jul. 1792. Book 16 p. 266

735. May 18, 1792 Nathaniel Alexander (Lincoln Co) to Michael Shell (same); for 100£ NC money sold [ac omitted] in Lincoln formerly Burke Co on S side of Jacobs R and both sides of Camp Cr; border: Henry Whitenar on E side of a small branch and Robert Orr's field. Signed Nat Alexander. Witness W. Alexander & Wm McCasland. Rec. Jul. 1792. Book 16 p. 267

736. May 17, 1792 Lodowick Proups (Lincoln Co) to Sapphira Proups (same); for 10£ NC money sold 100 ac on waters of Haywards Cr; border: old lines; part of grant Dec. 9, 1768 to Lodowick Proups. Signed Ludenteg(?) Probst (or Peeobst) (german). Witness David Ramsey & John Probst. Rec. Jul. 1792. Book 16 p. 269

737. Sept. 1, 1787 John Seffret (Lincoln Co) to Jacob Hain (same); for 50£ NC money sold 200 ac on both sides of Lick fork of Indian Cr above & joins Hugh Polock's; granted Dec. 16, 1769 to John Sloan and sold to "sundry persons" until John Seffret became legally vested in title. Signed John Seffrett. Witness Phillihh Antony (or Phil Anthony) (german) & Phillib Hen (german). Rec. Jul. 1792. Book 16 p. 270

738. Jan. 19, 1792 Daniel McKisick (Lincoln Co) to Elias Myars (same); for 100£ sold 250 ac on head "draughts" of Keeners Cr and on both sides of road from Beatey's ford & across W end of Little Mountain to Bullinger's Mill; border: Thomas Earwood; part of 525 ac granted Apr. 16, 1764 to James Thompson who sold Jan. 27, 1774 to William Bryson who sold Mar. 5, 1787 to James Bryson who sold Apr. 19, 1787 to Daniel McKisick. Signed Danl McKisick. Witness Thomas Earwood & Valentine Little. Rec. Jul. 1792. Book 16 p. 271

739. Dec. 29, 1791 John Doddorow, planter (Lincoln Co) to William Hammentree (same); for 50£ sold 213 ac; border: Costner Armstrong and Friday. Signed Johanes Dotters (german). Witness Jno Fulenwider & Phillib Null. Rec. Jul. 1792. Book 16 p. 272

740. Jun. 14, 1792 James Hillhouse (Lincoln Co) to Robert Black (same); for 150£ NC money sold 300 ac on both sides of Long Cr; border: Cowan and Hoyle "and part of two other tracts" joining aforesaid tract, McKnight & John Pinner; part of three grants to James Hillhouse (1) Feb. 28, 1775, (2) & (3) Mar. 25, 1780.

Signed James Hillhouse. Witness Arthur Graham & David Ramsey. Rec. Jul. 1792. Book 16 p. 274

741. Aug. 10, 1791 Absalom Bonham (Lincoln Co) to Jacob Havener (same); for 25£ NC money sold 100 ac on waters of Indian Cr; border: Abraham Havener; part of grant Aug. 7,1787 to Absalom Bonham.   Signed Absalom Bonham. Witness David Ramsey & John Cox. Rec. Jul. 1792. Book 16 p. 275

742. Mar. 3, 1792 Jacob Fifer (Lincoln Co) to George Rominger (same); for 80£ NC money sold 265 ac in Lincoln formerly Burke Co on E side of N fork of Long Br; border: Lutes, Alexander, George Hephner, James Wilson, & Daniel McKisick; granted Mar. 14, 1780 to Jacob Fifer.   Signed Jacob Phiffer's mark. Witness Rudolph Conrad & Elias Moyer (or Mayers) (german). Rec. Jul. 1792. Book 16 p. 276

743. Feb. 25, 1792 Awbry Noland (Newberry Co, SC) to Lewis Hill (Lincoln Co); for 70£ sold 350 ac on S side of Cataba R; border: John Beal late property of William Nixon, James Luckey, & old original lines; part of 950 ac granted Sept. 13, 1749 to Leonard Killian who sold to George Brown who sold 700 ac to Robert Wadkins & Francis Cost; being Cost's half of 700 ac which was sold to Awbry Noland.   Signed Aesbrey Noland. Witness Robert Hill, John Hunter, & Andrew Hunter. Rec. Jul. 1792. Book 16 p. 277

744. Dec. 8, 1789 Henry Landis (Rutherford Co) to Adam Mauny (Lincoln Co); for 130£ NC money sold 200 ac on Cornfield Br of Indian Cr; border: a hill; includes his mill; granted May 4, 1789 to Thomas Reynolds.   Signed Henry Landis's mark. Witness Vallentine Mauny & Antony Mauny. Rec. Jul. 1792. Book 16 p. 278

745. Apr. 6, 1792 Peter Yont, planter (Lincoln Co) to Adam Yont, carpenter (same); for 30£ NC money sold 200 ac on waters of Lyles Cr; border: head of a branch, said Peter Yont's "other" survey, Griffith Edwards, & Sifold; granted Oct. 29, 1782 to Peter Yont.   Signed Peder Yund (german). Witness Jacob Fullbright & Willem Duhl (german). Rec. Jul. 1792. Book 16 p. 280

746. Feb. 20, 1792 Robert McCashland (Lincoln Co) to Matthew McCashland (same); for 200£ sold 250 ac on waters of Mountain Cr; border: Francis McCorkle and crosses "the" creek; granted Dec. 16, 1763 to Francis McCorkle who sold to Robert McCashland.   Signed Robt McCasland. Witness Jos Henry & William McCasland. Rec. Jul. 1792. Book 16 p. 281

747. Feb. 20, 1792 Robert McCashland (Lincoln Co) to Matthew McCashland (same); for 100£ sold 200 ac on branches of Michaels Cr; border: Laum and new lines; granted Apr. 28, 1768 to Robert McCashland.   Signed Robt McCasland. Witness Jos Henry & William McCasland. Rec. Jul. 1792. Book 16 p. 282

748. Feb. 20, 1792 Robert McCashland (Lincoln Co) to Mathew McCashland (same); for 150£ sold 150 ac; border: his own land, Martin Friday, & Cansler; granted Sept. 12, 1787 to Robert McCashland.   Signed Robt McCasland. Witness Jos Henry & William McCasland. Rec. Jul. 1792. Book 16 p. 283

749. Feb. 20, 1792 Robert McCashland (Lincoln Co) to Matthew McCashland (same); for 50£ sold 15 ac on a branch of S fork of Cataba R; border: Philip Cansler's "second" corner, his own land, & Shell; granted Jul. 21, 1774 to Robert McCashland.   Signed Robt McCasland. Witness Jos Henry & William McCasland. Rec. Jul. 1792. Book 16 p. 284

October Court 1792
750. Dec. 28, 1787 Joseph Henry, sheriff (Lincoln Co) to Robert Wier (same); for 13£ 5s sold [ac omitted] on Beasons Cr of Buffaloe Cr; below Abraham Clark's entry; includes his own improvement; sold Dec. 28, 1787 due to writ from Lincoln Co Court to levy 16£ 6s 3p from William Morris due to suit of William Graham. Signed Jos Henry. Witness Jo Dickson. Rec. Oct. 1792. Book 16 p. 285

751. Oct. 2, 1792 Samuel Jarrett (Lincoln Co) to John Jarrett (same); for 50£ NC money sold 250 ac; part of grant to Elias Lagardere.   Signed Samuel Jarrett. Witness Andw Turner & Andrew Stockinger. Rec. Oct. 1792. Book 16 p. 286

752. Mar. 22, 1791 Samuel White (Lincoln Co) to Michael Hoyle (same); for 20£ sold 300 ac on SW side of S fork of Cataba R and on Lick Br; granted Apr. 6, 1765 to Peter Laboon who sold Mar. 2, 1779 to Samuel White.   Signed Samuel White. Witness Jno Fulinwider & Wm Temple Coles. Wit. oath Oct. 1792 by Jno Fulinwider. Book 16 p. 287

753. Aug.20, 1792 John Belck (Lincoln Co) to Isaac West (same); for 120£ sold 109 ac on S side of Doctors Cr; border: William Moore, Cobin's old line, an old School House Br, & the "fifth" line that crosses the creek; part of 200 ac granted to John Bealy, school master.   Signed John Bealk. Witness Stephen Weast & William Bealk. Wit. oath Oct. 1792 by S. West (sic). Book 16 p. 288

754. Apr. 23, 1792 George Patterson (Lincoln Co) to Nathan Harris (same); for 200£ NC money sold 250 ac on both sides of Indian Cr of S fork of Cataba R. Signed George Patterson. Witness Samuel Carpenter, Robert Glenn, & Francis Guthrie. Wit. oath Oct. 1792 by Francis Guthrie. Book 16 p. 289

755. Jan. 26, 1784 John Curry (Lincoln Co) to John Falls (same); for 250£ sold 300 ac on both sides of Kings Cr near the head; granted Sept. 26, 1766 to James Fanning and sold Jan. 19, 1780 by James Fanning, his son & heir, to John Curry. Signed John Curry's mark. Witness Thomas Ferguson, Gilbrath Dickson, & Jno Wilson. Wit. oath Oct. 1792 by Jno Wilson esq. Book 16 p. 290

756. Jul. 16, 1792 Daniel Warlick (Lincoln Co) to Henry Bingal (same); for 55£ NC money sold 150 ac on both sides of "said" Warlicks Mill Cr; border: "second & third" corners of the grant and an old line of another survey; part of 200 ac granted Oct. 26, 1767 to Daniel Warlick sr.   Signed Daniel Warlick. Witness John Fegel & Adam Statler. Rec. Oct. 1792. Book 16 p. 291

757. May 10, 1792 Henry Whitener, planter (Lincoln Co) to Henry, Catey, John, Joseph, & Barbara Dellinger, minors and sons & daughters of John Dellinger (same); for 10£ sold 460 ac on Jacobs fork of S fork of Cataba R; border: John Mull, Conrod Yoder, Daniel Whitener (or Whitaker), & an old line; part of two grants to Henry Whitener (1) in 1751 and (2) in 1780.   Signed Henerh Weitner (german). Witness Heneriy Weitner (german) & John Carruth. Wit. oath Oct. 1792 by Henry Weitner. Book 16 p. 292

758. Mar. 31, 1792 James Holland (Rutherford Co) to James Henderson (same); for 163£ "in money & ready money notes" sold 3,750 ac in the "Middle" District [Tenn.] on both sides of Duck R; border: Joseph Hinds, a branch, a small creek, & Fountain Cr; part of 5,000 ac granted (#74) Jul. 10, 1788 by Gov. Samuel Johnston to James Holland.   Signed Jas Holland. Witness Js (or Is) Holland, Jonn Gullick, William Huggins, & Lawson Henderson. Wit. oath Oct. 1792 by Lawson Henderson.   Book 16 p. 294

759. Aug. 20, 1792 Conrad Adams (Lincoln Co, Ky) to William Hermon (Lincoln Co, NC); for 60£ sold 320 ac on both sides of the forks of Lyles Cr; border: the mill shoal fork, Waggoner, Conrad Adams, Saml Steel, & Boston Cline; granted Nov. 9, 1784 by Gov. Alexr Martin to Henry Adams desc "in his minority" and said Conrad Adams is Henry Adams' only brother.   Signed Conrad Adams' mark. Witness Joseph Steel & William Reather. Rec. Oct. 1792. Book 16 p. 295

760. Jan. 17, 1792 Paul Anthony (Burke Co) and Daniel & David Shuford, heirs of John Shuford desc (same), to John Boste (same); for 8£ NC money sold 37 ac on Clarks Cr waters of S fork of Cataba R; border: Coonce, William Bost, & said Anthony's old line; granted (#461) Dec. 22, 1768 to Paul Anthony & John Shuford and John Shuford in his will appointed his sons Daniel & David Shuford as his executors.   Signed Peaülüs Antoni (german), Daniel Sufert (german), & David Shuford (in English). Witness George Wilfong & John Wilfong. Rec. Oct. 1792. Book 16 p. 297

761. Feb. 7, 1792 Michael Fladder Miller (Lincoln Co) to Conrad Weaver (same); for a "bond for maintainance" give to him by Conrad Weaver sold 200 ac on a branch of Leonharts fork; border: Howard; granted Apr. 25, 1767 to Valentine Mauney.   Signed Michael Flader Miller (german). Witness Frederick Aderhold & Jacob Blank. Rec. Oct. 1792. Book 16 p. 298

762. Jul. 14, 1792 James Henderson (Lincoln Co) to John Douglas (same); for 30£ sold 200 ac on waters of Little Cataba Cr; border: James Holland and Thomas

Henderson's survey.   Signed James Henderson. Witness Jn Henderson, Wm Dickson, & Lwsn Henderson. Rec. Oct. 1792. Book 16 p. 299

763. Oct. 12, 1790 Christian Nigh (Lincoln Co) to Martin Speagle & John Hawn, trustees of Lutheran congregation on Jacobs R a Southern branch of S fork of Cataba R; for 5£ NC money sold 10 ac for building a "convient" church or "Stiled" Meeting House for Dutch Lutheran congregation & school house "to instruct Youth besides Publick Worship" and for burial of dead of said congregation; land is near head of a branch running into Jacobs R; part of 250 ac "warranted" then in Burke Co Feb. 20, 1779 for Christian Nigh and granted May 18, 1789 in Lincoln Co & registered in Lincoln Co Aug. 18, 1790.   Signed Kristian Nei (german). Witness Michael Cline, Johannes Silier(?) (german), & Andrew Stockinger. Rec. Oct. 1792. Book 16 p. 301

764. Mar. 16, 1792 Walter Beaty (Mecklenburg Co) to James Luckey (Lincoln Co); for 55£ sold 125 ac; border: James Luckey.   Signed W Beaty. Witness Nat Alexander & Clem Nance. Rec. Oct. 1792. Book 16 p. 302

765. Sept. 1, 1789 Samuel Fisher (Lincoln Co) to Jackson Harwell (same); for 80£ NC money sold 150 ac on W side of Cataba R; border: Barkley and Lockman; granted from "the" governor to Samuel Fisher.   Signed Samuel Fisher. Witness Samuel Harwell & Robert Abernathy. Rec. Oct. 1792. Book 16 p. 303

766. Sept. 16, 1791 Adam Killion (Lincoln Co) to Frederick Shell (Sullivan Co, NC (sic)); for 100£ NC money sold 166 ac on waters of Keenors Cr; border: Valentine Cline, Thomas Earwood, Wm Earwood, & his own land; part of two tracts: one a king's grant & second a state grant.   Signed Adam Killion. Witness Valentine Little & Jno Bodine. Rec. Oct. 1792. Book 16 p. 304

767. Jan. 30, 1786 Joseph Henry esq (Lincoln Co) to George Graham (same); for 40£ sold 190 ac; border: Kuykendal; granted Sept. 24, 1754 to John Moore who sold Feb. 10, 1778 to James Graham and sold Aug. 12, 1784 due to suit of William Moore by sheriff's deed to Joseph Henry.   Signed Joseph Henry. Witness Jno Barber, Henriy Wellenger(?) (german), & Jno Wilson. Rec. Oct. 1792. Book 16 p. 305

768. Sept. 6, 1789 Doctor John Member & wife Hannah Margret and George Hide & wife Magdalene (all of Berks Co, Pa) to George Graham (Lincoln Co); for 20 [£] paid to each sold their 2/3rds interest in 202 ac on S side of Cataba R in fork of said river on Doctors Cr; granted Sept. 24, 1754 to Frederick Hambright who sold Jan. 11, 1757 to Conrad Sailor who died and left only three daughters: Hannah Margret Member, Magdalene Hide, & Susanna Cloves.   Signed John Member and marks of Hanna Margret, Gerg Heit, & Magdelanna Heit. Witness Jas Graham, Jacob Ritter, & Georg Kitter (german). Rec. Oct. 1792. Book 16 p. 306

769. Dec. 26, 1789 John Cloves & wife Susannah (Washington Co, Md) to George Graham (Lincoln Co); for 20£ sold their 1/3rd interest in 202 ac on S side of Cataba R on Doctors Cr; granted Sept. 24, 1754 to Frederick Hambright who sold Jan. 11, 1757 to Conrad Sailor who died and left only three daughters: Susannah Cloves, Hannah Margaret Member, & Magdalena Hide.   Signed John & Susannah Cloves' marks. Witness Jas Graham, _?_ Hörner, & Johannes Hünnl. Rec. Oct. 1792. Book 16 p. 308

770. May 2, 1788 Tobias James, planter (Lincoln Co) to Christian Sputt, farmer (same); for 45£ NC money sold 300 ac on both sides of Reynolds Mill Cr. Signed Tobia James' mark. Witness Christopher Acre & Thos Norman. Rec. Oct. 1792. Book 16 p. 309

771. Aug. 10, 1792 Jacob Carpenter (Lincoln Co) to Henry Carpenter (same); for 100£ NC money sold 222 ac on E side of Clarks Cr; border: an old tract; part of grant Sept. 3, 1753 to Peter Broyl who sold Jun. 3, 1758 to Derick Ramsour who sold Sept. 27, 1779 part to Boston Cline and part to Jacob Carpenter and Boston Cline sold Jun. 6, 1771 to Jacob Carpenter.   Signed Jacob Zimmerman (german). Witness Jo Dickson. Rec. Oct. 1792. Book 16 p. 310

772. Apr. 8, 1789 John Hiltebran (Rutherford Co) to John McGaughy (Lincoln Co); for 10£ NC money sold 100 ac on both sides of Howards Cr; granted Aug. 6, 1787 to John Hiltebran.   Signed John Hildebrand. Witness Andrew Turner & David Ramsey, jurat. Rec. Oct. 1792. Book 16 p. 312

773. Dec. 20, 1783 Peter Henley (Burke Co) to Caleb Phifer (Mecklenburg Co); for 127£ 10s NC money sold 200 ac in Burke Co on both sides of Haggins fork; border: David Lorance & Peter Lorance.   Signed Peter Henley's mark. Witness Rd Trotter & Martin Phifer jr. Wit. oath Oct. 1792 by Martin Phifer esq. Book 16 p. 312

774. Nov. 24, 1790 William Hinnan (Iredell Co) to Henry Kehler (Lincoln Co); for 100£ NC money sold 223 ac on waters of Clarks Cr; border: West's field; part of 777 ac granted (#488) Oct. 28, 1782 to James Hennan who sold Jan. 19, 1784 to Elisabeth Hennan who married John Baxter and sold Sept. 22, 1790 by John Baxter to William Hennan.   Signed William Hennan. Witness Thomas Puntch & Joseph Hartle. Rec. Oct. 1792. Book 16 p. 313

775. Aug. 20, 1792 Conrad Adams (Lincoln Co, Ky) to William Herman (Lincoln Co, NC); for 60£ sold 320 ac on both sides of branch of Lylses Cr; border: Henry Adams' SW corner, Samuel Steel, & John Summers; granted Nov. 9, 1784 by Gov. Alexander Martin to Conrad Adams.   Signed Conrad Adams' mark. Witness Joseph Steel & William Reather. Rec. Oct. 1792. Book 16 p. 314

776. Aug. 9, 1792 Frederick Graff (Lincoln Co) to William Herman (same); for 100£ sold 183 ac on S side of Mecklins Cr; border: Jacob Deal, SW corner of tract

from which "it is taken", & old lines; part of 550 ac granted Oct. 28, 1782 to Frederick Graff.   Signed Fradrick Graff. Witness Joseph Steel & Jacob Troffle. Rec. Oct. 1792. Book 16 p. 315

777. Aug. 22, 1792 John Pitts, heir of his father George Pitts (Iredell Co), to James Crawford esq (same); for 100£ sold [ac omitted] on both sides of Haggins fork; border: on S side of Long Br, Matthew Wilson, Hugh Brevard, & Isaac Robinson; granted (#338) Oct. 28, 1782 to George Pitts, father of John Pitts.   Signed John Pitts' mark. Witness John Nisbit, Jas Byers, & John Crawford. Book 16 p. 317

778. Jan. 2, 1792 Wireley Rudisell (Lincoln Co) to John Crouse (same); for 15£ NC money sold 128 ac on Indian Cr; border: Peter Carpenter, Adderhold, & Mauney; granted in 1784 to Wireley Rudisell.   Signed Wirey Rudisell. Witness Sam Givens & Jonas Rudisell. Wit. oath Oct. 1792 to Sam Givens. Book 16 p. 318

779. Sept. 29, 1792 Robert Wier (Lincoln Co) to James McDonald; for 20£ sold a bay gelding about 14 hands high about 6 or 7 years old branded on nigh buttock "AP".   Signed Robert Wier. Witness Jeremiah Elders. Rec. Oct. 1792. Book 16 p. 319

January Court 1793
780. Dec. 25, 1790 (sic--17th year of independence) Francis McCorkle & wife Elisabeth (Lincoln Co) to Frederick Mires (same); for 100£ NC money sold 150 ac on waters of Halls Cr on W side of Cataba R in Lincoln formerly Burke Co; border: Robert McCashland and James Fleming; granted (#529) in Oct. 1782 to Francis McCorkle and registered in Burke Co Book 3 p. 15.   Signed Fras McCorkel & Elisabeth's   mark. Witness Elias Moyer (german) & Juhur (or Jahar) Henrich Hatter (german). Rec. Jan. 1793. Book 16 p. 319

781. Oct. 29, 1792 George Reel sr (Lincoln Co) to George Reel jr (same); for 40£ sold 195 ac on both sides of Leepers Cr; part of grant to Lawrence Snapp sr who willed it to son Lawrence Snapp jr who sold to George Reel sr.   Signed Georg Rill (or George Reel) (german). Witness Lemuel Saunders & Dendel Driehl (german). Wit. oath Jan. 1793 by Lemuel Saunders. Book 16 p. 320

782. Jan. 3, 1793 Peter Dunkin & wife Mary (Lincoln Co) to Aaron Forman (same); for 25£ NC money sold 25 ac on both sides of Mountain Cr; border: John Snider (Anderson--lined out) on E and John Bullinger on W.   Signed Peter Dunkin & Mary's mark. Witness John Bodine & Peter Bodine. Wit. oath Jan. 1793 by John Bodine. Book 16 p. 321

783. Dec. 2, 1792 John Beale (Lincoln Co) to John Robertson (same); for 80£ NC money sold 170 ac on waters of Catawba R and E side of Killions Cr; border: a waggon raod from George Heagers to Tool's ford on Catawba R and Heager's

open line.   Signed John Beale. Witness Jones Abernathy, John Edwards, & William Heaker. Rec. Jan. 1793. Book 16 p. 322

784. Mar. 6, 1787 Elias Myars (Lincoln Co) to Jacob Link (same); for 1£ 17s sold 103 ac on both sides of Cilins Cr; border: lower side of Myars' meadow field, Myars' old corner, & David Crits; part of grant from the king to Francis Beaty and sold to Elias Myars.   Signed Elias Miÿer (german). Witness Devolt Krits & Frederick Link. Rec. Jan. 1793. Book 16 p. 323

785. Dec. 29, 1792 Samuel McMin (Lincoln Co) to Charles Regan (same); for 5s NC money sold 150 (180--lined out) ac on W side of Catawba R; border: William Kinkaid, Abner Wamock, & Beaty; granted to Samuel McMin.   Signed Samuel McMin. Witness Abner Womack & Isaac Bond (or Rond). Wit. oath Jan. 1793 by Abner Womack. Book 16 p. 324

786. Apr. 12, 1792 David Ramsey (Lincoln Co) to son James Ramsey (same); for love and affection and 5£ NC money sold (1) 200 ac on waters of Howards Cr; border: old lines; and (2) 25 ac on Howards Cr; border: tract 1 and old lines. Signed David Ramsey. Witness Adam Reep & Henrich Bellinger (german). Rec. Jan. 1793. Book 16 p. 325

787. Mar. 31, 1792 Daniel Kingeray (Richmond Co, Ga) to Philip Anthony (Lincoln Co); for 100£ NC money sold 130 ac on waters of Indian Cr and both sides of road from Moses Moore's to Broad R; border: Henry Reynolds and a hill nigh a swamp; part of 350 ac granted by the king to David Huddleston who sold to Herman who sold Nov. 29, 1792 to Daniel Kingeray; money received Sept. 18, 1792.   Signed Daniel Kingry. Witness Wiegls Reh(?) (german) & Jacob Miller (german). Wit. oath Jan. 1793 by Jacob Miller. Book 16 p. 326

788. Nov. 28, 1791 John Badley (Lincoln Co) to George Lance (same); for 12£ NC money "in gold or silver" sold 100 ac on forks of Long Br of Howards Cr and on both sides of "the" road; includes the meadows "of both branches".   Signed John Bradley's mark. Witness Paul Anthony & Frederick Dietz. Wit. oath Jan. 1793 by Paul Anthony. Book 16 p. 327

789. Dec. 27, 1792 Matthias Killian (Lincoln Co) to Archibald Young; for 30£ NC money sold 150 ac; border: Leonard Killian; granted Sept. 24, 1785 to Matthias Killian.   Signed Mathiaes Killien (german). Witness John Fullbright & David Quillien. Rec. Jan. 1793. Book 16 p. 328

790. May 22, 1790 Thomas Salter, merchant (Northern Liberties of city of Philadelphia, Pa): an oath (sort of); on Feb. 19 & 20, 1768 Peter Harpell sold to Thomas Salter 420 ac in Anson now Lincoln Co on N fork of Indian Cr; border: black oak marked "PH"; Thomas Salter intended to give the land to his cousin Isaiah Liming and step-brother John Cox: on May 25, 1787 the South part (210 ac) to Isaiah Liming and on May 30, 1787 North part (210 ac) to John Cox; but

the division line was called out wrong in Isaiah Liming's deed so there's an argument between Isaiah Liming & John Cox; so now for the original consideration, Thomas Salter describes the division line between the two tracts. Signed Tho Salter. Witness Arthur Graham & Richd Whitehead. Wit. oath Jan. 1793 by Arthur Graham. Book 16 p. 330

791. Jan. 4, 1793 John Dellinger (Lincoln Co) to John Fulenwider (same); for 40£ sold 230 ac on both sides of Shoal Br of S fork of Catawba R; border: black oak marked "FB" Phiffer's corner and Lip.   Signed John Dellinger. Witness Henrich Bollinger (german) & Henrich Smitt(?) (german). Rec. Jan. 1793. Book 16 p. 331

792. Oct. 20, 1791 Jacob Cotner (Lincoln Co) to Josiah Angel (same); for 50£ NC money sold 55 ac on W side of S fork of Catawba R; border: Rockey ford; part of grant Mar. 14, 1780 to Jacob Cotner. Signed Jacob Cotner's mark. Witness John Cotner & Robert Blackburn. Wit. oath Jan. 1793 by Robt Blackburn. Book 16 p.332

793. Jul. 28, 1790 Basil Dorsy (Lincoln Co) to John Dorsy (same); for 25£ NC money sold 175 ac; border: Richard Harris' "second" corner and edge of an old field; part of grant Oct. 28, 1782 to William Craig.   Signed Bassell Dorsey. Witness David Falls & William Harbison. Wit. oath Jan. 1793 to David Falls. Book 16 p. 333

794. Nov. (blank), 1792 Richard Venables jr (Lincoln Co) to Richard Venables sr (same); for 150£ NC money sold 200 ac on S side of Catawba R on middle fork of Crowders Cr; border: post oak marked "RV" Wilson's corner; part of grant to Ephraim McLean who sold to Richard Venables sr who sold to Richard Venables jr.   Signed Richard Venabls. Witness Jno Barber, Sarah Barber, & Isabel Barber. Wit. oath Jan. 1793 by John Barber esq. Book 16 p. 334

795. Sept. 24, 1790 Martin Gortner & wife Mary (Lincoln Co) to Frederick Ryder (same); for 200£ NC money sold 240 ac in Lincoln formerly Mecklenburg Co on both sides of Hope(?) Cr; border: George Iker and a conditional line; part of grant Apr. 25, 1767 to Nicholas Fry and sold Feb. 11, 1786 by Peter & Elisabeth Fry, executors of Nicholas Fry, to Martin Gortner.   Signed Martin & Mary Gortner's marks. Witness Conrod Hawn & John Wilfong. Wit. oath Jan. 1793 by John Wilfong esq. Book 16 p. 336

796. Nov. 3, 1792 John Dawsey (Lincoln Co) to George Musconnonck (same); for 50£ sold 175 ac on S side of Mecklins Cr; border: William Sloan, Richard Harris' "second" corner, a meadow branch, & edge of an old field; part of grant Oct. 28, 1782 to William Craig who sold Jul. 28, 1790 to Basil Dawsey.   Signed John Dorsey. Witness David Falls & Rich Haris. Wit. oath Jan. 1793 by David Falls. Book 16 p. 337

797. Oct. 11, 1792 Joseph Dickson, commissioner in trust for Lincolnton, (Lincoln Co), to John Roney (same); for 40s sold [ac omitted] lot 18 in SW square of Lincolnton; lot is 6 by 14 rods.   Signed Jo Dickson. Witness Ad Brevard. Rec. Jan. 1793. Book 16 p. 338

798. Jn. 15, 1790 Henry Carlock (Rutherford Co) to Thomas Norman sr (Lincoln Co); for 80£ NC money sold 400 ac on both sides of Little Cr of Buffaloe Cr above Fisher's; includes a cabin on W side of the creek.   Signed Henry Carlock. Witness Forney Green Norman & Thomas Norman jr. Wit. aoth Jan. 1793 by Thomas Norman jr. Book 16 p. 339

799. Apr. 20, 1786 James & William Ker (Rowan Co) to Philip Bollinger (Lincoln Co); for 400£ NC money sold 336 ac on W side of Catawba R and both sides of Little Mountain Cr; granted three hundred and (blank) ac Feb. 22, 1784 (sic) by Earl Granville to Thomas Anderson who sold May 3, 1782 (sic) to John Work who sold to James & William Ker.   Signed Jas & Wm Ker. Witness Valentine Little & Johannes Bollinger (or Jno Bollinger) (german). Wit. oath Jan. 1793 by John Bollinger. Book 16 p. 340

800. Jun. 13, 1791 James Smith (Lincoln Co), administrator of Henry James desc, to Nathan Mendinghall (same); for 25£, paid by Thomas West to Henry James, sold 117 ac on waters of Crowders Cr; border: Anthony Clark's old line; includes Kymball's old improvement; granted (#267) Aug. 7, 1787 to Henry James; Henry James gave a bond of 50£ to make a good deed for Thomas West; Thomas West assigned his rights to Nathan Mendinghall, and Henry James died without making a deed; James Smith has given administration bond in open court to administer Henry James' estate.   Signed James Smith. Witness Jas Wilson & Jno Wilson. Wit. oath Jan. 1793 by John Wilson esq. Book 16 p. 341

801. Jul. 23, 1789 William Henry jr (Lincoln Co) to Nathan Mendinghall (same); for 21£ NC money sold his half of 202 ac on both sides of Falls Br of Crowders Cr; includes William Henry jr's improvements; granted Apr. 28, 1768 to Wm Henry who died intestate and land went to eldest son Moses Henry who sold Feb. 13, 1773 to John Henry who by will Dec. 24, 1779 gave land to his brothers Joseph Henry & William Henry jr equal shares.   Signed Wm Henry. Witness Robert Wilson, Jno Barber, & Jn Wilson. Wit. oath Jan. 1793 to John Wilson esq. Book 16 p. 342

802. Aug.3, 1791 Charles Hamilton (Maddison Co, Ky) to Nathan Mendinghall (Lincoln Co); for 30£ NC money sold (1) 100 ac on branch of Crowders Cr; border: Gingles and new lines; granted to Wm Henry who died intestate and land went to eldest son Moses Henry who sold to Charles Hamilton; and (2) 45 ac; border: tract 1 and Gingles; granted May 18, 1789 to Charles Hamilton.   Signed Charles Hamilton. Witness James Wilson & J. Wilson. Wit. oath Jan. 1793 by John Wilson esq. Book 16 p. 344

803. Aug. 17, 1790 Samuel Hollingsworth (Burke Co) to David Wilcockson (same); for 70£ sold 300 ac in Lincoln formerly Burke Co on both sides of waters of Mountain Cr; border: on N by Aaron Forman, on S by Isaac Lollar, & road "to" Ramsour's mill to Sherrill's ford on Catawba R; granted Oct. 28, 1782 to [omitted]. Signed Samuel Hollingsworth's mark. Witness John Snider & Frederick Ward. Wit. aoth Jan. 1793 by John Snider. Book 16 p. 345

804. Oct. 5, 1792 Joseph Henry (Lincoln Co) to Arthur deBardeleben & Andrew Turner (same); for 25£ sold [ac omitted] lot 4 in SE square of Lincolnton; lot is 6 by 12 poles.   Signed Joseph Henry. Witness W. Alexander. Rec. Jan. 1793. Book 16 p. 346

805. Jul. 3, 1792 John Reynolds (Lincoln Co) to William Magness (same); for 60£ NC money sold 250 ac on both sides of Buffaloe Cr of Broad R; border: the old survey; part of grant Aug. 9, 1755 to Thomas Reynolds who sold Jan. 18, 1759 to John Reynolds.   Signed John Reynolds' mark. Witness David Ramsey & Francis McNemar. Rec. Jan. 1793. Book 16 p. 346

806. Oct. 8, 1789 Michael Buff (Lincoln Co) to Peter Moyars (same); for 60£ sold 300 ac on the dividing ridge between Leonards fork and Indian Cr.   Signed Michael Buff. Witness Waightstile Avery, John McGaughey, & Wm Bates. Wit. oath Jan. 1793 by Waightstile Avery esq. Book 16 p. 347

807. "This deed is to be executed in compliance with a Bond of performance to convey the premises dated Apr. 15, 1789 in penal sum of 200£ W. A."
Oct. 11, 1791 William Bonner (Lincoln Co) to Christian Hegar (same); for 150£ sold 250 ac on middle fork of Killions Cr; granted Mar. 24, 1754 to Leonard Killion. Signed William Bonner. Witness John Beale & Richd Beale. Wit. oath Jan. 1793 by John Beale. Book 16 p. 348

808. Jan. 9, 1793 William Rankin, sheriff (Lincoln Co) to David Miller (Rutherford Co); for 16£ sold 150 ac on waters of Howards Cr; border: Johnston's old line, Nicholas Friday, Jacob Rinehart, & Valentine Lower; previously sold Jun. 30, 1792 by John McGaughey to Joseph Paxton; now sold due to writ from Lincoln Co court to levy 25£ 17s 5p from Joseph Paxton due to suit of John McGaughey; sold on Jan. 8, 1793.   Signed W. Rankin. Witness Jo Dickson. Rec. Jan. 1793. Book 16 p. 349

809. Sept. 13, 1792 Wallace Alexander (Lincoln Co) to Henry Cline (same); for 50£ sold 72 square poles lot 3 in SE (NE--lined out) square of Lincolnton; lot is 6 by 12 poles; "refer to p. 429" [see end of this book; relates to change from NE to SE in deed].   Signed W. Alexander. Witness Andw Turner. Rec. Jan. 1793. Book 16 p. 351

810. Jul. 28, 1791 William Deal (Lincoln Co) to Nicholas Hillerman (same); for 50£ sold 250 ac on head of Sheegles Cr and on upper side of Philip Cloninger's

land; includes his improvement; granted Jul. 21, 1774 by Gov. Josiah Martin to William Deal. Signed Willem Diehl (german). Witness Joseph Steel & Jacob Dalb. Wit. oath Jan. 1793 by Joseph Steel esq. Book 16 p. 351

811. "The verdict of the jury appointed to value and lay off the land among the heirs of Michael Rudissell desc; the E tract on waters of Michaels Cr at a white oak the beginning corner of the Woal survey we allow to be 10£ more than the Weast tract."
"Jan. 7, 1793 Judgement of jurors appointed to lay off a tract on both sides of Long Cr belonging to heirs of Michael Rudissell desc; we allow NE tract to be 10£ more than the SW tract." Signed David Ramsey, Christian Renhart, Saml Givens, Jhenoy Benn (or Denn) (german), & Henrich Dillinger (german). Rec. Jan. 1793
"course of the first tract of heirs of Michael Rudissell desc" on both sides of Long Cr: 100 ac tract [only various trees are mentioned].
"second tract" [ac omitted] surveyed by David Ramsey.
"Most Northerly part" of this tract or #1 goes to Philip Rudissell; "Most Southerly part" of this tract or #2 goes to Henry Rudisell; decided by lot. Signed Saml Givens, Jhonoy Dinn(?) (german), David Ramsey, Christian Renhart, & Henrich Dillinger (german); plat attached. Rec. Jan. 1793
Jan. 7, 1793 surveyed for heirs of Michael Rudissell desc on waters of Michaels Cr 225 ac divided in two parts (plat attached: the two parts are labeled #3 & #4; "first" part borders: an old field, "beginning" corner of an old survey, & second part; "second" part borders: Conrad Gilbert's field, "second" corner of an old survey, Nicholas Deutor's field, & "second" corner of "first" part. Signed David Ramsey D. Surv.
"Most Northerly part" of the tract or #4 goes to Jacob Rudisell and "Most Southerly part" of the tract or #3 goes to Henry Rudisell, son of John (sic) Rudisell desc; decided by lots. Signed Saml Givens, Jhonoy Din(?) (german), David Ramsey, Christian Renhart, & Henrich Dillinger (german). Rec. Jan. 1793. Book 16 p. 353

812. Nov. 17, 1792 Lewis Warlick, farmer (Lincoln Co) to Wallace Alexander, esq (same); for 40£ sold 400 ac on both sides of Potts Cr; border: Frederick Wise's pasture, line of 1,000 ac grant mentioned hereafter, Sherrill, & edge of a meadow; part of 1,000 ac grant Sept. 3, 1753 to Daniel Warlick desc who sold Dec. 16, 1769 to son Philip Warlick who dies in 1789 and land went to his "full" brother Lewis Warlick. Signed Lewis Warlick. Witness Christian Renhart & Jas Abernathy. Wit. oath Jan. 1793 by Christian Renhart. Book 16 p. 355

April Session 1793
813. Sept. 4, 1792 Philip Killian, planter (Lincoln Co) to Lewis Lowman (Burke Co); for 110£ NC money sold 135 ac; border: Andrew Killian, Bostion Cline, John Hayet, Crawder, & Samuel Killian. Signed Philib Killion. Witness Robert Craig, Jacob Crib (or Crils), & John Dietz. Wit. oath Apr. 1793 by John Dietz. Book 16 p. 356

814. Jul. 30, 1790 William Ozborn (96 Dist, SC) to William Fikes (Lincoln Co); for 20£ sold 100 ac on Battle Run waters of Mountain Cr; border: Henry Lollar, William Bridges, & William Handbus (or Handleus); granted Oct. 29, 1782 to William Ozborn.   Signed William Ozborn's mark. Witness John Fike, Isaac Lollar, & Henry Lollar. Wit. oath Apr. 1793 by John Fike. Book 16 p. 357

815. Feb. 9, 1793 Christian Bear (York Co, SC) to Christian Horse (Lincoln Co); for 100£ NC money sold 200 ac on a branch of Howards Cr; border: Nathaniel Ewing, Waddel, & Alexander; includes William Thompson's improvement; granted Nov. 1, 1784 to Henry Houser.   Signed Christian Bear's mark. Witness _?_ Banr (? ink blob), Niclas Auris, & Michael Buff. Wit. oath Apr. 1793 by Michael Buff. Book 16 p. 358

816. Jan. 10, 1793 Anthony Holman (Lincoln Co) to Jacob Trurebough (same); for 7£ 10s sold 7.75 ac on waters of Howards Cr; border: Andrew Lorouts; part of larger tract belonging to Anthony Holman.   Signed Anthony Hollman. Witness David Ramsey & Michel Drerbach. Wit. oath Apr. 1793 by David Ramsey. Book 16 p. 359

817. Dec. 21, 1792 John Jenkins (Lincoln Co) to Philip Rhyne (same); for 70£ NC money sold 200 ac on N side of Little Long Cr; border: said Rhyne and Palmer; granted Jun. 12, 1789 to John Jenkins.   Signed John Jenkins. Witness Peter Hoyl and Jacob Rhyne. Wit. oath Apr. 1793 by Peter Hoyl. Book 16 p. 360

818. Aug. 25, 1790 George Cockburn (Wilks Co, Ga) to William Graham (Rutherford Co); for 25£ (26--lined out) NC money sold 100 ac on S side of Beastons Cr; border: widow Collins and his own land; granted to George Cockburn.   Signed Geo Cockburn. Witness Abm Collins, Arthur Graham, & Archibald Graham. Wit. oath Apr. 1793 by Abm Collins. Book 16 p. 361

819. Aug. 25, 1790 George Cockburn (Wilks Co, Ga) to William Graham (Rutherford Co); for 65£ NC money sold 200 ac on N side of Beastons Cr and on both sides of widow Collins' path; granted Jun. 7, 1785 to George Cockburn. Signed Geo Cockburn. Witness Abm Collins, Arthur Graham, & Archibald Graham. Rec. Apr. 1793.   Book 16 p. 362

820. Jan. 2, 1792 David Wilcockson (Lincoln Co) to John Bodine (same); for 100£ sold 300 ac on both sides of waters of Mountain Cr; border: on N by Aaron Fermon, on S by Martin Miller, & a road to Ramsour's mill and Sherill's ford on Catawba R; granted Oct. 28, 1782 to [omitted]. Signed David Willcokson & Cannah's mark. Witness Aaron Forman & Peter Bodine. Wit. oath Apr. 1793 by Peter Bodine. Book 16 p. 363

821. Jul. 29, 1792 George Selly (Burke Co) to Nicholas Chapman (Lincoln Co); for "good causes & valuable considerations" sold 100 ac on S side of Jacobs R a

fork of S fork of Cataba R above Alexander's land on both sides of Camp Cr; includes fork of said creek and his improvements; surveyed Mar. 28, 1789 for "said" Robert Orr.   Signed George & Alice Selly's marks. Witness Daniel Wartman & Thomas Sligdon(?). Wit. oath Apr. 1793 by by George Selly. Book 16 p. 364

822. Jun. 26, 1788 James Wilson sr & Daniel McKisick (Lincoln Co) to John Moore (same); for 350£ sold 606 ac in Lincoln formerly Anson Co on waters of Clarks Cr; border: John Welch of E side Clarks Cr and John Ramsour; includes William Mills' improvement; granted Apr. 23, 1768 to John Mills and sold Mar. 16, 1784, due to writ from Lincoln Co Pleas & Quarter Sessions Court, by Joseph Henry, sheriff, to Daniel McKisick (sic).   Signed James Willson & Danl McKisick. Witness Jas Wilson & Jn Patton. Wit. oath Apr. 1793 by James WIlson jr (sic). Book 16 p. 365

823. Jan. 24, 1793 John Reed & wife Lettice (Lincoln Co) to Peter Lineberger (same); for 35£ NC money sold 250 ac on W side of Cataba R on Flat rock Br of Mountain Cr above McCorkle; granted Oct. 26, 1767 to John Littel and at his death it went to Lettice Little as her part in division of her first husband's estate and she is now wife of John Reed.   Signed John Reed & Lettice's mark. Witness Fras McCorkle & Cornelius Clark. Wit. oath Apr. 1793 by Francis McCorkle. Book 16 p. 366

824. Dec. 14, 1792 John & Joseph Cronkleton (Lincoln Co) to Joshua Sherrill (same); for 50£ sold 200 ac; border: Little's old line and McCorkle; granted by the state to Joseph Cronkleton sr and John & Joseph Cronkleton are not proprietors by heirship "it" bearing date Aug. 7, 1787 [probably the grant].   Signed John & Joseph Cronkleton. Witness Jas Holsclaw & Henry Partain. Wit. oath Apr. 1793 by Henry Partain. Book 16 p. 368

825. Feb. 1, 1792 Robert Carrithers (Lincoln Co) to William Maskel (same); for 100£ NC money sold 184 ac; border: Archibald Lyttle.   Signed Robert Carrthers. Witness William Rose Sadler & Lewis Hill. Wit. oath Apr. 1793 by William R. Sadler. Book 16 p. 368

826. Jun.27, 1788 John Moore (Lincoln Co) to Alexander Moore (same); for 50£ sold 75 ac; border: tract where Alexr Moore lives on waters of Hoyls Cr, Shutley, & a branch.   Signed John Moore. Witness Benj Smith. Wit. oath Apr. 1793 by John Moore esq. Book 16 p. 369

827. Apr. 28, 1792 Paul Sippe sr (Lincoln Co) to Daniel Woodringer (same); for 50£ NC money sold 100 ac on waters of Lyles Cr; part of grant Oct. 28, 1782 to Philip Siffala who sold Oct. 24 & 25, 1787 to Paul Sippe sr.   Signed Paul Sippe's mark. Witness Abraham Yont & Robt Blackburn. Wit. oath Apr. 1793 by Robt Blackburn. Book 16 p. 370

828. Apr. 1, 1793 Hannah Bentley (Lincoln Co) to daughter Margert Bentley; for love and affection gave all goods & chattels, my land and "plantration", my Debts, plate, jewels, working tools, a Negro man Sam, & all "my substance".   Signed Hannah Bentley's mark. Witness Francis McNemar & Lydia McNemar. Wit. oath Apr. 1793 by Francis McNemar. Book 16 p. 371

829. Jul. 10, 1792 Thomas Buckhannan (Lincoln Co) to Adam Stroup (same); for 50£ NC money sold 150 ac; border: Adam Stroup, Henry Dellinger, & Jacob Stroup.   Signed Thos Buchannan. Witness Joseph Neel, William Ryndles, & Miles Abernathy. Wit. oath Apr. 1793 by Miles Abernathy. Book 16 p. 372

830. Jan. 20, 1782 Jesse Featherstone (Lincoln Co) to James Hanks (same); for 40£ NC money sold 200 ac on branches of S fork of Cataba R; border: Palmer, Sterrett, & Lamkin; granted Mar. 2, 1775 to William Alston.   Signed Jesse Featherstone. Witness Ralph Cobb & George Lamkin. Wit. oath Apr. 1793 by Jesse Featherstone. Book 16 p. 373

831. Apr. 23,1788 Boston Best (Lincoln Co) to Peter Best (same); for 50£ sold 100 ac on N side of S fork of Cataba R; border: top of a hill, John Hoyl, & "the" river bent.   Signed Bassian Best (or Bess) (german). Witness Stephen Senter & Jacob Beest. Wit. oath Apr. 1793 by Stephen Senter. Book 16 p. 374

832. Feb. 9, 1793 Henry Howser & Nicholas Havener (Lincoln Co) to Christian Horse (same); for 20£ NC money sold 132 ac on waters of Leonards fork; border: Peter Plunk.   Signed Henerih Hoüher & Nicholas Havener's mark. Witness Jacob Hevener & Michael Buff. Wit. oath Apr. 1793 by Michael Buff. Book 16 p. 375
833. Sept. 17, 1792 Peter Smith (Lincoln Co) to Peter Best (same); for 50£ sold 35 ac on waters of South fork; border: Peter Best, John Hoyle, Boston Best, & an open line; granted May 18, 1789 to Peter Smith.   Signed Petter Smith. Witness Jo Dickson. Wit. oath Apr. 1793 by Peter Smith. Book 16 p. 377

834. Apr. 9, 1791 Robert Abernathy (Lincoln Co) to Benjamin Walker (same); for 30£ NC money sold 109 ac on waters of Leepers Cr; border: Morrison and Stroud; part of grant to John Stroud who sold to Peter Dunkin who sold to John Brown Shrimshire.   Signed Robt Abernathy. Witness Hugh Millen & William Abernathy. Wit. oath Apr. 1793 by William Abernathy. Book 16 p. 377

835. Mar. 28, 1793 Robert Blackburn (Lincoln Co) to Daniel Earnest (same); for 10£ sold 100 ac; border: on E of said Blackburn's old tract and by John Wilson's corner; part of grant Aug. 7, 1787 to Robert Blackburn.   Signed Robt Blackburn. Witness Wm Blackburn, Abm Loyman, & Elias Blackburn. Wit. oath Apr. 1793 by Robt Blackburn. Book 16 p. 378

836. Nov. 8, 1783 David Elliott (Lincoln Co) to George Galbraith (same); for 150£ sold 300 ac where David Elliott lives; "granted" by George Patterson to

David Elliott.   Signed David Elliott. Witness Edward Hunter, James Faris, & John McGill. Wit. oath Apr. 1793 by James Faris. Book 16 p. 379

837. Nov. 15, 1792 George Seitz & John Bower (Lincoln Co) to Bostian Edleman (same); for 5£ sold 200 ac on "a" N fork of Leepers Cr; border: Lorentz Snap. Signed George Seitz's & John Bower's marks. Witness Jacob Seitz & John Edleman. Wit. oath Apr. 1793 by John Edleman. Book 16 p. 380

838. Apr. 4, 1793 John Sloan (Spartanburg Co, SC) to Patrick OBrian (Lincoln Co); for 50£ NC money sold 250 ac on waters of Lick fork of Indian Cr and waters of Muddy fork of Buffaloe Cr; border: Thomas Curwell; granted (#256) Nov. 11, 1774 to Thomas Calrsell (or Calwell).   Signed John Sloan. Witness Jno Moore & Jno Leeper. Wit. oath Apr. 1793 by John Sloan. Book 16 p. 380

839. Apr. 9, 1791 Peter Shoup (Lincoln Co) to martin Speegle (same); for 5£ NC money sold 50 ac on both sides of Jacobs fork of S fork of Cataba R; border: Downs; granted Dec. 29, 1791 to Peter Shoup.   Signed Peter Shoup's mark. Witness Robert Blackburn & Daniel Hodson. Wit. oath Apr. 1793 by Robert Blackburn. Book 16 p. 381

840. Aug. 12, 1779 William Alston (Orange Co) to Jesse Featherston (Lincoln Co); for 400£ NC money sold 200 ac on branches of S fork of Cataba R; border: Palmer, Sterrett, Lamkin, & Newton.   Signed Wm Alston. Witness Richard Featherston, Solomon Alston, & Obey Johon.   Wit. oath Apr. 1793 by Robert Alexander esq (sic). Book 16 p. 382

841. Jul. 30, 1790 Thomas Lyttle (Burke Co) to John Cunningham (Lincoln Co); for 40£ NC money sold 250 ac on W side of Cataba R; border: crosses Flat rock Br; granted May 22, 1772 by Gov. Richard Caswell to Thomas Lyttle.   Signed Thomas Little. Witness Isaac Lockerman & James Clark. Wit. oath Apr. 1793 by Isaac Lockerman. Book 16 p. 383

842. Mar. 14, 1789 Ulrick Crowder (Wilks Co, Ga) to John Yoder (Lincoln Co); for 30s NC money sold 12 poles square (or 144 square poles) on a branch of Whiteners Cr waters of S fork of Cataba R; land is lot 6 in SE square of a town newly laid out by Ulrick Crowder.   Signed Ulrick Crowder. Witness Robt Blackburn & Johanes Boley (or Olez) (german). Wit. oath Apr. 1793 by Robt Blackburn. Book 16 p. 384

843. Feb. 25, 1793 Samuel Martin (Lincoln Co) to James Martin (same); for 48£ NC money sold 180 ac; border: John McCall, William Newton, John Taylor, Joseph Dickson, top of hill near a "deep Draft", Kuykendall, Moore formerly (now Dickson's line, & "the" creek.   Signed Samuel Martin. Witness Joseph Dickson & Iaac Moreland. Wit. oath Apr. 1793 by Joseph Dickson. Book 16 p. 385
844. Feb. 25, 1793 Samuel Martin (Lincoln Co) to James Martin (same); for 5£ NC money sold 6 cows & 5 yearling calves, 3 yearling heifers (being all the cattle

I own), a sorrel mare, a 2 year old colt of bay color, 10 sheep, 4 beds & bedsteads & their furniture (being all the beds I own), a big plough, a jack plough, 3 iron pots, a Dutch oven, 2 chests, a trunk, a table & 6 chairs, & 3 sows & 18 pigs. Signed Samuel Martin. Witness Joseph Dickson. Wit. oath Apr. 1793 by Joseph Dickson. Book 16 p. 386

845. Jan. 31, 1793 John Crawford (Iredell Co) to Thomas Bell (Lincoln Co); for 67£ NC money sold 67 ac on W side of Cataba R and S side of Mountain Cr; border: the low ground; part of tract sold by Abraham Collett to Henry Thompson sr who sold to Alexr Thompson and sold by Alexr Thompson & Henry Thompson sr (sic) to Henry Thompson jr who sold to Thomas Wheeler and sold, due to execution against Thomas Wheeler, by Joseph Henry, sheriff, to John Crawford. Signed John Crawford. Witness Jas Crawford, Robert Knox, & William Means. Wit. oath Apr. 1793 by Robert Knox. Book 16 p. 386

846. Jul. 15, 1791 William Falls (Iredell Co) to William Harman (Lincoln Co); for 60£ sold 320 ac on head branch of Mecklins Cr; border: Adam Bolick, Peter Deal, Jacob Myars, & my other survey; include an improvement where Christopher Beckman lived; granted Mar. 14, 1780 to Galbraith Falls desc and by "legal hereditary descent" to his son William Falls. Signed William Falls. Witness Joseph Steel & David Falls. Wit. oath Apr. 1793 by Joseph Steel esq. Book 16 p. 387

847. Jul. 20, 1789 William Crocket (Lincoln Co) to Richard Featherston (same); for 85£ sold 227 ac on S side of Cataba R and S side of S fork of Cataba R about 3 miles below the "lower mound"; granted Nov. 16, 1764 to Allen Alexander who sold to Nathan Henderson who sold to James Patterson who sold to David Elder who sold to Andrew Floyd who sold to William Crocket. Signed William Crocket. Witness John Patterson & Robert Patterson. Wit. oath Apr. 1793 by Robert Patterson. Book 16 p. 389

848. Mar. 29, 1793 Samuel Kehely, planter (Lincoln Co) to Adam Cronister (same); for 50£ NC money sold 200 ac on waters of Buffaloe & Little Creeks; border: Alexander Reynolds and Guthrie. Signed Samuel Kehely's mark. Witness Forney Green Norman & William Welsh. Wit. oath Apr. 1793 by Samuel Kehely. Book 16 p. 390

849. Feb. 2, 1793 Christian Carpenter (Lincoln Co) to Peter Carpenter (same); for 10£ NC money sold two tracts joining each other on waters of Mountain Br waters of S fork of Catawba R: (1) 200 ac; border: a hollow; granted Feb. 28, 1775 to [omitted]; and (2) 200 ac; border: Lick Br and Mauney; granted Dec. 21, 1763 to Jacob Cook who sold to Michael Hoiel who sold Sept. 22, 1779 to Christian Carpenter. Signed Christian Carpenter's mark. Witness David Ramsey & Frederick Carpenter. Wit. oath Apr. 1793 by Christian Carpenter. Book 16 p. 391

July Court 1793

850. Apr. 26, 1793 Nathaniel Ewing & wife Rebecca (Iredell Co) to James Sullivan (Lincoln Co); for 120£ sold 250 ac; border: Peter Harpill on NE side of a run.   Signed Nathl & Rebecah Ewing. Witness Adlai Osborn. Wit. oath Jul. 1793 by Adlai Osborn. Book 16 p. 392

851. Jul. 2, 1793 Rudolph Conrad (Lincoln Co) to Henry Bullinger (same); for 100£ sold 62 ac on waters of Pinch gut Br and Bullinger's mill Br; border: "supposed to be" Muskenunck's or Stockinger's corner, Tibbald, Conrad, said Bullinger, & Slinker; granted Aug. 7, 1787 to Rudolph Conrad.   Signed Rudolph Conrde. Witness W. Rankin & Ad Osborn. Rec. Jul. 1793. Book 16 p. 393

852. Mar. 9, 1789 Ulrick Crowder (Wilks Co, Ga) to Mary Magdalane Stricker (Lincoln Co); for 30s NC money sold 144 square poles or 12 poles square on branch of Whiteners Cr waters of S fork of Cataba R; land is lot 34 in NW square of town of Ulricksburgh.   Signed Ulrich Crowder. Witness Wm Temple Coles & Absalom Bonham. Wit. oath Jul. 1793 by Absalom Bonham. Book 16 p. 394

853. Mar. 9, 1789 Ulrick Crowder (Wilks Co, Ga) to Daniel Stricker (Lincoln Co); for 30s NC money sold 144 square poles or 12 poles square on waters of Whiteners Cr of S fork of Cataba R; land is lot 29 in NW square of Ulricksburg. Signed Ulrick Crowder. Witness Wm TempleColes & Absalom Bonham. Wit. oath Jul. 1793 by Absalom Bonham. Book 16 p. 395

854. May 20, 1789 Ulrick Crowder (Wilks Co, Ga) to Michael Miller (Lincoln Co); for 3£ NC money sold tow lots of 144 squre square poles or 12 poles square each on waters of Whiteners Cr of S fork of Catawba R; (1) is lot 7 in NW square and (2) is lot 6 in SE squre of Ulricksburgh; part of grant Dec. 21, 1764 to Ulrick Crowder. Signed Ulrick Crowder. Witness John Keenor & Magdalina Keenor. Wit. oath Jul. 1793 by John Keenor. Book 16 p. 396

855. Jun. 29, 1793 Philip Burns (Burke Co) to Jacob Fhy, sadler (Lincoln Co); for 40s NC money sold two lots of 144 square poles or 12 poles square each on branch of Whiteners Cr of S fork of Cataba R; (1) is lot 29 in SE square and (2) is lot 40 in SE square of town laid out by Ulrick Crowder desc; part of grant in 1764 to Ulrick Crowder and Ulrick Crowder sold these two lots Mar. 13, 1789 to Philip Burns.   Signed Philip Burns' mark. Witness David Miller & Jacob Miller. Wit. oath Jul. 1793 by David Miller. Book 16 p. 397

856. Jul. 4, 1793 Daniel McKisick, farmer (Lincoln Co) to Philip Hoyar (same); for 100£ NC money sold 200 ac on both sides of Allens Cr and Maiden Cr; border: on W side of Island ford Road and N of a hill; part of grant Mar. 14, 1789 to Daniel McKisick.   Signed Danl McKisick. Witness Joseph Morris & Jo Dickson. Rec. Jul. 1793. Book 16 p. 398

857. Jul. 1, 1792 John Boyd (Lincoln Co) to Daniel Stricker (same); for 15£ sold 72 square poles lot 5 in SW square of Lincolnton; border: lot 6; lot is 6 by 12

poles.   Signed John Boyd. Witness Wallace Alexander & W. Atkinson. Wit. oath Jul. 1793 by Wallace Alexander. Book 16 p. 399

858. May 13, 1792 John Colter (Lincoln Co) to George Cevits (Rowan Co); for 180£ sold 157.5 ac; border: Gasper Shell, George Wilfong, & Martin Colter; part of 424 ac granted Oct. 11, 1783 to Peter Mull who sold Jan. 29, 1786 to John Grossby who sold Nov. 2, 1792 to John Colter.   Signed John Colter's mark. Witness Joseph Steel & Henrih Bollinger (german). Rec. Jul. 1793. Book 16 p. 400

859. Dec. 22, 1792 Jacob Rhodes sr (Lincoln Co) to John Jackson Moor (same); for 60£ NC money sold 300 ac on S fork of Howards Cr; border: Thomas Welch and Potts; "except" a "piece" taken by Christian Rhinhart's in fork of said creek. Signed Jacob Rolh (german). Jacob Wetsel (german) & Thomas Sharp. Wit. oath Jul. 1793 by Thomas Sharp. Book 16 p. 401

860. Jun. 27, 1793 Robert Johnston sr (Lincoln Co) to Robert Johnston jr (same); for 40£ sold 200 ac on both sides of Doctors Cr; border: William Moore, "said" Millican, Hogan, & John Moore; sold by William McEwin to Robert Johnston sr. Signed Robert Johnson (sic). Witness Andrew Johnson. Rec. Jul. 1793. Book 16 p. 402

861. Apr. 7, 1789 Ulrick Crowder (Wilks Co, Ga) to Andrew Crysel (Lincoln Co); for 3£ NC money sold two lots [ac omitted] on a branch of Whiteners Cr of S fork of Catawba R; (1) is lot 30 in NE square and (2) is lot 31 in NE square of newly laid off town; part of grant in Dec. 1764 to Ulrick Crowder.   Signed Ulrick Crowder. Witness David Ramsey & Wm Temple Coles. Wit. oath Jul. 1793 by David Ramsey. Book 16 p. 403

862. Jan. 28, 1789 John Hawn & wife Agenay (Lincoln Co) to Joshua Hawn (same); for 5£ NC money sold 300 ac on both sides of Henrys R; border: an old tract; part of grant Apr. 8, 1768 to John Hawn.   Signed Johannes Hawn (german) & Agnes' mark. Witness John Fisher & Burhil(?) Hahn (german). Wit. oath Jul. 1793 by John Fisher. Book 16 p. 404

863. Dec. 3, 1792 Philip Rudisell (Lincoln Co) to Henry Longcryer, planter (same); for 80£ NC money sold 250 ac on E side of Clerks Cr about a mile E of Ramsour's land; border: a branch; granted Nov. 15, 1762 to William Welch who sold Jul. 23 & 24, 1768 to George Shipe who on Sept. 13, 1773 gave power of attorney to Henry Hollman who sold Mar. 7, 1782 to Michl Potts who sold Apr. 4, 1786 to Philip Rudisell.   Signed Philipp Rudisil. Witness Wm Blackburn & Elias Blackburn. Rec. Jul. 1793. Book 16 p. 405

864. Jun. 4, 1793 Philip Rudisell (Lincoln Co) to Henry Longcryer (same); for 10£ sold 94 ac on both sides of Ramsour's mill pond Cr; border: Caun and Philip Rudisell's old line; granted Aug. 7, 1787 to Philip Rudisell.   Signed Philipp

Rudisil. Witness Nicholas Deetor & John Ramsour. Rec. Jul. 1793. Book 16 p. 407

865. Dec. 25, 1792 William Rose Sadler (Lincoln Co) to John Boldrige (same); for 100£ sold 0.9 ac; includes a saw mill; border: "the" creek.   Signed W. R. Sadler. Witness Alexdr Baldrige & Richard Williams. Wit. oath Jul. 1793 by Alexdr Badlrige. Book 16 p. 408

866. Mar. 25, 1793 Francis McNemar (Lincoln Co) to wife Lydia McNemar; for love and affection gave all goods, chattels, land, debts, plate, jewels, working tools, a Negro wench Edea, & all "other substance".   Signed Francis McNemar. Witness Tempe McNemar and Uell (or Wll) McNemar. Rec. Jul. 1793. Book 16 p. 409

867. May 11, 1793 Thomas Lowe (Lincoln Co) to Henry Hite (same); for a bond of 24£ NC money, for Thomas to pay Henry 12£, due on Dec. 11 "next" and for $1 sold 400 ac; border: James Wilson, John Bradley, & George Shuffert; deed void if Thomas Lowe pays the debt.   Signed Thomas Lowe. Witness Frederick Deitz & Willim Baily. Wit. oath Jul. 1793 by Frederick Deitz. Book 16 p. 410

868. Jan. 25, 1789 John Hawn sr & wife Agnay (Lincoln Co) to John Hawn jr (same); for 5£ NC money sold 156 ac on both sides of Henrys Cr; border: Joshua Hawn; part of grant Apr. 8, 1768 to John Hawn sr.   Signed Johannes Hahn (german) & Agnes' mark.   Witness Johen Fisher & Bertis Hahn (german). Wit. oath Jul. 1793 by John Fisher. Book 16 p. 411

869. Jun. 20, 1793 Joseph Dickson (Lincoln Co) to Jonathan Greaves; for 5£ sold a Negro boy Adam 8 years old.   Signed Jo Dickson. Witness J. Wilson. Rec. Jul. 1793. Book 16 p. 412

870. Oct. 19, 1787 John Perry, attorney for John Yarbrough, to James Henderson, attorney for Samuel Caldwell; "said" James has paid or will pay cost of a suit in Halifax Superior Court where John Yarbrough was plaintiff and Samuel Caldwell was defendent, and said suit to be dismissed and releases John Yarbrough's right & title to following slaves in Samuel Caldwell's possession: Hannah a girl, Rachel a girl, Ned a boy, Jacob a boy, & Sarah an old woman & mother of aforesaid Negroes.   Signed John Perry. Witness Ralph Cobbs & John Henderson.
Oct. 19, 1787 (Franklin Co) John Yarbrough "confirms & approves" within bill of sale for slaves to Samuel Caldwell. Witness Henry & Thomas Yarbrough and John Henderson. Rec. (Lincoln Co) Jul. 1793. Book 16 p. 412

871. Jan. 14, 1793 Job Robinson (Lincoln Co) to John Wilson; for 100£ sold a Negro girl Nell about 12 year old.   Signed Job Robinson. Witness John Barber & Jo Wilson. Wit. oath Jul. 1793 by John Barber. Book 16 p. 413

October Court 1793

872. May 22, 1792 Jacob Mauny (Lincoln Co) to Christian Mauny (same); for 5£ sold 150 ac on waters of Beaverdam Cr; border: Christian Mauny. Signed Jacob Mauny's mark. Witness J. Wilson & John Moony. Rec. Oct. 1793. Book 16 p. 414

873. Aug. 22, 1793 Zachariah Spencer to Ann Hannah; for 70£ NC money sold 100 ac on E side of S fork of Cataba R below Spencer's ford; includes his improvements. Signed Zachariah Spencer. Witness Jas Dickson, Alexr Hamilton, & Joseph Dickson. Wit. oath Oct. 1793 by Joseph Dickson. Book 16 p. 415

874. Jul. 13, 1793 James Wilson sr (Lincoln Co) to Thomas Wilson (same); for 100£ NC money sold 250 ac on both sides of Potts Cr of S fork of Cataba R; border: Samuel Jarrett, Martin Speegle, Jacob Witsill, Philip Anthony, Henry Neiff, & head of a branch; half of grant Nov. 9, 1784 to James Wilson sr. Signed James Wilson sr's mark. Witness Jas Wilson & Christian Braneman. Rec. Oct. 1793. Book 16 p. 416

875. Aug. 16, 1793 Daniel Warlick (Lincoln Co) to Anthony Holman (same); for 150£ sold 200 ac; border: on S side of Clarks Cr and the old survey; part of 1,000 ac granted in 1751 to Daniel Warlick. Signed Daniel Warlick. Witness David Ramsey & Andrew Turner. Rec. Oct. 1793. Book 16 p. 417

876. Oct. 9, 1793 John B. Davis (Lincoln Co) to John Sloan (Spartanburg Co, SC); for 25£ sold 200 ac on waters of Persiman Br of Buffaloe Cr below said Davis' land; granted (#119) in 1784 to John B Davis. Signed John B. Davis. Witness Willey S. Brown & John Carruth. Wit. oath Oct. 1793 by John Carruth esq. Book 16 p. 418

877. Oct. 8, 1793 Robert Ferguson (Lincoln Co) to John Sloan (same) (sic); for 100£ sold 20 ac on waters of Crowders Cr; border: Ferguson's old line; being NW part of tract Robert Ferguson lives on; part of grant to Jonathan Newman. Signed Robert Ferguson. Witness John Carruth & Willey S. Brown. Wit. oath Oct. 1793 by John Carruth esq. Book 16 p. 419

878. Oct. 10, 1793 Jacob Plunk (Lincoln Co) to John Sloan (Spartanburgh Co, SC); for 30£ sold 150 ac on waters of Big Long Cr; border: Espey, Plunk, White, & Carruth; part of grant Sept. 24, 1785 to Jacob Plunk. Signed Jacob Plunk's mark. Witness Willey S. Brown & Danl McKisick. Wit. oath Oct. 1793 by Willey S Brown. Book 16 p. 420

879. Jan. 9, 1792 John Drake (Lincoln Co) to Alexander Hamilton (same); for 100£ NC money sold 100 ac "on" fork of Catawba R on head of Wyatts Branches of S fork of Catawba R; border: McKnitt and "said" Wyatt; granted Nov. 10, 1784 to Daniel Wyatt who sold to Stephen Senter who sold Oct. 6, 1786 to John Peter Baker and sold Jun. 2, 1788, due to Lincoln Co court case, by Joseph Henry, sheriff, to Richard Vandike who sold to John Drake. Signed John Drake.

Witness Andrew Taylor & Daid. Cobbs. Wit. oath Oct. 1793 by Andrew Taylor. Book 16 p. 421

880. Jan. 10, 1792 John Gillespy (Lincoln Co) to Samuel Gillespie (same); for 200£ sold 200 ac on S side of S fork of Catabaw R; border: William Glen; granted Apr. 23, 1767 to William Glen who sold to John Gillespy sr who willed it to John Gillespy jr.   Signed John Gillespie. Witness Jos Henry & John Staret. Wit. oath Oct. 1793 by Joseph Henry. Book 16 p. 422

881. Jul. 15, 1793 William Rankin, sheriff (Lincoln Co) to Peter Mosdeller (same); for 9£ sold 100 ac on waters of Balls Cr; border: Abraham Robison, William Simpson, Archibald Hamilton, & Jacob Gabriel; granted Oct. 28, 1782 to Wm Simpson who sold Oct. 20, 1787 to Rudolph Conrad; now sold due to execution from Lincoln Co court to levy 11£ 10s 5p from Rudolph Conrad due to suit of John Deeds.   Signed W. Rankin. Witness W. Alexander. Rec. Oct. 1793. Book 16 p. 423

882. Jan. 10, 1792 John Gillespy (Lincoln Co) to Samuel Gillespy (same); for 100£ sold 74 ac on S side of S fork of Cataba R; border: William Glen, Gilmore, & said Gillespy; granted to John Gillespy sr who willed it to John Gillespy jr. Signed John Gillespie. Witness Joseph Henry & John Staret. Wit. oath Oct. 1793 by Joseph Henry. Book 16 p. 425

883. Sept. 1, 1793 Philip Gyer (Lincoln Co) to Joseph Mehafey (same); for 52£ sold 100 ac on head branches of Clarks Cr; border: Jacob Hiddle, Conrad Adams, Samuel Steel, & James Kennan.   Signed Philip Jujer (or Giyer) (german). Witness Joseph Steel & John Wilson. Wit. oath Oct. 1793 by Joseph Steel esq. Book 16 p. 426

884. Jul. 10, 1793 Philip Kenchler sr (Lincoln Co) to Philip Deuebaugh (same); for 5£ sold 27 ac on S fork of Catawba R; border: Philip Kenchler, "the" wagon road, & Philip Kenchler's old survey.   Signed Philip Gänotler (german). Witness Wallace Alexander. Wit. oath Oct. 1793 by Wallace Alexander. Book 16 p. 427

809A. [refer to deed #798 on p. 351 of this book]. [no date] "for deed" dated Sept. 13, 1792 to Henry Cline for lot 3 in SE square of Lincolnton, change "North" to "South"; then it will read SE square.   It is consented this is a mistake [in original deed].   Signed Wallace Alexander & Henry Cline. Witness John Wilson, register.   Oct. 6, 1795 Wallace Alexander certified this change.   Book 16 p. 429